002

The Boundaries of Utopia

The Boundaries of Utopia

Carol Weisbrod

Pantheon Books
New York

LIBRARY OF CONGRESS CATALOGING IN PUBLICATION DATA
Weisbrod, Carol.
The boundaries of Utopia.
  Includes bibliographical references and index.
  1. Collective settlements—Law and legislation—United States. 2. Freedom of association—United States. 3. Utopias. I. Title.
         KF1390.C6w44   340′.02′40693   79-1898
         ISBN 0-394-50781-9

Manufactured in the United States of America

FIRST EDITION

About the Author

Carol Weisbrod attended Vassar College and graduated from Columbia Law School. She is Professor of Law at the University of Connecticut.

To my mother
and
to the memory of my father

Starting, as from one terminus of history, from a condition of society in which all the relations of Persons are summed up in the relations of Family, we seem to have steadily moved towards a phase of social order in which all these relations arise from the free agreement of individuals. . . .

We may say that the movement of the progressive societies has hitherto been a movement *from Status to Contract*.

Sir Henry Sumner Maine, *Ancient Law**

---

*Epigraph sources can be found in the Notes section preceding the numbered notes.

Contents

Acknowledgments

Research for this work was done in a number of collections, but largely in Sterling Memorial Library, Yale University, and the Yale Law Library. I am grateful to both of these for their courtesy and assistance.

In its early stages, this research was aided by a grant from the Johnson Fund of the American Philosophical Society. I would also like to acknowledge the institutional support received at later stages from the law school of the University of Connecticut, under Dean Phillip I. Blumberg.

I owe special thanks to Ellen Ash Peters for her encouragement and assistance. I would also like to thank Susan Gyarmati, Jane Isay, Richard Kay, Dorothy Lipson, Leon Lipson, Mark Sheingorn, Pamela Sheingorn and Aviam Soifer for help of various kinds. Errors are my own.

Finally, I would like to thank David Weisbrod, and Stephen and Eva Weisbrod, for their support throughout.

c.w.

Introduction

As a system of case law develops, the sordid controversies of litigants are the stuff out of which great and shining truths will ultimately be shaped. The accidental and the transitory will yield the essential and the permanent.

Benjamin Cardozo

This essay offers a legal perspective on nineteenth century American utopianism, a movement which took the form of self-contained communities established throughout the United States. The narrative focuses on controversies between former members of the societies and the societies themselves, and treats in detail a number of lawsuits involving four of the most famous of the nineteenth century American utopian communities: the Shakers, the Harmony Society, Oneida, and Zoar. These lawsuits were initiated by former members claiming, on one legal theory or another, to be entitled to a portion of the wealth of the societies to which they had belonged. Although the four societies involved in this litigation were in ways quite different from each other, they also shared certain characteristics. All four of these communities were committed to religious communism and a communal life apart from the world, and all four were relatively long-lived.[1] Three of the four lived in domestic arrangements different from those of the outside society: the Shakers and the Harmonists living in celibacy; the Oneida Perfectionists, rejecting property in persons as well as in things, living in a system of group marriage called "complex marriage." These four communities had a variety of interactions with the American legal system. Of these, the lawsuits brought against them by their former members are particularly interesting, since they reveal the way in which four of the most successful of the utopian societies used an orthodox framework—the idea of freedom of contract—to create and defend their quite unorthodox institutions.

The nineteenth century American utopias were voluntary associations.[2] The joining of these societies was, broadly speaking, a contractual act. In the case of some of the communities, including the four major communistic societies discussed here, the act of joining the group was also marked by an explicitly legal contractual undertaking. The formal contracts of the major communistic societies served a number of different functions. One of those functions was the protection of the societies against the claims of former members.

The model of the contract developed by the major communistic utopian societies was this: Under the terms of the agreement, on joining the communistic society a member would give everything he had to the community and would accumulate nothing privately by way of property or wages during the period of association. In return, he would be supported by the group. He would be entitled to withdraw whenever he liked, but his support by the group would continue only during the period of association. The community might choose to provide a departing member with a donation or a settlement. As a matter of right under the contract the member would be entitled neither to return of property brought in nor to wages, no matter how rich he had been when he entered, no matter how rich the community was when he left, no matter how long or faithful or productive his service.[3] As a matter of right the member had been entitled to support during membership, and that he had already received. A contract with this overall orientation is referred to here as a utopian contract.

Contracts like this—differing in range and detail but with the same outline—were used by the four communistic societies at a time when ideas of contract, and particularly of freedom of contract, were held in especially high esteem by the courts and indeed the world at large.[4] Freedom of contract was perceived as a fundamental right, the right of individuals to create relationships between themselves and have the state honor the resulting obligations through the legal enforcement of the contract. Associated with the idea of freedom of contract were two secondary propositions: first, that the right to contract should be generally available, restricted only in those highly unusual instances in which, for example, individuals lacked sufficient age or understanding to make contracts that would adequately protect their interests; and second, that the state should enforce contracts with only minimal supervision of their terms. The role of the state was perceived, in general, as one of enforcement. Courts were not to make contracts for the parties. The bargain might turn out to be badly conceived, disadvantageous, and finally even disastrous; even so, the individual's original freedom of choice would be respected. A contract that no longer reflected his judgment of where self-interest lay would be enforced against him. If he were a plaintiff, seeking somehow to avoid the contract he had made, a court might find that the contract he had freely signed would bar his action. If he were a defendant, in a suit in which the other party alleged a breach of contract, a court might find that he was held to his contract and would have to pay damages for breach. (The remedy was limited ordinarily to money damages. Only rarely, under special circumstances, would a court order an actual or specific performance of the contract.) There were limits on the doctrine of freedom of contract. Contracts would not be enforced, for example, where there had been fraud or duress in the making, or where the substance of the contract was illegal or otherwise opposed to public policy. But the general overriding principle was that the private ordering of individual relationships which the contract represented would be honored.

Freedom of contract was a particularly useful idea in nineteenth century America. Legally enforceable contracts are a device for transferring wealth, and the transfer of wealth was a central aspect of the economic system. The proposition that individuals were free to make their own arrangements in their own interest meshed neatly with the assumptions of a market economy. Individual initiative, energy, and responsibility found their correspondences in specific doctrines of the law of contracts emphasizing individual volition, will, and intention. Contract, it is widely said, and laissez faire capitalism went together. "The individualism of our rules of contract law," Friedrich Kessler wrote, "of which freedom of contract is the most powerful symbol, is closely tied up with the ethics of free enterprise capitalism and the ideals of justice of a mobile society of small enterprisers, individual merchants and independent craftsmen."[5]

But contract was also understood to have a wide range of functions that were not centrally economic. Through contract one created status: man and wife, master and servant, clergyman and parishioner. And through contract one built institutions: families, churches, businesses, and even, if one accepted the theory of the social contract, states themselves.

By the mid-nineteenth century, the proposition that the contracts of the communistic utopian societies were not, in principle, against public policy had been clearly decided in a group of cases which, as a body, stood as specific authority for that point. Thus, the Supreme Court noted in 1914 that "the validity of agreements providing for community ownership with renunciation of individual rights of property during the continuance of membership in the community, where there is freedom to withdraw, has repeatedly been affirmed."[6]

But the fact that there are cases on the point, and that they can be cited so clearly for the statement that the contracts are not against public policy, is a sharp indication that somewhere, at some time, it was urgently argued that there was something very wrong with these contracts. The courts of the state and federal judiciaries upheld the utopian contracts over the arguments that they were against public policy because they were procured by fraud, were violative of religious liberty, and had a tendency to enslave.

In presenting a discussion of the litigation brought by dissident utopians, this essay focuses on a dark side of the American communitarian experience. But through the distortion of this presentation one reaches something central. The history of the relationships between these four communities and their former members—including that part of the history which is found in the case reports—instructs us on the relation between the communitarian movement and the outside society. It reveals that the four communities not only identified a legal device through which they might be accommodated within the American system, but that they tended to use that device with considerable sensitivity. Often the communities did not press their contracts to their formal limits. Often they tried to avoid litigation, as a matter of both principle and expediency. And where settlement and compromise failed, and litigation was unavoidable, they defended their contracts on the basis of entirely familiar legal ideas. Oneida's John Humphrey Noyes suggested once that "extensive revisions of the old code of English law" might have to be undertaken when utopian communism got to court.[7] In fact, it was not necessary. The contracts of the communistic utopians created a legal status which was as clear in its way as corporate status. That status, the contractual nexus, was the essential defining relationship between the communities and the world.

It is conventional, in works on the utopian movement, to offer discussions of the utopians and the world, including sometimes accounts of these cases.[8] But the subject "relations with the world" is often handled in terms of points of tension and the way in which the particular deviations of the community caused adverse responses from the outside world. The communities may be viewed as isolated from the world—they failed, one writer argued, because of an error in their fundamental ideas, since the time for Robinson Crusoes had passed.[9] Even for those who suggest that the communities were in many ways engaged in the world—those who point for example, to the widespread commercial activity of some of the utopians—the image is largely one of limited points of contact. By contrast, the interpretation here stresses that the utopians lived in a continuous relation to the outside world. That relationship is explored first where it is obvious, in the case of the Mormons—too large to be classed with the utopians, though sharing some of their characteristics—whose battle with the federal government is a well-known part of nineteenth century American history. The relationship is explored again in the case of the communistic utopians, who had validated by the law of the state a legal status simultaneously conforming to their beliefs about themselves and conformable to the legal categories of the outside system.

This essay stresses the specific recognition—clear to

some of the nineteenth century utopians—that the cases involving the different communistic societies belong together. The litigation was an occasion for the expression of state sentiment regarding the communistic societies, and there can be little doubt that the cases facilitated, if they did not actually make possible, the development of those societies as stable, though not ultimately permanent, institutions. A nineteenth century lawyer, James Towner, a member of the Oneida community, synthesized the major cases this way:

1st. That Community contracts are not against public policy, nor contrary to any principle of law or morals.

2d. That they are not in derogation of the inalienable right of liberty or conscience, but are really an exercise of that right.

3d. That they are supported by a good and sufficient consideration, *viz.*, one's support, etc., from the common fund while a member.

4th. That they are maintainable and should be supported on the principles of the law of trusts and charitable uses administered by courts of chancery.

5th. That in adopting community of property persons are but following the example of the Apostles and adopting a rule ordained by them. Though this point might be claimed to be an *obiter dictum*, it is sustained by judges of the standing and fame of Justice McLean of the Supreme Court of the United States and Chief Justice Gibson of the Supreme Court of Pennsylvania.

6th. That if such contract were illegal and void, a party to it could have no recovery against others, on the principle that they are in *pari delicto* and the law leaves them where it finds them.[10]

Towner offered a concise statement of the role of the contracts and the litigation in the histories of the communistic societies. "Communism conserves contract," Towner wrote, and "contract supports Communism."[11]

But the litigation over the utopian contracts has an importance beyond its role in the history of the utopians and raises matters of interest to much broader discussions of American law and American society. In detail the cases differ from each other: different parties, different contracts, different points at issue, technically different resolutions. A single case might, for example, decide only that an individual because he had signed a contract which barred wage claims (and because the contract he signed was valid) could not make a claim for wages after he left the society. The particular case involves a victory for the society and a defeat for the withdrawing member. A group of cases involving similar victories and similar defeats in relation to a single society would tend to show that the outside world believed that one society at least had a right to exist unmolested by claims of former members. A number of such cases resulting in victories for different societies must begin to speak to structural questions involving the relationship between the outside society and internal associations of any kind. Thus, in the utopian litigation, participants are seen as standing for more than themselves. Individual plaintiffs are sometimes seen as surrogates of factions in communities, individual societies as surrogates for all societies, and the courts of a single state in a complex federal system as surrogates of the greater State in relation to internal associations. The utopian contract cases raised questions which are current in part because they are never resolved in the abstract, but only in particular cases. Thus the utopian societies have their contemporary counterparts both in the modern commune movement and in what are called the religious cults; and certain issues of mind control, free will, and religious freedom discussed today were foreshadowed, at least in part, by the litigation over the nineteenth century utopian contracts. The conflicts between the communities and their members over property and wages raised issues of private government and private autonomy that are very much alive today as to religious groups and other kinds of organizations, and the desirability of state intervention is as much debated today as it was in the last century.

The contract between the individual and the nineteenth century communistic society was a number of things. It was a private moral obligation, the constitutional document of a voluntary association, and the church covenant of a religious body. But, as well, it was always, in form and intent, an ordinary legal contract. It is as a contract that it came into litigation in the civil courts. At the level of manifest content, a lawsuit by a former member against a communistic society is about a private contract and a point of law relating to that contract; at the level of latent content the case is precisely about the recognition the outside system would give to alternative worlds, represented by the utopian societies. Through an examination of the litigation over the utopian contracts—contrasted with some of the legal experiences of the Mormons—we can explore the capacity of the civil state to tolerate nonconforming collectivities inside the state structure. The utopian contract cases demonstrate the extent of the pluralistic accommodation that was permitted in the nineteenth century through the device of contract. The Mormon encounters with the legal system indicate some limits.

The interpretation of the utopian materials offered here, while dominantly legal, is not doctrinal. Within the legal system a case is less an event in an ongoing associational history—which is the way a community might see it—than the statement of a legal principle applied to particular individuals or groups before the court. The focus of an exclusively legal analysis here would be on the doctrine of law affecting religious communistic soci-

eties and the relations between these societies and their
individual members. Such an approach would treat the
cases, their holdings, and their discussions in relation to
each other, reconciling differences, flattening irregulari-
ties in the pattern, and emerging finally with a statement
of general propositions that would constitute, then, the
law. Such a reading was given by Towner in the 1870s
and again by Zollmann in the discussion of the communistic societies that he offered in his 1917 treatise, *American Civil Church Law*.* The ideals and the way of life of
the religious communities may be peculiar, Zollmann
said, but they are not for that reason illegal, and contracts by which persons agree to work for such societies
without wages, surrendering their property to the group,
are valid.[12]

The present work does not undertake a legal synthesis
along these lines. It is concerned not so much with the
law relating to the communistic utopias as with the communistic utopias as illustrative of a legal doctrine in
practice.

The doctrine of freedom of contract is in considerable
disrepute,[13] associated in the twentieth century more
with inequality than with egalitarianism, and more with
coercion than with freedom. Contract was the device

---

*There is no attempt here to offer a list of cases on utopian contracts. One list
of authorities can be found in Carl Zollmann, *American Civil Church Law*
(1917; reprint ed., New York: AMS Press, 1969, pp. 315-17. A revision was
published in 1933; see pp. 409-10.) The length of a list of relevant cases would
depend, of course, on what was being counted. Nineteenth century cases?
Twentieth century cases? Cases involving communities classified (by whom?)
as "utopias"? Cases involving groups not so classified but raising related problems? Cases brought by former members? By heirs? Strangers? Cases focusing
on the relation between living communities and their members? Cases dealing
with the windup of community affairs? These and other questions could be
raised and answered for the purposes of the creation of a list, but that enterprise is not pursued here. The cases discussed raise questions other than contract questions, but the emphasis here is on issues relating to freedom of
contract. The contracts themselves sometimes deal with matters beyond the
rights of withdrawing members, but the focus here is on that issue to the
exclusion of others.

through which industrial workers, as the theoretical equals of their employers, were permitted to work long hours for low wages. Under the banner of contract a variety of social reforms were invalidated by the courts. Grant Gilmore writes:

> The legislatures, stirred by populist discontents, experimented with social legislation—regulating the hours and conditions of employment, restricting the exploitation of women and children and so on. The courts routinely struck down these statutes on one or another ground—the most amusing ground having been the great principle of freedom of contract. That is to say, if a ten year old child wants to work twelve hours a day in a textile mill, by what warrant is the legislature empowered to deprive the child's parents of their right to enter into such a contract on his behalf?[14]

More recently we know freedom of contract as an argument offered when a lender seeks enforcement of an abusive and burdensome credit term against a low-income consumer. In contexts like these, the abuse of freedom of contract in the service of economic gain is so large as to make it difficult to empathize with the nineteenth century understanding of the law of contracts. It was an understanding that included the idea that limits on freedom of contract were degrading to the protected class, reducing the status of grown men to that of children, and the proposition that restrictions on freedom of contract were infringements on basic and inalienable liberties.

The essence of it is that while the nineteenth century conceived freedom of contract as genuinely involving liberty and autonomy, this is for us a somewhat difficult point. Our experience of the law of contracts seems to lie too heavily in the marketplace,[15] but perhaps we have other experiences to look at. The utopian contracts are an example of a political, religious, and social use of the

contractual instrument. Although the communistic utopias also used contract for purely economic purposes—
some of them in fact accumulated great wealth—their
own membership contracts were used primarily to create
new families and new societies. Their contracts brought
together two great myths, that of the beginning of social
organization—the social contract—and that of its ideal
end—the utopia.[16] In the litigation over these contracts
we see these myths before the courts.

Part 1

New Worlds

We had left the rusty iron frame-work of society behind us.
Nathaniel Hawthorne

1

Experiments
and Institutions

This Preliminary Society is particularly formed to improve the character and conditions of its own members, and to prepare them to become associates in independent communities, having common property.

The sole objects of these communities will be to procure for all their members the greatest amount of happiness, to secure it to them and to transmit it to their children to the latest posterity.

> Constitution for The Preliminary Society of
> New Harmony (1825)

"Forty years ago," the economist Richard Ely wrote in 1885, "men of high education and large ability thought that communistic villages would revolutionize the economic life of the world."[1] The world to be revolutionized was compared by Edward Bellamy, in his utopian novel *Looking Backward* (1888), to a "prodigious coach," driven by hunger and dragged along by the mass of humanity. The top of the coach was covered with passengers who sat in comfortable places where they could "enjoy the scenery at their leisure or critically discuss the merits of the straining team."[2] Bellamy's description stressed that coach seats were not permanently assigned and that a major preoccupation of the passengers was to retain their seats.[3] As the rich might lose their seats the poor might—somehow—obtain seats. This mobility was central to the system.

Bellamy's coach represented a reality to which at least one segment of America was explicitly opposed. A part of the commitment of the communistic utopians in particular was to the creation of environments in which distinctions of wealth would be eliminated. Within a political state based on economic inequality and uncertainty—in republican establishments, Chancellor Kent remarked, "wealth does not form a permanent distinction"[4]—the communistic societies were devoted to economic equality and security. A member's transfer of property to such a society was not primarily conceived of as a gift, given without expectation of return; on the contrary, as Oneida's John Humphrey Noyes explained, those "who give their property to the Community receive in return a guaranty of maintenance for themselves and their families for life in this world."[5]

If some of the utopian enterprises were thought of as adventures, noble but possibly transitory efforts, others were envisioned in a different temporal frame. Oneida was "never in our minds, an experiment," an Oneida Perfectionist said; "we believed we were living under a system which the whole world would sooner or later adopt."[6] George Rapp's Harmony Society was intended to last until the second coming and beyond.[7]

Despite the survival of some groups into the twentieth century, the utopian movement discussed here is on the whole a nineteenth century phenomenon. It was obvious to contemporary observers of the communities that they were reporting on a development which, however important, was not to last. When A. J. Macdonald circulated his printed questionnaire to the leading socialists of 1851 he formulated his questions about the communities in the past tense: "How long did they keep together?" "When and why did they break up?"[8] and then, as if suddenly recalling that success too was at least a theoretical possibility, "If successful, what were the causes of success?"[9] In 1900 William Hinds visited Zoar but found that it was no longer a community.[10] The two revisions (1902, 1908) of his 1878 work on the *American Communities* chronicle the dissolution of a number of the utopian societies. By 1902, when Richard Ely published an article on the Amana Society, he was able to say that "unless I am mistaken, in studying Amana we are examining the history of altogether the largest and strongest communistic settlement in the entire world."[11]

But in the mid-nineteenth century, the utopian communities were visible worlds inside the world—active, industrious, and sometimes even thriving. It is difficult now even to say how many communities there were, although most accounts are agreed that the number is well over one hundred. "No exact list exists or can be made because of the great latitude in definition and the unlimited variety in the nature and constitutions of communities. Many are born and die with no public record, except, perhaps, a deed buried in some remote courthouse."[12] A "flower of reform," Ambrose Bierce wrote of a California attempt, "gorgeous, exuberant and ephemeral."[13] Morris Hillquit concluded that "several hundred communities existed in different parts of the United States during the last century, and that the number of persons who at one time or another participated in the experiments ran into hundreds of thousands."[14] And over and above those who directly participated, there were those who sympathetically watched, subscribing to community newspapers and generally supporting community endeavors, as friends still in the world.

From one point of view, the utopian societies were less a large number of independent communes than a system of fraternal and sometimes actually cooperating organizations.[15] The Zoar and Harmony communities cooperated in the processing of membership applications,[16] and there was once a discussion of a merger of

Economy, Zoar, and the Shakers.[17] Individuals passed from one community to another, sometimes because of some dissatisfaction, sometimes because a group had dissolved and the former member now had to find a new communal home. In this sense, the communitarians were part of a single enterprise, sharing what Professor Arthur Bestor has called "the communitarian point of view."[18] Within that enterprise, however, the diversity of the utopian communities remains striking. There were, as Edmund Wilson summarized the movement,

> communities entirely Yankee and communities, like the French Icarians and the German religious groups, made up entirely of immigrants. There were sectarian communities, communities merely Christian and communities full of Deists and unbelievers. There were communities that practiced complete chastity and communities that practiced "free love"; communities that went in for vegetarianism. Some aimed at pure communism of property and profit and some—notably the Fourierist phalanxes—were organized as joint stock companies. Some, entirely discarding money, lived by barter with the outside world; some by building up industries and driving a good bargain. One follower of Owen, a Scotch woman, Frances Wright, founded a community on the Wolf River in Tennessee, which was intended to solve the Negro problem: it was partly made up of slaves whom she had begged or bought from their masters and whom the white members were to educate and set free.[19]

In addition to Frenchmen and Germans, the societies included Swedes, Poles, Norwegians, and Russians, and it was common to categorize the communities in terms of national origin. The Germans "make better communists than any other people," Nordhoff wrote, "unless the Chinese should some day turn their attention to communistic attempts."[20] Some communities died very quickly. Others, formed early in the century, lived to see

Jacksonian Democracy, the Civil War, Reconstruction, and the Gilded Age. The movement as a whole began to develop in the decades when America was young and optimistic; when the struggle for existence was, in W. D. Howell's language, a free fight;[21] when there was so much land that its availability was sometimes seen as the solution to the problem of poverty. Thus, Horace Greeley advised the poor of the cities to "go straight into the country—go at once!"[22] Some of the strongest representatives of the utopian movement survived to the end of the century, by which time the land was taken and the economic world was "an encounter of disciplined forces," with the free fighters that were left "ground to pieces between organized labor and organized capital."[23] The poor remained.

At the time of Nordhoff's writing, in 1875, some of the utopian societies had seen the death of their patriarchs (Zoar, Harmony) and were maintaining themselves under new leadership. Others, like Oneida, were still living under the authority of their original founders. Some of the communities were incorporated (Zoar in Ohio, Amana in Iowa, Icaria in Illinois at Nauvoo, the former site of the Mormons). Others, like the Shakers, the Harmonists, and the Perfectionists, rejected the corporate form, in part because it seemed to require too much recognition of the forms of the world. Some of the utopians were pacifist, and, notably in the case of the Shakers,[24] had a history of encounters with the law on that subject. Others were willing to fight. The Bishop Hill Colony, for example, furnished soldiers for the North in 1861, sending both officers and privates.[25] Although some of the communities were established in areas far from the center of American life, as common was the creation of a community quite close to mainstream America. Brook Farm, in fact, could hardly have been closer. We want "to bring Brook Farm before the public," their announcement said, "as a location offering at least as great advantages for a thorough experiment as can be found in the vicinity of Boston."[26]

The nineteenth century American utopian communities existed as part of American culture, not on the whole outlawed or hidden but, on the contrary, legal and open to visitors. The groups were well known in their own time, and communistic villages in particular were regularly described by American and European writers and travelers. The Harmonists appear in Byron's *Don Juan*, and the Shakers provide the theme for two of Hawthorne's stories. The history of the American communities was told and retold, and finally would be regularly summarized as background to the history of the socialist movement in America.

The fundamental point is that the communitarian enterprise itself was legal. Perhaps the communities died because of "general depravity,"[27] as Noyes suggested, but they were not suppressed by government. This is perfectly clear in Edmund Wilson's summary of their demise.

> A very few of these communities lasted longer than a decade, but a great many never completed two years. They had against them sources of dissension within and pressure of public opinion from without, incapacity of lower class groups to live up to socialist ideals and incapacity of upper class groups to adapt themselves to manual labor. And all kinds of calamities befell them: fires and typhoid epidemics. A creek would overflow on swampy ground and they would all come down with fever and ague. They would be baffled by land which they had had the bad judgment to buy while it was under snow. They would start off with inadequate equipment or insufficient supplies and never be able to make them go round; or with debts that would get heavier and heavier and finally drag them down. They would get

into legal difficulties about their land titles; they would be unbusinesslike and make messes of their accounts. They would be disrupted by the bigotries of the religious and by jealousies among the women. They would suffer, as was said by a member of the Marlboro Association in Ohio, from "lack of faith in those who had the funds and lack of funds in those who had the faith"; and from "accepting the needy, the disabled and the sick." They would end up in acrimonious lawsuits brought by members against the association; or in the event of their actually having been able to increase the value of their property, there would be members unable to resist the temptation to speculate and sell the community out.[28]

The point that the utopians were engaged in enterprises that were legal must be stressed precisely because it is not self-evident that communities so different from the larger society would have been tolerated by the outside system. In their most radical form, the major utopian communities were communistic in a society so devoted to the individual accumulation of property that finally a religious leader would urge upon his listeners a "duty to get rich."[29] Some communities were celibate in a society committed generally to marriage, and others were nonmonogamous in a society committed not only to monogamous marriage but also to the belief that monogamous marriage was the foundation of civil society. Communities were sometimes hierarchical, if not tyrannical, in their internal governments, stressing order, obedience, and renunciation of self-interest in a society dedicated not so much to the ideal of equality as to the legitimacy of the pursuit of individual interest by free men. And finally, the communities tended to foster potential, and sometimes even actual, political dissidence. They interposed the authority of the community and its leader between the individual and the state, often in the name of a higher law, the appeal to which, Bentham pointed out, justifies civil disobedience and is, therefore, in its nature, an attack on the law of the state.[30]

The communities primarily discussed here are the Shakers, the Harmony Society, Zoar, and Oneida, and a very brief outline of the history of these groups may be useful at this point.

1. *The Shakers* (United Society of Believers). Founded in 1776 in Watervliet, New York, by the Englishwoman Ann Lee, the Shakers (Shaking Quakers) grew to their largest in the mid-nineteenth century, having then a membership of five or six thousand. The group was always communistic and celibate, living under a regime of strict discipline and order, coexisting with mysticism and spiritualism. Their society was noteworthy for parallel equal hierarchies of men and women. The Shakers published many works describing their religious beliefs and form of church organization, and were the subject of books and tracts written by their opponents. In the course of their long history the Shakers encountered mob violence, as well as a variety of legal difficulties. Shaker societies were formed in New York, Massachusetts, Connecticut, New Hampshire, Maine, Ohio, Kentucky, and Indiana. Branches and short-lived communities existed also in Pennsylvania, Georgia, and Florida. At this writing, two societies still exist, one at Canterbury, New Hampshire, the other at Sabbathday Lake, Maine.[31]

2. *The Harmonists.* Led by George Rapp of Württemburg, Germany, more than seven hundred Harmonists came to America in 1804 to escape religious persecution. They settled first at "Harmony" in Pennsylvania, moved in 1814 to "Harmony" in Indiana, and then (selling their Indiana site to Robert Owen for his New Harmony experiment) moved back to "Economy" in Pennsylvania. The group suffered a substantial split in 1832 and also had difficulty with seceding individual members. The

Harmonists adopted the principle of celibacy in 1807. The Harmony society was very prosperous in its long history, and had at its largest a membership of about a thousand. The society dissolved, after protracted litigation, in 1904.[32]

3. *Zoar* (Society of Separatists). Like the Harmonists, the Zoarites were from Württemburg, Germany. They emigrated in 1817 under the leadership of Joseph Baumler (Bimeler), who arrived in the New World with several hundred followers. They received the assistance of American Quakers and settled in Ohio where they adopted community of goods in 1819. Originally celibate, the Zoarites later permitted marriage. The community was unusually democratic in internal structure and was incorporated in Ohio in 1832. At its largest, the community had about five hundred members. Zoar disbanded in 1898.

4. *Oneida (Perfectionists)*. John Humphrey Noyes founded the Oneida community in upper New York State in 1848 following trouble in his home state of Vermont, and the Perfectionist community lived relatively peacefully there for some thirty years. The group was well known for its domestic institutions: *complex marriage*, a system of group marriage derived from the idea that there should be no private property in either goods or persons; *male continence*, a method of birth control; and *stirpiculture*, a form of human genetics through which reproduction was controlled by the community. The Oneida Perfectionists published a newspaper for many years, as well as various tracts. Internal and external pressures in 1879 resulted in the abandonment of complex marriage, and soon after the community became a joint stock company. Oneida, including branch communities, had about three hundred members in the 1870s. The most long lived branch was at Wallingford, Connecticut.

These four communities were among the most promi-
nent and successful of the American utopian communities, and in our discussion these four will for certain
purposes represent the others. The communities developed in an environment that was entirely prepared to
receive them, not because there was approval of specific
programs, but because the environment contained ideas
of social and individual freedom that permitted growth
of collective forms. The associative principle, the nineteenth century publicist Francis Lieber suggested, is an
aspect of progress and liberty. The more free a nation,
he said, the more developed is the idea of association,
while "the more despotic a government is, the more ac-
tively it suppresses all association."[33] Lieber referred ap-
provingly to the freedom that a government may grant
to groups of all kinds, provided that they were moral
and did not injure the rights of others.[34] The associative
principle was fully implemented in the nineteenth century United States, and de Tocqueville's well-known description of an "immense assemblage of associations, . . .
religious, moral, serious, futile, general or restricted,
enormous or diminutive"[35] was an accurate description
of American life. Civil rights and a great deal of land
made the country seem a "functioning Utopia to people
elsewhere and [it] was the scene of most of the Utopian
experiments of the period."[36] The two are linked.

In addition to freedom of association, America was
committed (in principle) to religious toleration and to
the idea that religious beliefs (and some degree of religious practice) would be given legal protection. A Maine
court in an early Shaker case declared itself plainly on
the point: "With us modes of faith and worship must
always be numerous and variant; and it is not the province of either branch of the government to controul [*sic*]
or restrain them, when they appear sincere and harmless."[37] Freedom of conscience in America was cele-

brated in a Shaker hymn: "Now free toleration to conscience is given—we're saved from the terror of tyrants and kings."[38] The Shaker example, Noyes wrote, has demonstrated "not merely that successful communism is subjectively possible, but that this nation is free enough to let it grow."[39] "Who can doubt," he added, "that this demonstration was known and watched in Germany from the beginning, and that it helped the successive experiments and emigrations of the Rappites, the Zoarites, and the Ebenezers?"[40] The Shaker Elder Frederick Evans repeatedly emphasized the importance of religious freedom. "The Shaker Societies," he wrote, "have not yet extended beyond the boundaries of the Model Republic, which is accounted for by the Shakers themselves thus:—they say their religion can not exist and flourish except under such governments as secure freedom of person, freedom of speech and of the press, liberty of conscience & perfect separation between church and state."[41] Certainly Elder Evans believed that America was one of those governments. "The American government and the Shaker order came up together; they belong together. Their history has run, and will run parallel."[42]

Noyes was correct in his assessment of the influence of freedom of conscience on other groups. When the Harmony Society sent a petition to Jefferson, then President, they wrote that "having been persecuted & punished in every manner for sake of the Truth which they perceived and confessed," they were now forced "to look for a place, where [there] is liberty of Conscience & where they may exercise unprevented the Religion of the Spirit of Jesus"[43] Their understanding was that "America would be such a place," and so the entire Society had "unanimously resolved to send their Leader George Rapp . . . to inquire about the country."[44] Rapp wrote to his people from Lancaster, Pennsylvania, on September

12, 1803: "There is no tithe here. . . . There is religious freedom enough here. Here they laugh at a person who speaks of parties. They want you to think and believe what you wish, only be an honest man, that is esteemed."[45]

As a legal matter it is important to note two points: First, the protection of religious liberty in the nineteenth century did not revolve only around the First Amendment to the federal Constitution ("Congress shall make no law respecting an establishment of religion or prohibiting the free exercise thereof"). According to nineteenth century legal theory, the First Amendment did not apply to the states. (What the law calls the incorporation of the First Amendment through the Fourteenth Amendment—that is, the application of the provisions of the Amendment to actions of the states—was the result of a process of judicial interpretation that took place in the twentieth century.) State law on the subject of religion was, therefore, of considerable importance.

Second, while fundamental ideas of association and religious liberty were immensely important, they were not finally unlimited, even in principle. Freedom of association was permitted unless the association was immoral or a threat to the state. Religious liberty was protected, but the law would not protect illegal or immoral acts claimed to be exercises of religion. There was always the idea that the state must screen all groups and ascertain that their existence is not harmful either to their members or to society as a whole. The law and the courts drew the boundaries of utopia.

The Latter-day Saints may be seen as a utopian community of heroic dimensions. The Mormons were, as John Humphrey Noyes suggested, a "gathering which grew to be a nation."[46] The Mormons raised some issues for the society that were similar to those raised by the utopians. They were a religious group led by a prophet who claimed to have received a new revelation. They practiced, in addition to polygamy, a high degree of economic collectivism and had a system of internal government whose sanctions, it was sometimes thought, extended to the death penalty. Control of the Latter-day Saints was a national obsession in the nineteenth century, and the struggle between the Mormons and the legal system is recounted here as a counterpoint to the story of the American utopias.

2

"A Painfully Interesting Problem": The Case of the Mormons

> Nothing was more characteristic of the entire group of exaggerated movements in America than the history of the Mormons. We find in it . . . a talent for spontaneous social organization independent of government and resisting its authority linked to enthusiastic Americanism.
>
> Johan Huizinga

Mormonism was to the nineteenth century a fascinating popular spectacle. The London *Times* (1855) noted that Mormonism is a "combination of Judaism, Mohammedanism, socialism, despotism, and the grossest superstition," and that these, together with practical good sense, combined to "make it the most singular phenomenon of modern times."[1] The early history of Utah was familiar to its readers, *Harper's* noted in 1871: "It constitutes one of the most wonderful chapters in the religious annals of the world."[2]

The Mormon community in Utah had its origins as a part of the religious ferment of the early nineteenth century. "A circle described on a radius of one hundred and fifty miles around such a center as Pittsfield, Massachusetts," Bernard DeVoto suggested, "would include the birthplaces of ninety percent of the American sects and of an even greater percentage of their prophets."[3] Among the prophets born in Vermont was Joseph

Smith, who organized the Church of Latter-day Saints in New York in 1830. The community founded by Joseph Smith moved from New York, from Ohio, from Missouri, and from Illinois, often involuntarily.

The early Mormon persecution had a variety of causes. The non-Mormons of Missouri, for example, had religious and secular grievances against the Mormons. The list of charges against the Mormons (Missouri, 1833) described them as either "fanatics or knaves." They claim "to hold personal communication and converse face to face with the most High God . . . to heal the sick by laying on hands; and . . . to perform all the wonder-working miracles wrought by the inspired apostles and prophets of old." The Mormons were also a threat to certain secular interests in Missouri. The Latter-day Saints were accused of "tampering with our slaves and endeavoring to sow dissensions and raise seditions amongst them." The Mormons had to leave, and if they refused to leave the settlers agreed to "use such means as may be sufficient to remove them." To that end, the old settlers of Missouri pledged to each other their "bodily powers . . . lives, fortunes and sacred honors."[4]

Finally the expulsion was under public and not private authority. In 1838, responding to a Mormon offensive and the possibility of civil war, the governor of Missouri wrote to his general: "The Mormons must be treated as enemies and must be exterminated or driven from the State if necessary, for the public good."[5]

Expelled from Missouri, the Mormons built a new home in Illinois at Nauvoo, chartered by the state of Illinois in 1840. The city grew, its numbers vastly increased by the emigrants from abroad brought by Mormon missionaries. The Mormons formed a militia, the Nauvoo Legion. A United States artillery officer wrote in the New York *Herald*: "What does all this mean? Why this exact discipline of the Mormon corps? Do they intend to conquer Missouri, Illinois, Mexico?" It was true, he said, that Joseph Smith's troops were part of the militia of the state of Illinois, but still they were somewhat troublesome. "The time will come," the observer predicted, "when this gathering host of religious fanatics will make this country shake to its center. A western empire is certain."[6] He was quite right; Nauvoo did contain the seeds of empire.

Joseph Smith did not live to see the great Mormon kingdom; in 1844, he and his brother were murdered in the jail at Carthage, Illinois.[7] In 1845 the city charter of Nauvoo was revoked and Brigham Young led the Mormons to Utah where the western empire became a reality. The site at Nauvoo became the home of the Icarians. In 1850 the Mormon state of Deseret applied for statehood, but Utah was not admitted to the Union until 1896.

Although polygamy is the best known of the deviant institutions of the Latter-day Saints, in fact the Mormon community, even in its early period, was highly unusual as well in economic and political structure. Professor Arrington has summarized the critical points of opposition to the Mormons. Plural marriage was "an unspeakable vice," the "theocratic economy interfered with the spread of capitalistic institutions," and "supposed church control of political life was thought to be inconsistent with democracy."[8]

ECONOMIC ORGANIZATION

In economic terms, early Mormon life in Ohio and Missouri was characterized by a high degree of collectivism and, indeed, is often referred to as communistic. The system was, however, quite different from the communism of the religious utopias. As Professor Arrington has noted, while the "United Order" of the Mormons (also called the "Order of Enoch" or the "Law of Consecration and Stewardship") was designed to produce an economic equality, it was also designed to preserve individual free enterprise.[9] It seems to have been directed more to an egalitarian redistribution of wealth than to the abolition of private property. The Order's essential feature was a consecration of property to the church followed by a stewardship over the property given back to individuals.[10] It was assumed that some consecrations would be greater than the allocated stewardships, and that the stewardships of some persons would come from the excess.[11]

After the initial consecration of wealth, there was also to be consecration of surplus products, for distribution to the needy. Beyond this, however, there was to be considerable freedom of enterprise in production and in the management of properties held as stewardships. As Professor Arrington notes, "There was no provision for the minute and intimate regulation of economic activity which prevailed in some contemporary communitarian societies."[12]

There are some indications that there was trouble with early Mormon apostates over property transferred to the group. Originally, the steward received a "life lease" in his newly assigned property, subject to cancellation. But this arrangement, Professor Arrington notes, was changed "because of legal and other difficulties" to a system (1833) under which stewardships were given out in fee simple.[13] Thus a system under which rights to the leasehold would be forfeited—leaving the steward with nothing—was changed to a system in which the steward owned the property assigned to him, although not the property originally consecrated.

We are told that when a Mormon revelation "commanded the Ohio converts to impart of their lands to their eastern brethren," Leman Copley (a former Shaker) at first volunteered to sell land at half its value but later renounced his offer.[14] And, finally, a contemporary Mormon report indicates that a man who subscribed fifty dollars for the purchase of lands and necessaries for the Mormons sued and obtained a judgment.[15] The basis for the court's judgment in favor of the apostate is not clear.

The spirit of the early Mormon collectivism survived the difficulties of Missouri and Illinois. "While unity and cooperation characterized the early church," Professor Arrington notes, "it remained for Brigham Young to develop the technique of unified action and combined endeavor to its fullest extent."[16] Brigham Young began the program, which included "cooperative arrangements for migration, colonization, construction, agriculture, mining, manufacturing, merchandising—and, in fact, for every realm of economic activity."[17]

PLURAL MARRIAGE

One of the most important differences between the Mormons and the surrounding community involved family organization. Rumors of polygamy among the Mormons resulted in denials of the charge by the Mormons as early as 1835, and these denials continued until 1852, when the official announcement was made in Salt Lake City that the Latter-day Saints were practicing plural marriage.[18] The first federal legislation against polygamy in the territory of Utah was passed in 1862. Mormon polygamy was associated with the harems of the Eastern despotisms. The common assumption was that women were either forced into polygamy or entered it "voluntarily" under conditions so terrible that their actions could not be said to be truly their own. Although

Utah's women were given the franchise in 1870 and were among the first women in the United States to vote, the question of woman suffrage in Utah was largely either ignored in the debate over polygamy or considered essentially without significance. Woman suffrage in Utah did little to change the popular image of Utah's Mormon women as victims of male lust and tools of the Mormon hierarchy. This was true even for some of those who supported the highly controversial cause of woman suffrage. Polygamy, said Henry Blackwell in the *Woman's Journal*, was "social barbarism," and "as long as it exists the equality of women is impossible."[19]

A modern writer has summarized the charges against polygamy, which was thought by its enemies to have

> bred vice, incest, forced marriages, sexual slavery, degenerate children, and unbridled male lust. The situation of the Mormon women was as bad as the position of female slaves under Southern planters. The morality of the Mormons was a fiction. . . . Polygamy was merely instituted to gratify the lechery and avarice of the Mormon leaders and to perpetuate their power. With the system of the harem came the vices of Turkey and Asia.[20]

Bigamy and polygamy were "crimes by the laws of all civilized and Christian countries," the Supreme Court said in 1890. They were crimes that "tend to destroy the purity of the marriage relation, to disturb the peace of families, to degrade woman and to debase man."[21] To call the advocacy of plural marriage "a tenet of religion," the Court concluded, "is to offend the common sense of mankind."[22]

To the nineteenth century, the Mormon revival of polygamy was astonishing and, finally, outrageous. "Is nothing ever to be settled?" *Harper's* inquired in 1857. "Are we to be discussing in America and in the nineteenth century and so forth whether a man ought to have forty wives?"[23] A writer in the *Woman's Journal* expressed fundamental inability to understand the attitude of the Mormon women toward polygamy. We can pity and sympathize with our "fanatical sisters among the Mormons," she said, "just as we do with the Hindoo widows who throw themselves on the funeral piles of their husbands," but "the spectacle of women in this age and country accepting and defending polygamy is a phenomenon we are utterly unable to comprehend."[24]

But there were some in the nineteenth century who offered moderate accounts of the Utah community and even attempted to separate the issue of polygamy from other aspects of Mormonism. Thus, a legal journal said in 1871 that much could be said "in praise as well as in blame" of the Mormons. "They have, no doubt, trampled upon one of the strongest traditions of civilization," the journal conceded, but at the same time the Mormons had done "some service to the State." If one put aside the question of polygamy, the Mormons had "obeyed the laws quite as well as most new western communities," and they had "never failed to respond promptly to any calls made upon them to aid in defending the country or in prosecuting its wars." Indeed, as to plural marriages, they had been tolerated for a quarter of a century, "so long, indeed, as to justify [the assumption] that they had become legalized by prescription."[25]

Some understood that the popular image of the Mormon women was distorted, at least in some part. Thus, George Tichnor Curtis, arguing before the Supreme Court on behalf of the Mormons, rejected the stereotype of the victims of polygamy:

> . . . unless we meet the Mormon women of Utah half way, and recognize who and what they are, we cannot accomplish anything useful. It is unphilosophical, it is

absurd, it is dangerous to deal with the subject in any other way. The idea of treating these women, many of them women of New England birth, people, at least, of intelligence, educated in the public and private schools of our older States, as if they were a set of degraded beings, bearing a yoke under which they bend, and from which it is our duty to emancipate them by any and every means . . . if we do not lay aside this idea we can never do anything successfully with this terrible problem.[26]

The campaign against polygamy formally began in 1862 and did not succeed finally until 1890 when the church was forced to capitulate. The Mormons succumbed to the widespread sentiment expressed, for example, by Dudley Haskell of Kansas when he said in 1881 that "polygamous Mormonism [is] treasonable at heart to the Republic. . . . Its civil and religious creed is diametrically opposed to the institutions of any free Republican system."[27] The federal victory is reflected in provisions in the constitutions of several states, explicitly banning plural marriage.[28]

THEOCRACY

"Wherever the Mormons went," Joseph Smith's biographer, Fawn Brodie, has commented, citizens "resented their self-righteousness, their unwillingness to mingle with the world, their intense consciousness of superior destiny."[29] Those who were closest to the Mormons in Illinois were "desperately afraid of being crushed" by them, hating Joseph Smith "because thousands followed him blindly and slavishly."[30] An early nineteenth century Methodist circuit rider, Peter Cartwright, described an argument with the founder of Mormonism, that reveals the threat of Joseph Smith: "His wrath boiled over, and he cursed me in the name of his God, and said, 'I will show you, sir, that I will raise up a government in these United States which will overturn the present government, and I will raise up a new religion that will overturn every other form of religion in this country.' "[31] In 1885, clergyman Josiah Strong objected to Mormonism as "an *imperium in imperio* ruled by a man who is prophet, priest, king and pope, all in one." Strong forcefully described the threat of Mormonism when he quoted a speech by a Mormon bishop (1881) that described the solidity of the Mormon vote, stressed that the balance of power would be to the Mormons, and looked to the admission of Utah to the Union as a polygamous state, along with the "other territories we have peacefully subjugated." The bishop said that Mormon principles were of sacred origin, and would "spread throughout the United States." The Mormons, he said, "possess the ability to turn the political scale in any particular community we desire. Our people are obedient. When they are called by the church, they promptly obey."[32] The issue of bloc or controlled voting was clear in regard to the Mormons and was used as an argument for disfranchisement of Utah's women as part of the campaign against the Mormon priesthood. Mrs. Angelina Newman, in her petition to the Senate and House of Representatives in 1886, quoted Mrs. Stenhouse: "I have often seen one solitary man driving into the city a whole wagon load of women of all ages and sizes. They were going to the polls and their vote would be one."[33] For some, the idea of women voting was insupportable in itself. But even for those who endorsed the franchise for women in principle, the fact of woman suffrage in a polygamous territory sometimes conveyed not the vision of a new form of social organization, but only images of the travesty involved in forcing an enslaved population through a democratic form. The women of Utah lost the vote in 1887 with the passage of the Edmunds-Tucker Act.

The control of the theocracy was believed to extend to vastly more than the vote, and the internal sanctions of the Mormons were thought to go far beyond the conventional sanctions of churches and voluntary associations. J. G. Shea, writing in the *American Catholic Quarterly Review*, described the Mormons as "practising polygamy, and murdering with impunity any whom they condemn in their secret councils."[34] It seems possible that the image of the avenging Danite bands—evident, for example, in A. Conan Doyle's *A Study in Scarlet*—was as potent as the image of the victims of polygamy in arousing the nation against the Utah community.[35] It "must be said of the Mormons," J. H. Beadle wrote in 1870, that "they have always treated their own people worse than outsiders; and . . . they have visited apostates and dissenters with extreme vengeance." It would be a "wearisome and disgusting task," he said, to give accounts of those who left or tried to leave the territory, and to describe the "bloody fate which has overtaken many, even of the tools of the Church, when suspected."[36]

The evil was in theocracy itself, Beadle said. Even before polygamy, "the priests ruled the ignorant people with spiritual terrors, and that made them dangerous neighbors and troublesome citizens wherever they lived." It might be, Beadle noted, that some evils grew out of polygamous marriage, or perhaps had been strengthened by it. But the real problem was that ecclesiastical policy held sway, not law, and that Gentiles (non-Mormons) were "subjected to all the annoyances of petty tyranny" and "in their business and social life [were] constantly subjected to the secret espionage of the Church." "Friends and fellow-countrymen have been secretly murdered; and the Church prevents them from obtaining justice." In short, non-Mormons were "exposed to the tyranny of an unopposed majority, and that majority controlled by a small and compact hierarchy working out its Star Chamber decrees against liberty by secret and to the people irresponsible agents." This was the thing, Beadle said, that "grinds the feelings of American citizens." It was not the "social, immoral or polygamic features" of Mormonism that were of concern, "but the hostile, the treasonable and the mutinous."[37]

In connection with his discussion of Mormon-Gentile conflict Professor Thomas O'Dea referred to the desire of the Mormons to increase group loyalty and to strengthen church authority. He described the doctrine of "blood atonement," quoting Brigham Young: "There are sins that men commit for which they cannot receive forgiveness in this world, or in that which is to come, and if they had their eyes open to see their true condition, they would be perfectly willing to have their blood spilt upon the ground, that the smoke thereof might ascend to heaven as an offering for their sins." O'Dea suggested that while blood atonement was "rarely practiced," the "atmosphere" among the Mormons was one of "inordinate group loyalty to the point of fanaticism."[38]

These were the problems encapsulated in the term "theocracy," and there is no surprise in the fact that the debate in Congress over federal antipolygamy legislation in the 1880s was not limited altogether to the issue of domestic institutions. "The government of Utah to-day has no semblance to republican government," one legislator said. "All that was intended to be conserved of republican institutions and theory has been displaced by a system of theocracy. And therefore for the purpose of obtaining the spirit and meaning and principle of republican government it is necessary that that theocracy shall be displaced."[39] And in 1890, when the Supreme Court condemned the Mormon church for its immorality, it also noticed its attempt to set up an autonomous political community in Utah. "It is unnecessary here," Justice Bradley said, "to refer to the past history of the sect, to their defiance of the government authorities, to their attempt to establish an independent community, to their efforts to drive from the territory all who were not connected with them in communion and sympathy."[40]

The threat of the Mormons was not only in their organization and structure, but also in their refusal to yield to the authority of the outside state. "We have before us," Justice Bradley said, an organization wielding "immense power in the Territory of Utah," which employed its resources and power "in constantly attempting to oppose, thwart and subvert the legislation of Congress and the will of the government of the United States."[41] The threat Justice Bradley saw was not merely a deviant religious institution but a deviant state within the sovereignty of the United States.

SANCTIONS

The history of the Mormons and the law establishes the larger general proposition concerning the role of the law of the outside system in relation to the unconventional practices of any group claiming religious sanction. "However free the exercise of religion may be, it must be subordinate to the criminal laws of the country, passed with reference to actions regarded by general consent as properly the subjects of punitive legislation."[42] The Mormons insisted that polygamy must be lawful—despite legislation to the contrary—as it was an exercise of religious belief protected by the First Amendment. They were not successful.

The constitutionality of the antibigamy act of 1862 was established in the 1878 term of the Supreme Court in the case of *Reynolds* v. *United States*.[43] Brigham Young's secretary, George Reynolds, married twice, in violation of the federal statute. He argued (on behalf of himself and polygamous Utah) that his act was protected by the First Amendment to the federal Constitution as an exercise of his religious faith. Writing for a Court that was unanimous on this issue (Justice Field dissented on a point of evidence), Chief Justice Waite rejected Reynolds's argument. The Morrill Act was constitutional, he said. While Congress could not pass an act that violated the First Amendment, the antibigamy act did not violate the amendment.

The Supreme Court said very little about the particular evils of polygamy, but there can be no doubt that in the minds of the members of the Court the evils of polygamy were very great. Regulation of marriage was a critical state function, and while Congress was "deprived of all legislative power over mere opinion," Chief Justice Waite said, it was "left free to reach actions which are in violation of social duties or subversive of good order." The most explicit comment on the precise danger of polygamous institutions to the social order is found in a citation to Francis Lieber:

> . . . according as monogamous or polygamous marriages are allowed, do we find the principles on which the government of the people, to a greater or less extent, rests. Professor Lieber says, polygamy leads to the patriarchal principle and which [*sic*] when applied to large communities fetters the people in stationary despotism, while the principle cannot long exist in connection with monogamy.[44]

There could be no exemption from the statute on account of religious belief. To create an exemption would be "to make the professed doctrines of religious belief superior to the law of the land, and in effect to permit every citizen to become a law unto himself." Government, Chief Justice Waite concluded, "could exist only in name under such circumstances."

The *Reynolds* case made plain that the federal government was fully entitled to act against polygamy. Indeed, the tone of its opinion, its references to the odiousness of polygamy, and its approval of lower court jury instructions referring to the "innocent victims of polygamy," might have supported the suggestion that Congress had a moral obligation to act against polygamy in the territories. But the institution was not defeated, despite the direct intrusion of the state through the criminal law. Plural marriages were difficult to prove. Other federal legislation was enacted and other criminal proceedings instituted under the new legislation. Hundreds of Mormons were imprisoned, others denied the right to vote, and finally the escheat of church property to the United States government was upheld. The institution of polygamy, the Supreme Court said in 1890, was in effect a "return to barbarism."[45] It would not be tolerated. The Morrill Act, which forbade polygamy, contained also a form of mortmain statute.* The act limited the property the Mormon church could acquire and hold, and also moved against polygamy by annulling the act that incorporated the church, as well as all laws maintaining polygamy. If the Morrill Act of 1862 did not "absolutely repeal the charter of the corporation," the Supreme Court said in 1890, "it certainly took away all right or power which may have been claimed under it to establish, protect, and foster the practice of polygamy."[46]

---

*Mortmain acts were designed to limit the holding of lands by religious groups, whose ownership would be perpetual. The concern was that the land would be held by a dead hand (mortua manu). In England members of religious orders were regarded as civilly dead.

These provisions of the Morrill Act were examples of familiar forms of state control of religious bodies.

Richard Ely spoke of the mortmain problem in terms of concentration and fluidity. "Some people fear only the concentration," he said, but it is the "concentration without fluidity, without being amenable to control, which is the large part of the evil."[47] State control over the amount of land (or other property) held by religious groups reflects not only concern over the free alienation of land, but also over the degree of independence that the group can attain. Property is accumulated so that independence can be assured, for if property may be theft, and if it may control power, it may also guarantee liberty, in this case the liberty of association of those committed to the communal religious life. Too great a degree of liberty or autonomy in groups can be threatening to certain views of state sovereignty. The mortmain statute may be used to set the limits.

For related reasons, the state guards the privilege of incorporation, and insists that the corporation is merely a creature of the state subject to regulation by the state. Again, the history of the Mormons demonstrates the potential for state control, in that the dissolution of the corporation and seizure of church property were the final stages of a battle against Mormon polygamy that lasted nearly three decades from the passage of the Morrill Act in 1862.

Mormonism was perceived as antithetical to and subversive of American ideals and values. The Mormons were not alone in being viewed in this way. As historian David Brion Davis has noted, similar concerns were widely expressed as to the Freemasons and the Catholics. "During the second quarter of the nineteenth century," Professor Davis wrote, "when danger of foreign invasion appeared increasingly remote, Americans were told by various respected leaders that Freemasons had infiltrated the government and had seized control of the courts, that Mormons were undermining political and economic freedom in the West, and that Roman Catholic priests . . . had made frightening progress in a plot to subject the nation to popish despotism."[48] When one could not be certain of what the public interest was, and when "no one could take for granted a secure and well-defined place in the social order," it was difficult, Professor Davis suggests, "to acknowledge legitimate spheres of privacy."[49] Americans of the Jacksonian period "appeared willing to tolerate diversity and even eccentricity, but when they saw themselves excluded and even barred from witnessing certain proceedings, they imagined a 'mystic power' conspiring to enslave them."[50]

But if Mormonism was somehow like the hidden subversive evils of Catholicism and Masonry, it was also clearly like the religious communal enterprises of the utopians. Thus, Beadle (1870) suggested that Mormonism was properly viewed as an enormous and highly centralized version of religious pathology that was evidenced also by the Shakers and Harmonists. A few such groups, Beadle suggests, coming originally from Europe, have maintained "a sort of sickly life through two or three generations in America." Groups like the Shakers and Harmonists, Beadle said, were, however, "comparatively innocent and harmless."[51]

It was because of the obvious similarities between the Mormons and the Oneida Perfectionists that it became critical for the Perfectionists to differentiate themselves from the Latter-day Saints. They published a detailed list of the differences:

> The Mormons are supposed to be defiant of civil authority; the Oneida Community claim to be its peaceable subjects.
> The Mormons have their drilled soldiers; the Oneida Community are non-resistants.

The Mormons send out evangelists and compass sea and land for proselytes; the Oneida Community use no such means to increase their numbers.

The Mormons establish themselves in places remote from the centers of civilization; the Oneida Community seek those centers and shun the wilderness and the desert.

Mormonism is supposed to degrade woman; Oneida Communism elevates and ennobles her.

The Mormons insist that every man has a right to as many wives as he can win and support; the Oneida Community insist that, in the highest form of society, rights in the sense of ownership and social bondage do not exist.

The Mormons are supposed to recruit their numbers largely from the lower classes; the Oneida Community claim to represent the best classes in the churches and society.

Mormonism is based on a new revelation, and has a new Bible; the Oneida Communists have no new Bible, and base their system on the teachings and examples of Christ and his Apostles.[52]

In 1857, it was not difficult for *Harper's* to perceive the difficulties of Utah as remote. "Utah is so far away that we think of it as we do of Japan."[53] But if Utah were Westchester, *Harper's* concluded, "it would not be tolerated for a moment."[54] The Perfectionists of upper New York State had reason to be concerned.

Variations of the Oneida argument might have been offered by other utopias. But the differences between the utopians and the Mormons were to a significant degree involved with scale. When we speak of hundreds of Perfectionists or a thousand Harmonists, we see in the case of the Latter-day Saints at Nauvoo a group estimated at eleven thousand.[55] Their economic development was so successful that Bernard DeVoto suggested in 1936 that Mormonism had developed not in the direction of Brook

Farm or Oneida "but in the direction of Standard Oil."[56] The substantive issues raised by the Mormons were fundamentally of three kinds—relating to domestic, economic, and political arrangements; and these issues were very much like those raised on a much smaller scale by the communistic utopians.

The Mormon experience has been reviewed here not as an example of a fifth utopian community treated by the state like the other four, but rather as a counter example to be set against the others. The Mormon history reveals both the substantive issues that might move the state to action and the range of instruments available to a government in dealing with a deviant group. The state could impose criminal penalties (fine or imprisonment) or civil and political disabilities (disfranchisement). It could limit permissible land holding (mortmain) and it could reward dissidents and seceders at the expense of the collective. In the case of the Mormons, it was finally disincorporation and the taking of property as much as criminal penalties that succeeded in containing and domesticating the Utah community. In the case of the utopians, it was first the refusal of the state to act legislatively to suppress the communities and second the refusal of the state to favor the seceders in civil litigation that reflected the state's willingness to accept the existence of these tiny nonconforming groups.

3

The Dark Side

From time to time strange sects arise which endeavor to strike
out extraordinary paths to eternal happiness.

Alexis de Tocqueville

The utopian societies were created inside another system, and their dependence on that system, and particularly on its laws, was sometimes quite clearly perceived.
"These little communities exist in the very heart of the
old Society," a nineteenth century newspaper editor
said. "They are surrounded on every side by its laws, its
habits and its atmosphere," finding around them "mar-
kets for their produce; laws for the repression of crime;
penalties for attempted fraud . . . and a place into which
they may expel all troublesome members."[1]

But each of the protections available to the communities from the outside society was also a potential threat,
for as the communities could invoke the law in their own
behalf, others could invoke the law against the communities. Laws to punish crimes, penalties for fraud, and
places into which the communities might expel members—all might be turned around: The utopians might
be the criminals, they might be the ones accused of
fraud, and their expelled members might have assorted
grievances to present to the courts of the outside world.

There are indications in the law reports of a considerable range of litigation involving the utopians. The necessity of living a daily life in the world was common to

all the societies and gave rise to a quite ordinary sort of civil litigation. We find commercial litigation involving the Shakers (one case is still cited in legal discussions of contract damages),[2] and a suit for failure to pay for goods delivered (Icaria).[3] Reports of civil litigation of this type may illuminate the activities or conditions of the utopians, but in the decisions themselves it seems to hardly matter that utopian communities were involved at all. There is also a range of legal activity in which it very much mattered that utopians were parties. In legislative investigations, certain civil actions, and certain criminal actions, it was precisely the essential features of the community that were under attack.

We are accustomed to thinking well of the utopians, seeing them as sincerely motivated individuals working collectively to accomplish fundamentally commendable objectives.[4] But in their own time the communities were viewed more critically. In his unsigned review of the Nordhoff account of the societies, Henry James noted that Nordhoff had written in a "friendly spirit." It would have been possible, James suggested, "for an acute moralist to travel over the same ground as Mr. Nordhoff and to present in consequence a rather duskier picture of human life at Amana, Mount Lebanon, and Oneida."[5] Some of the objections were aesthetic. "One is struck, throughout Mr. Nordhoff's book," James wrote, "with the existence in human nature of lurking and unsuspected strata, as it were, of asceticism, of the capacity for taking a grim satisfaction in dreariness." As to the Shakers, he notes that Nordhoff has explained everything except how "twenty-five hundred people . . . can be found to embrace a life of such organized and theorized aridity."[6] But some of his other objections were moral. James's observations on Oneida, for example, go far beyond concerns about asceticism and dreariness. Oneida's "industrial results are doubtless excellent," James wrote, "but morally and socially it strikes us as simply hideous."[7]

SOCIAL FORMS

The idea that there was something fundamentally wrong about Oneida, for example, is not altogether uncommon. Like the Mormons, the Perfectionists formed a new family pattern, in this case called "complex marriage." The celibate Shakers were able to find something positive to say about complex marriage. "While it is far from Shakerism," they wrote, "it is, we truthfully believe, vastly purer than some of the most respectable marriages of today."[8] But few others who observed it seem to have found much good in Oneida's system of group marriage. The *Woman's Journal* denounced it as based on polygamy and incest and leading to the subjection of women.[9] Complex marriage was linked with Mormon polygamy as a horror of the age, to be suppressed if at all possible.

In the case of Oneida there was an additional problem in the group's practice of human genetic engineering. Oneida was in some respects, a nineteenth century gynecologist commented, a "great physiological experiment."[10] The enterprise was called stirpiculture, and the idea was that the community itself would approve applications for parenthood, so that people could be bred as animals were, for better traits. The world's "best thinkers," Hinds explained to an imaginary questioner, "are now demanding that at least as much scientific attention shall be given to the physical improvement of mankind as has been given to the sheep, the horse, cow, and hog."[11] Perhaps so, but the practices of Oneida aroused a certain outrage. "Nothing is surer," *The Nation* wrote in

1879, "than that the Oneida system of complex marriage was a reversion to barbarism"; "pretensions" concerning stirpiculture "did nothing to extenuate it."[12] T. W. Higginson identified the idea as Greek, though noting that it was held by the Perfectionists as Christian, and then the well-known reformer indicated that he abhorred the theory since it would result in suffering and would "defeat its own end, by omitting from these unions all deep personal emotions."[13] Women were as degraded at Oneida as in Utah, argued Professor John Mears, a leader in the anti-Oneida campaign. There is no question, he said, of the "effect of both these systems upon the unfortunate creatures who have been drawn into their toils." Despite the claim of the utopians to be opening possibilities for the future, it was clear to Mears that "the path of progress and of social evolution does not lie across those bogs of uncleanness."[14]

Underlying the attacks on Oneida was the idea that the practices of the community were not only immoral but also unnatural, and violative of the rules of familial relationships.

Questions were also raised concerning the Shakers. All who become Shakers must lead lives of celibacy, the Ohio legislature said in 1811, "in consequence of which women have been abandoned by their husbands, robbed of their children, and left destitute of the means of support."[15] And even aside from the claims of the mother, there was concern about the welfare of children placed in Shaker custody.[16] For some, the underlying thought was that the environment provided by the celibates was inherently unsuitable. Perhaps it might be better for any child to be raised outside the system of the Shakers, rooted, as it concededly was, in the rejection of the conventional social ties viewed by the outside world as the basis of society.

COLLECTIVISM

In their maintenance of common property, the communistic utopians carried to its furthest point a conception of economic relations which, sociologist Ferdinand Toennies suggested, is in some degree characteristic of all Gemeinschaft (communal) forms. "In all relationships of this kind," Toennies noted, "the strict exclusiveness of private property is frequently broken and modified, for instance, through gifts, hospitality, interest-free loans, and many kinds of unilateral or mutual aid."[17] But the communistic societies carried the cooperative idea to the point of total renunciation of private interest in property, rejection of the value of private accumulation of wealth, and total reliance on the collective for the provision of individual needs.

Even so, it seems that the communism of even the most successful communities was not particularly troublesome to the outside world. To begin with, their teaching of communistic doctrine was religious, explicitly based on the New Testament and the precedent of early Christianity. This was seen as unusual but essentially legitimate, since there could be disagreement among believers over whether the economic arrangements of the Apostles[18] should be taken as a direct model. Further, practical apostolic communism as presented in the religious utopias was neither revolutionary and directed toward a change in the outside system nor, on a mass basis, particularly attractive. Shaker celibacy, or Noyes's view that the Second Coming had already occurred in A.D. 70, as concomitants of the idea that wealth should be held in common, tended to reduce the threat of widespread emulation. But much more important, the communities did not seem a threat to the outside world, because they functioned as businessmen and capitalists in their relations with the external system, and not as communists at all. In the world of nineteenth century America the societies bought, sold, and accumulated like everyone else. Not only did they defend the idea of contract, but they linked it to the individual right to property, meaning the right of the individual to dispose of his property as he wanted to, by transfer, for example, to a communistic society. In recognition of this aspect of the communistic societies, the socialist Morris Hillquit carefully noted that the communism of the Harmonists, like that of the Shakers, was "limited to the members of their own community and church."[19] The Harmony Society, Hillquit wrote, "had practically evolved into a limited partnership of capitalists owning lands, oil-wells and stocks in railroad, banking and mining corporations."[20] We may note here that the economic success of the Harmonists is in a familiar tradition. Thus, Max Weber wrote of the Quakers and Baptists that they "believed their religious merit to be certified before all mankind by such practices as their fixed prices and their absolutely reliable business relationships. . . ." This reliability encouraged others to deal with them, and thus "the religious sectarians [became] wealthy, even as their business practices certified them before their God."[21]

Other communities also had an active economic life and were familiar to the outside world for their products as well as their doctrines. "The Shakers are widely known as an industrious and frugal sect," the *New York Times* commented in 1875, "believing in celibacy and garden seeds. . . . They present a sharp contrast to the Oneida Communists who believe in a great deal of marriage and who prefer rat traps to garden seeds."[22]

Still, these utopians were practicing communists, and by the time of the labor disorders of the mid-1870s Hinds found it necessary to include in his 1878 account of the American communistic communities a section distinguishing American communism from "European" and "international" communism. The latter was a communism of force and violence, he said, while the "Communism which has been practically illustrated in the United States during the last fourscore years is voluntary, peaceable, conservative." There is no violence to be feared from American communism, and if there were a strike or uprising or disorders or destruction "anywhere or of any kind, it may be safely assumed that communism, in the true American sense of the word, is in no manner responsible for it."[23] (Hinds may have been anticipating, rather than answering, an attack on this point. Professor Mears, for example, was careful to limit his denunciations of Oneida to issues of morality, and made plain that he had no objection in the case either of the Mormons or the Perfectionists to their existence "as experiments in the great problem of cooperation."[24])

The general point, however, is clear. The communistic societies offered themselves as models to the world, and believed, as a Zoarite expressed it, that "in Heaven there is only communism."[25] They simultaneously adopted the categories of the outside society in a peaceful accommodation to the American economic system.

AUTONOMY

But there was another important issue. Beliefs and practices aside, the mere existence of such communities, the simple fact of associations organizing separately, with systems of internal regulation, allegiances, and penalties, could itself cause concern. The Americans laugh at those who speak of parties, George Rapp suggested; but they did not always laugh. The concern with factions, parties, and secret societies is a constant theme, and not a simple one. For example, George Washington, who denounced factions and "self-created societies,"[26] was also a Mason.[27] Freedom of association—the multitude of associations that de Tocqueville noted—could present, at points, an obvious danger. Historian David Brion Davis concludes that American nativists tended to divide groups and denominations into those that demanded only "partial loyalty from their members, freely subordinating themselves to the higher and more abstract demands of the Constitution, Christianity and American public opinion,"[28] and those that "dominated a larger portion of their members' lives, demanded unlimited allegiance as a condition of membership and excluded certain activities from the gaze of a curious public."[29] It is apparent that the utopians fell rather on the wrong side of this line. At Oneida they tried to deal with the secrecy issue, and to reach the public for various purposes, through an intense program of publication. If it is the case that we are not known, Noyes wrote to an English newspaper in 1851, "it is not our fault."[30] The Perfectionists had published three annual reports, "several books and pamphlets,"[31] and a weekly newspaper. The Shakers also published widely. But no amount of publicity would finally answer the argument that the communities demanded a loyalty from their members beyond that given to most societies or churches. They were separated from the rest of society, and that itself was dangerous. Where the issue involved communitarians who participated in the civil system and who voted, the distress over the communities reached issues of political democracy and republicanism. Although the question of exercise of the franchise was one on which communities might differ, bloc voting itself was entirely consistent with some utopian ideas. As Professor Arndt has noted, "Since the aim of the Harmonists was to achieve perfect harmony and brotherly love in all things," they would finally agree also on the candidate to endorse.[32] But bloc voting—perceived as voting under direction—was anathema to the outside world. This concern with separatism was reinforced by assimilationist ideas, common in nineteenth century America. Thus, the *New York Times* argued in 1854 that the new immigrants should Americanize themselves. "They should imbue themselves with American feelings. They should not herd themselves together for the preservation of the customs, habits, and languages of the countries from which they came."[33]

The Germans, for example, were associated with ethnic preservation, and some tried at times to create a kind of new Germany in America.[34] A German asked in 1813: "What would Philadelphia be in forty years if the Germans there were to remain German and retain their language and customs?" The answer was that it would be "a German city, just as York and Lancaster are German counties. What would be the result throughout Pennsylvania and Maryland?" The result would be "an entirely German state" where the "beautiful German language would be used in the legislative halls and the courts of justice."[35] This ethnic separatism was carried through in the communities of the German utopians.

Separatism raised visible problems in the course of the immigration of the Russian Mennonites (they were originally Dutch, but spoke German after a stay in Prussia), who in 1874 wanted to enter the United States as a group of forty or fifty thousand, and asked for a separate tract of land to develop. They tried to be certain that their separateness would be preserved in America as, until shortly before, it had been in Russia. They approached both the Americans and the Canadians with their request, giving the following instructions to their delegates: They were to secure, if possible, guarantees including "religious freedom, and exemption from military service," and the "right to live in closed communities, with their own form of local government; and the use of the German language as they had been permitted to practice it in Russia."[36] The bill providing for land for the Russian Mennonites was extensively debated in the United States Congress in 1874. Finally no action was taken and the bill failed. The speech by Senator Edmunds of Vermont demonstrated that the objections to the Mennonite bill were, in his mind, fundamentally linked to the issues of association and group separatism. American history did not furnish a precedent for a bill of this type, he said. It never "occurred to the founders of this Government, or to those who have administered it heretofore, that the highest public policy—by which I mean the best progress of the Republic—would tolerate a species of legislation of this character, either for Mormon, or Shaker or Baptist or Episcopalian, or any religious or political sect or band of people whatever." The problem for Senator Edmunds had nothing to do with particular religious or political beliefs. Rather it was the idea "fundamental to successful republicanism," of a "homogeneous unity of the whole body of the citizens of a State divided into political parties, divided into sects, divided into social grades," but with everyone "in the body of the community living as friends and neighbors" and not separated by territorial or other distinctions. What sort of country would America be, Edmunds persisted, "if distinctions prevailed such as this bill proposes to set up, of locating men of special religions or special political or social ideas exclusively in one place?"[37] Others denied Edmunds's characterization of the bill and insisted on the good character of the Mennonites and their intention of becoming American citizens, but still the land bill did not pass.[38]

In the case of the Mennonites, issues of separation were linked to issues of land. Landowning, and particularly contiguous compact landowning, has a clear political significance since the "possessor of the surface to a certain degree 'owns all.' "[39] The landowners of a small independent self-contained community may, in fact, "practically control local politics, the schools, roads, churches, and community life." Landowning communities "may determine the religion, language and social customs" and may, finally, be "relatively impervious to outside influences."[40]

Land and separatism, together with religious fanaticism, might result in abuse of power. It was on this basis that Samuel Tilden attacked the Shaker society: "If its internal police extends to the supervision and control of the minutest personal concerns; if its fundamental law is an unqualified submission of its members to their irresponsible rulers, and if the penalty with which those rulers are armed is a forfeiture of all he possesses by any member who shall be ejected from or shall leave the association,—can it be that a society so constructed and possessing such powers shall not frequently work great individual wrong and oppression?"[41] In fact there were individuals in the nineteenth century who believed that the societies worked wrong and oppression, and these individuals sometimes appealed to the agencies of the state, seeking a remedy against the communities.

SANCTIONS

A culture may express itself in quite different ways on the acceptability of an internal community. It may express itself outside the law, through riots and mob violence, or it may in a variety of ways declare its views as the law. A legislature might declare the community practice invalid—by creating a new crime, for example. It might declare that children could not be apprenticed to the group, or hold that the transfers of wealth to such a group were invalid, or that societies could not possess more than a certain amount of land. Courts might act against such societies, independently of legislative action, in particular cases at the request of plaintiffs claiming to have suffered some particular injury. Courts might find that a particular transaction was void for one reason or another, or that an individual child was better placed outside the community than in it. Tests of acceptability might take the form of a struggle over conscientious objector status—an issue in the case of the Shakers particularly—or involve questions of corporate status.

Where a society had chosen to incorporate, and was able to do so under the laws of the state, it did so in the belief that the advantages of incorporation—perpetual existence as a corporate person—outweighed the disadvantages of state scrutiny. For what the state had granted it could take away. In the case of Icaria, Cabet himself, the founder of the community, petitioned the legislature asking for a repeal of the Icarian charter. (He was expelled by the community and soon after died.[42]) Disincorporation was a part of the story of the campaign against polygamy (see pp. 127-30), and the Amana litigation of 1906[43] was focused on the question whether the Amana community as a corporation should be dissolved because it had exceeded its corporate powers.

The nineteenth century utopians were familiar with the attempts of individuals to seek remedies against them through the legislatures. In the case of those asking for remedies against the Shakers, these attempts were to some degree successful, and the anti-Shaker activity of the early nineteenth century left its mark on the legislation of several states. Two different problems were presented to the legislatures regarding the Shakers. The first was the issue of the aggrieved member. Such problems arose, for example, early in the nineteenth century, when a petition was presented to the New York legislature by a group of seceders from the Shakers, who "complained that while they were living in the Community they could not see their relatives."[44] The second issue related not so much to the member as to his wife and children. The image here was of a wife abandoned by a now celibate husband; she is left to her fate in the world, while he, in the exercise of his piety, gives all his property to the religious group, and conceals their children in hiding places provided by the sect.

Ohio in 1811 and Kentucky in 1812 passed laws responding to what they saw as the problem of the abandoned wife. The Ohio law envisioned a man who "having joined in the marriage relation" then renounced the marital covenant or refused to live in the conjugal relationship by joining the celibate sect. The law voided any grants from such a man to the sect that "may tend to deprive his wife and children of that support to which they are entitled" and authorized an award of custody and control of children to a mother or guardian. The law also included a criminal provision (a $500 fine) directed at those who "with intent" to cause a married individual to "renounce the marriage covenant" entice or persuade a married man or woman to join a celibate sect, provided however, that the act was not to be construed as extending to "any person for delivering any public sermon, exhortation or address."[45]

Kentucky's law authorized divorce, removed custody of the children from the father, and provided that no conveyance by the father to the sect "would prevent the property . . . so given . . . from being subject to any decree . . . in favor of any wife, child or children." There would be no property decreed to the wife where she had either been "amply and fully provided for by the husband according to the full extent of his estate" or lived in "open adultery." There was also a provision for the issuance of a writ of habeas corpus in cases challenging the detention of a wife or child.[46]

One well-known encounter in New York arose out of the efforts of Eunice Chapman to obtain a legislative divorce from her Shaker husband and custody of her children. In 1817, New York debated a law to declare members of the Shaker sect "civilly dead." Such a law, a legislative committee said in recommending it, "would do little more than carry into effect the principles they profess to believe; and appears to be the only way of providing effectually, for the welfare and maintenance of the remaining part of the family who do not choose to join them."[47] The New York Shakers protested the recommendation: "As free citizens of a free state, and under a free constitution, we have an undoubted right to worship Almighty God as we believe to be most agreeable to his will, and to live such a life as our faith directs, for which we are answerable to God alone, so long as we do no moral injury to others." They denied that they had done injury. "We shrink not from investigation," they said. "Let them find those many women abandoned by their husbands and left to suffer, while their property is carried among the Shakers—Let them find those children who are abused and brought up in ignorance. With all the slanders of our enemies, they have never been able to prove a fact of this nature; for none exists."[48]

Jefferson thought that the search for a parallel to the anti-Shaker proposal would "carry us back to the times of darkest bigotry and barbarism." New York's Council of Revision (which reviewed the laws of the state of New York from 1777 to 1821) generally agreed. The legislation granting the Chapman divorce, together with its anti-Shaker provisions, was found inconsistent with the religious liberty guarantees of the New York State constitution. The Shaker tenet of celibacy might "be pitied as a delusion," the council said, "but it ought not to be regarded as a crime." The law was vetoed by the council although a less stringent version granting the divorce was ultimately adopted.[49]

The Shakers were again before the New York legislature in 1849, resisting an act to rescind the 1839 law that regulated the trusts under which they held land. Various petitions were presented to the "Select Committee on the subject of the Shakers" to the effect that the 1839 act "worked a serious evil to society" in that it permitted the Shakers to unite in a dangerous monopoly of the lands of New York, and that by its "teaching to the youthful minds who are placed among them," Shakerism tends "to lead into darkness rather than light." Witnesses were called who testified that the children of the society were "required to make open confession of their past sins, and were severely admonished against repetitions; that the general teaching of the Society is to convince the young that a departure from the Society or its faith, will be followed by disgrace and ruin." Thus, "deep-rooted fears" were created, and "many whose natural inclinations would lead them to leave the Society, after learning its general principles are deterred, lest the horrible consequences taught them, may follow."[50] After considering these charges, and testimony to the effect that the society lived strictly up to its principles of celibacy, frugality, temperance, and honesty, the committee concluded that the Shakers should be left alone. The Shakers were a religious society. Their "principles of religion and mode of worship may be sneered at, scorned or regretted," the committee said, but all must deny that the Shakers "are inhuman, and do not possess moral feelings." Thus the "panoply of our laws are over them, and they must be allowed, unmolested, to enjoy the free exercise of their religious devotions." The committee asked to be discharged from further consideration of the subject.[51]

An act of the Kentucky legislature was passed in 1828 at the request of former Shakers "aggrieved by the fraudulent conduct of those who hold the reins of government among the Pleasant Hill Shakers (see below, pp. 100–101)."[52] The act permitted those aggrieved to sue the Shakers as an entity, and to give notice by posting. The act was called "an act to regulate civil proceedings against certain communities having property in common" (1828) and provided that anyone having a claim in excess of fifty dollars against the Shakers could sue the community without naming the individuals in the community or serving process on them. Subpoenas founded on such bills were to be fixed on the door of the meeting house of the community and delivered to a member of the community. The legislation specifically stressed that it addressed only the procedure of the litigation and not its substance. No member would have any rights that he "would not have had if this act had not passed." Such rights would "depend upon and be determined by the laws, covenants and usages of such society, and the general laws of the land."[53]

The Shakers protested the law, noting that "almost the first notice" they had of the existence of the legislation "was from a display of its authorities on our house of worship."[54] They wondered how any legislature could "claim a right . . . to intrude into the sacred asylum of our church order," inasmuch as "even 'Congress shall make no law concerning [respecting] an establishment of religion or prohibiting the free exercise thereof.' "[55]

Robert Wickliffe of Fayette County, Kentucky (who was considered the "most successful real estate lawyer and the wealthiest member of the bar in the State"),[56] urged the repeal of the statute in a lengthy speech before the Kentucky General Assembly in January 1831.[57] He noted that the fourth section of the bill, to the effect that the act related to process and not substance, had been added late, and that the section "arrested the main design of the authors of this bill . . . [since] they intended by giving actions against the society to its discontented members, without reserve, to strip it of every vestige of support."[58] Wickliffe suggested that he saw a parallel between Kentucky's anti-Shaker legislation and legislation concerning "free people of color." If you attempt to put down vices, he said, "your very words and thoughts are weighed in scruples." Such nuisances are said to have their rights. "Take care of your constitution, take care of the rights of persons. But only introduce a bill to punish a poor negro, and it would seem as if we had neither mercy nor constitution." He concluded that "there is something so debasing in the thought of oppressing the weak, that my very soul revolts at it." The Shakers "are few in numbers; they do not vote; and hence it is that you trample upon them."[59]

In 1848, in New Hampshire, the Shakers faced another legislative attack.[60] Petitions had been submitted to the legislature that requested "the passage of a law prohibiting the binding of minor children to the Shakers, providing for the support of the wife and children of husbands joining the society, and for the remuneration of the services of persons leaving the same." The petition also requested provision for "notice to the friends of such persons belonging to that society of their illness and for the publication of the death of deceased persons belonging to the said society." Represented by General Franklin Pierce, the Shakers resisted. Dramatically suppressive legislation was not enacted, while a moderate remedy (reduction in the waiting period for divorce) designed largely to protect the spouse of a Shaker, rather than the Shaker himself, was adopted.

The Shakers were not, however, the only utopian group investigated. There were, for example, proceedings involving the Harmonists in the legislature of Pennsylvania, initiated by Jacob Schriber, a former member of the Harmony Society, whose lawsuit against the patriarch George Rapp formed only one part of his campaign against the society. Jacob Schriber's* petition (1827) indicated that he had entered the association at seventeen and stayed twenty years. He contributed no property, and the present claim was for compensation for service. His petition to the legislature urged that the inhabitants of the Harmony Society were "suffering the greatest injustice and imposition, contrary to the spirit of the constitution."[61] Schriber alleged that there were persons who "through ignorance [had] been drawn into the slavery of George Rapp," under the delusion of being joint partners. But when they wished to withdraw, "they found they were mistaken and were not allowed one cent for their services."[62]

The Pennsylvania committee noted that it would not presume to affirm or deny these charges. The committee believed that the charges "were clearly legitimate subjects of judicial inquiry."[63] "If Mr. Schri[b]er has, voluntarily, entered into a contract with Mr. Rapp individually, there can be no doubt of his obtaining redress in a court of law, if by the terms or nature of his contract he be entitled to it."[64] But, the committee said, if his agreement was with the society itself, it was "absolutely void," since the society "having no charter of incorporation, they have no legal existence," and could make no contract or sue or be sued.[65] (It was this point particularly that interested the Kentucky Shakers, who included an account of the Harmonist inquiry in the defense of their order that they "addressed to the political world" in 1828, noting some similarities between the groups at Economy and at Pleasant Hill.)

If Jacob Schriber had made a contract that turned out to be disadvantageous, the Pennsylvania judiciary committee said, "it is his own fault." That contract "can

---

*This name is variously spelled Schriber, Schriver, and Schreiber.

neither be cancelled by the legislature nor can they create a new one for him." That Jacob Schriber "should have spent twenty years in the prime of his life in the service of the society and then leave it, may perhaps be regarded as a serious evil; but it was one which was brought upon him by his own act."[66] The committee concluded that it would not say whether the cause of human happiness was advanced by associations such as that of the Rappites. Nor would they ask whether the society "has been brought together . . . through superstition, ignorance or design." If it were true, a Christian or philanthropist might lament, but "no power in this government can shackle the free operations of the mind, in its religious exercises, or prevent any free-man from disposing of his property or services as may seem to him right."[67] The committee asked that it be discharged from further consideration of the subject.

Oneida, too, was concerned late in its history with a demand for legislative intervention. The community insisted that its institutions violated no existing laws of the state of New York, but was well aware that these laws might be changed. In the case of Oneida, the demand was for the legislature to act against complex marriage, and the demand was made not by an aggrieved former member, but by some of the clergy of upper New York State.

"Complex marriage" had given trouble to the outside world from the start. Noyes and some others had left Vermont because Noyes had been arrested and charged with adultery. "As the pilgrim fathers fled from old England to New England," the Perfectionists said, telling their story in the *Circular*, "so in 1848 the leaders of the Oneida Community fled from New England to New York."[68] Shortly after in New York there were grand jury investigations of possible immorality at Oneida, but they came to nothing.[69] The Perfectionists "were much despised in the first years of their settlement," they wrote of themselves in the *Circular* in 1867, "but God prospered them, and they went steadily forward . . . until they are now after eighteen years, in a fair way to be as respectable as their Puritan forefathers."[70] They were too optimistic. The community felt the impact of federal law with the passage of the Comstock Act in 1873, forbidding the mailing of obscene material, including information relative to contraception. The act ended Oneida's distribution of material on male continence. Then, the campaign of the clergy against the community, with its emphasis on the desirability of legislative action against Oneida, intensified with the success of the anti-Mormon campaign and the *Reynolds* decision of January 1879. This external pressure, combined with considerable internal dissension, resulted finally in the voluntary abandonment of the institution of complex marriage in August 1879. The Perfectionists had seen "that the stubbornness of the Mormons had arrayed the whole power of the law and incited activity against them." While the Perfectionists disclaimed a likeness to Mormonism, they would not "be blind to the lessons which the Mormon conflict with the law affords."[71]

Immediately after the abandonment of complex marriage, it was apparent to some that the utopian Oneida had come to an end. *The Nation* commented that the compromise over complex marriage might soon be "succeeded by a crisis involving property rights in which no compromise will be possible." The spirit of individualism would operate to "convert the Community into a joint stock corporation, with liberty to withdraw and sell-out." With the end of complex marriage at Oneida, *The Nation* concluded, a "revolution has taken place: the Community as it was has suffered a mutilation which practically destroys its identity, and will by the coming historian be added to the list of extinct Utopias."[72] The prediction was accurate. By 1881 the community was a joint stock company.[73]

In 1879 a Mormon argued that the declaration by the government that Mormon polygamy was a crime might well have consequences for the practices of other religious groups. Once government entered the domain of conscience, he said, there was no way to predict where that intervention would stop. If the government could say to the Mormons that their marriages were not religious, it could conclude that the Shakers and Roman Catholic priests must marry, since celibacy was no more religious than polygamy.[74]

This in fact did not happen. Shaker celibacy was called delusion or fanaticism, but it was not labeled a crime.[75] The religious communism of the common-property societies was considered more or less admirable, but it was not suppressed. Sometimes legislators, when asked to act against the societies, refused to act at all. Sometimes, when they did act (notably in the case of the Shakers) the remedies they enacted were directed more to the protection of families left in the world than they were directed against the group itself. Thus, what did not happen is as important as anything that did happen. The legislatures did not force the utopias to reimburse seceders; they did not refuse the communities permission to raise children (subject to the discussion above concerning the Shakers); and they did not, even in the case of Oneida, move to close down the communities.[76]

But the failure of the legislatures to act definitively against the societies was not the end of the question. For example, the legislatures might not act generally on the issue of giving children to the Shakers, but specific courts would act in specific cases. Celibacy, or some other noncriminal behavior, might have been considered in some other forum—and in fact was—and action of some other kind might well have been taken against it.

One can illustrate the role of the courts with litigation involving child custody issues. Stephen Ball was a man who had become a Millerite.[77] His wife having died, Ball abandoned his children—two girls, eight and six—who stayed with his mother. The children were later taken to the mother of Ball's deceased wife. Ball then joined the Shakers and sued to get his children to live with him in the Shaker community. They did not want to go.[78] One court that dealt with the case—the Superior Court of Cincinnati—was particularly and detailedly concerned with the issue of natural affection. The "bonds of 'natural affection' would be cut asunder," the court said, "to be supplied by the mystic, may I not say the metaphysical tie of universal philanthropy, and the endearing relation of father and daughter dissolve in the cold and distant relation of fraternal brother and sister."[79] Thus the Ohio court left the children with their grandmother, over the claims of a Shaker father who, under the general rule of law, would clearly have been entitled to the custody of his children. The judge explained his deviation from the normal rule: "He seeks them that he may sever them from the bosom of their grandmother, and from his own bosom, and plant them in the cold ascetic bosoms of the 'female-caretakers.' " All this, the court said, "might be done by an honest man, and a pure man. But can it be done by a sane man? Does it not argue, at least, a morbid state of the amative and philoprogenitive faculties, bordering on insanity and totally inconsistent with a rational discharge of parental duty?"[80] Stephen Ball's case was seen as falling into an exception to the general custody rule to the effect that if a father were found "grossly immoral, intemperate, imbecile, insane, or otherwise disqualified to discharge the obligation of providing,"[81] the law would not award him custody of his children.

At about the same time, a case was decided in New York concerning the three sons of William Pillow, aged fourteen, eleven, and nine. The children had been bound to the Shaker Edward Fowler of New Lebanon as apprentices until the age of twenty-one. They stayed with the Shakers until December 1847, when their father took them to New York City. Edward Fowler initiated a petition of habeas corpus, seeking enforcement of the indentures. Counsel for the father, William Pillow, argued (*inter alia*) that the indentures of the children were in "violation and restraint of the rights of conscience of the infants, and of their freedom of religious belief."[82] The three boys were to be raised according to the principles of the Shakers. The apprentice system was "the means used by the shakers [*sic*] to augment their population and continue the existence of their community, while they do away with the marriage relation. Their association and all that upholds it, are contrary to good morals and void, and in this respect are repugnant to the laws regulating marriage." A "Rev. Mr. Lee" also spoke for the father of the apprenticed children, and the principles of the Shakers were again attacked. "The infants are to be brought up in a dark and fatal superstition, in the belief in verbal confession as the avenue to heaven, that spirits may be brought back and new revelations have been and will be made and in other nonsense."[83]

Justice Sandford responded. To begin with, there was no evidence on the point, but even if there had been, the result would be the same. "Whatever may be my own views of the principles and the supposed practices of that society, I have no right to act upon them in administering justice, so long as their practices do not infringe upon the municipal law." As to the religious beliefs of the Shakers, the court said that "fanaticism is no crime, nor subject to any punishment," and William Pillow "had as perfect a right to bind his children to a Shaker, with the intent to have them brought up in that sect, as he had to bind them with a similar intent to a Presbyterian or a Roman Catholic."[84] There was no legal objection to the existence of the Shaker community, and "I am admonished that it has the sanction of legislative enactments made for its protection in its rights of property, after an examination of its affairs and practices by a legislative committee."[85] The judge inquired into the wishes of the boys and, finding that the two younger children wished to stay with their father, he "directed them to be delivered to him; and the eldest wishing to return to the Shakers with his master, the judge ordered that he be permitted to do so, and that the officer in attendance protect him in his departure."[86]

In 1870, a New York court described again the objections that might be made to the Shakers as custodians of children, noting that the doctrines of the sect, "based upon what are regarded by the mass of Christians as erroneous and fanatical views of the gospel, lie at the foundation of the order, and have been taught and practiced from its first existence."[87] And yet, the court noted, "the legislature and the courts have not thought that these peculiarities of faith and practice were so obnoxious and detrimental to individual well-being or the public good as to deprive members of the community of the care, education and training of children legally committed to their care and custody by parents and guardians."[88]

Thus, two levels of sanction are involved in the child custody cases, legislative and judicial. Legislatures may refuse to say that, in general, children are not to go to the Shakers, yet in specific litigated cases the issue may arise and be debated again in the courts. So too in the question of the utopian contracts. Seceders had at various times approached legislatures asking in effect for statutes invalidating the forfeiture provision of the utopian contracts. In this they did not succeed, but the courts were still available as a forum to test the issue.

In the enforcement of contracts the state is involved in a function that is in one sense akin to minimal peace-keeping, like the prevention of theft and murder.[89] Yet in the enforcement of contracts judgments of the most serious political consequence are also sometimes made, judgments that approach questions of governance and go to the broadest questions of the nature of the state and the relationship of internal communities to the state.[90]

Part 2

Utopian Contracts

§1. Contract Defined

A contract is a promise or a set of promises for the breach of which the law gives a remedy, or the performance of which the law in some way recognizes as a duty.

Comment:

a. Other Meanings. The word "contract" is often used with meanings different from that given here.

Restatement of Contracts 2d (1973)

4

Free and Binding Contract

Whensoever a man transferreth his right, or renounceth it; it is either in consideration of some right reciprocally transferred to him; or for some other good he hopeth for thereby. For it is a voluntary act: and of the voluntary acts of every man, the object is some *good to himself*. . . .

The mutual transferring of right, is that which men call CONTRACT.

Thomas Hobbes

The utopian societies were created by voluntary acts, the acts of individuals who joined the societies. These acts were contractual, involving the volitional assumption of obligation. The contractual act is free and binding. Some of the utopians made formal use of the legal institution of contract, which they, along with many others, considered fundamental to Western society. Thus, Kessler and Gilmore note that "most of us take contract for granted. Together with family and property, as we feel, contract is one of the basic institutions of our social fabric."[1] The American utopians who would have disagreed as to property and the family, at least as conventionally defined, would have agreed as to contract. James Towner, a lawyer who became a member of the Oneida community, wrote, "Among the institutions that have been evolved in the progress of society is the institution of Contract." Contracts, he said, "form a large part of the transactions between men in civilized society, and upon their observance or enforcement the existence and improvement of such society in a great measure depends."[2]

The Shakers were also exponents of the view that contract lay at the foundation of society. Any act that would annul the Shaker contract, Shakers wrote, would be "wrong and altogether immoral in its tendency, as it would, in effect, destroy all covenants or agreements, deeds and obligations." Indeed, the "whole foundation of social compact or intercourse between man and man would be swept away," and "breach of promise would be no more wrong."[3] A former Shaker wrote along the same lines. Without the recognition of contract, he said, all contracts, deeds, and notes "would be mere scribblings, the loss of whose virtues would convulse, overturn and eventually destroy the monetary, social and moral world."[4] A similar loyalty to the idea of contract is evident in Article 35 of the Icarian constitution of 1851: "No one is free to violate an *agreement* freely made, an engagement freely contracted"[5]

The utopian defense of the principle of contract was focused on one particular kind of contract, called here a utopian contract. Towner called it a "Community contract" and defined it generally as "a contract between two or more to live in Community and to give up all they have or may earn to the Community."[6]

Not all utopian communities used contracts, and of those who did, some did not always use them. The utopian contracts that were used might be elaborate on matters such as conditions for admission or governance of the community; or they might be addressed almost entirely to the question of rights of withdrawing members. Communities that had contracts or constitutions governing relations with members might make changes in the instrument. Owens's New Harmony had, according to one account, seven constitutions or contracts in under two years.[7] Sometimes the changes drastically affected the rights of withdrawing members, as when the Harmony Society in 1836 replaced a provision for refund of property brought into the community by seceding members with language in which such claims were given up as a matter of right. The constitutions might deal with one class of member only, or might provide for several classes of membership, as at Zoar and among the Shakers, with different consequences attached to membership in different classes. In their agreements, utopian communities took a variety of approaches to the question of withdrawal and expulsion of members, and the actual practice of the communities might be different from the arrangement specified in the formal contracts.

An essential secular function of the contracts was to secure the property of the societies—property held as private wealth—against the claims of outsiders of any kind. There is no paradox, and no hypocrisy, in the simultaneous commitment of the common-property societies to a religiously based community of goods and to a legal defense of private property. Certainly property was necessary if they were to meet their covenantal obligations, but even more fundamentally, property was a necessary precondition of their existence. Charles Reich, writing in 1962, described property as a "legal institution, the essence of which is the creation and protection of certain private rights in wealth of any kind." One of the functions of property is to "draw a boundary between public and private power."

> Property draws a circle around the activities of each private individual or organization. Within that circle, the owner has a greater degree of freedom than without. Outside, he must justify or explain his actions, and show his authority. Within, he is master, and the state must explain and justify any interference. It is as if property shifted the burden of proof; outside, the individual has the burden; inside, the burden is on government to dem-

onstrate that something the owner wishes to do should not be done.[8]

The successful communistic societies wanted legally enforceable contracts. A statement of intentions and motives, standing alone, might satisfy religious purposes but still be too general and too undefined to be enforced in a civil suit. For example, one might see difficulty in judicial enforcement of the good intentions and imprecise commitments of the Covenant of the Christian Commonwealth,[9] a community of about three hundred that lasted four years. Members of the group were asked (though not required) to sign the following:

> I accept as the law of my life Christ's law that I shall love my neighbor as myself. I will use, hold, or dispose of all my property, my labor and my income according to the dictates of love for the happiness of all who need. I will not withhold for any selfish ends aught that I have for the fullest service that love inspired. As quickly as I may be able I will withdraw myself to the cooperative life and labor of a local Christian Commonwealth. As a member of this organization, I will work according to my ability in labor together with God, for the production of goods for human happiness.[10]

The communistic societies demanded both more specificity and more compliance with the demands of the legal system. The Shakers were clear about the reasons for legally enforceable contracts. Laws are "various in different states," they said, "but in all countries mutual agreements, and written contracts supersede the interference of civil authorities."[11] They concluded that "mutual agreements in things lawful is, therefore, our only resource for the defense of our civil rights."[12]

The right to contract was secured (and in this sense limited) to certain categories of persons, and the law provided certain additional requirements to transform mere agreements into legally enforceable contracts. Towner outlined the legal requirements:

> In order that a contract may be valid or binding it is requisite that it be made between parties that are capable, of sufficient age and understanding, and having the free exercise of their will at the time of making it. Idiocy, insanity, drunkenness, fraud, infancy and marriage to a limited extent, avoid contracts; and a party must not be under restraint, as by threats of personal injury or by imprisonment.[13]

Further, a contract "must be made upon sufficient consideration," which is a "price, motive, or inducement, which caused the promise to be made."[14] Thus, an "agreement to pay or do a thing, on one side, without any compensation on the other is wholly void in law," but, in general, any consideration, no matter how small, would be treated as adequate.[15]

For the contract to be valid, finally, the consideration could not be illegal, and the contract itself could not be contrary to public policy. "The object of the law being the repression of vice and immorality and the promotion of the welfare of society, all promises which originate in a breach or violation of its principles and enactments are void." The law will not "lend its aid to enforce any contract which will lead to the commission of crime or immorality or which is subversive of public morality."[16]

Although certain legal systems have adopted the view that promises of a serious nature ought to be enforced merely because they were seriously made, the American (and English) view came to be that the promise ought not to be enforced unless it was supported by some contribution coming (broadly speaking) from the other side. This theory, the so-called bargain theory of consideration (meaning that something bargained for is given in exchange) is a component part of traditional discussions in the Anglo-American law of contracts.[17]

The communists argued that "consideration" for their particular contracts existed without any doubt, since the central idea of the contracts involved exchange. The idea of exchange is clearly expressed in the explanation of the contract (quoted earlier) by John Humphrey Noyes: "Those who give their property to the Community receive in return a guarantee of maintenance for themselves and their families for life in this world."[18] And here is a discussion of the covenant by the Shakers: The signer is to be "devoted to the upholding and up-building of Society."[19] On its part, the society "does not invite this consecration without giving us a solemn assurance that it takes us 'for better or for worse, in sickness and in health,' in old age, and through unforeseen accidents and difficulties so long as we fulfill our part of the 'compact' to which we, at a mature age, have understandingly and voluntarily attached our signatures."[20] This extract refers explicitly to the requirements of the overriding state legal system—competency, voluntarism, and exchange—and also contains a significant echo of the marriage contract.

To say that the contractual form was intended to be legally binding is to say that, in principle, a member might sue a society for a breach of its part of the bargain. Thus it was said that while a member observes the Shaker covenant, "he has an absolute right to his support in health and in sickness, from youth to old age." His rights cannot, however, "be left in the mere voluntary keeping of his Covenant brethren."[21]

> Should the devil ever creep into these harmless villages as he once crept into Eden and fill the brethren with quile and selfishness so that they should deny protection and support to a worthy brother, however little of this world's goods he might have brought to the institution,

and though he may have for years lain helpless on their hands and be forever disabled from future labor; his right under the Covenant to his share of the consecrated property would be enforced, by any court, however little it might sympathize with the religious faith or practice of the believers.[22]

But there is always also the underlying notion that an unworthy member would not be entitled to maintenance, no matter how old, weak, or poor. Oneida's guarantee of support, John Humphrey Noyes wrote, could be forfeited only by "gross violations of the rights of the Community, such as personal withdrawal, or acts of insubordination and hostility that are equivalent to withdrawal."[23] But the point is that the right of support could be forfeited. And then the conventional lawyers' questions arise, substantive and procedural: Who is worthy? and Who will decide? A resolution of the second may eliminate the need, in any particular forum, to decide the first.

To say that the contractual form was intended to be legally binding is also to say that, in principle, a society might sue a member for breach. If the contract was not specifically enforceable (meaning that a court would refuse to compel a member to perform labor), damages could conceivably have been awarded, based, for example, on the value of the sustenance provided by a society to a member who had refused to perform his part of the arrangement.[24]

From the point of view of the law, the community was created by the agreement of individuals. The assumptions of the legal discussion were very much the same for the courts, the lawyers, and the communities. The general principle was that contracts freely made should be enforced. But even a contract freely made for good "consideration" could in some cases be avoided. A court might refuse to enforce it for a number of reasons, one being that the contract was against public policy. Here the utopian communists would be squarely up against the question whether the outside world viewed their arrangements as somehow detrimental to the public interest, or harmful to the individuals participating in the movements, so that, like the innocent victims of polygamy, the communitarians would have to be protected against themselves.

The utopian contracts were legal contracts, and thus fit into the mold of contracts between the parties called A and B, X and Y in the law books—buying and selling, promising and return promising.

But the legal face of these contracts was only one of several. In their legal aspect, the contracts would be measured by "pure" contract doctrine, an area, as Professor Lawrence Friedman writes, of "abstract relationships, . . . blind to details of subject matter and person." The doctrine of the law of contracts "does not ask who buys and who sells, and what is bought and sold. . . . Contract law is abstraction—what is left in the law relating to agreements when the particularities of person and subject-matter are removed."[25] In the case of the utopian contracts, although they had certain features of ordinary contracts, it seems likely that no judge entirely forgot—though he might choose to ignore—their very special nature: They were contracts binding on individuals, which created a collective property; they were the contracts of individuals, but also the covenants of churches and the constitutions of miniature states.

5

Covenant As Contract

I have set My bow in the cloud, and it shall be for a token of
a covenant between Me and the earth.

Genesis 9:13

The forms of the utopian societies were rooted in early
Protestantism, as well as early Christianity. H. Richard
Niebuhr, summarizing the characteristics of some institutional systems deriving from sixteenth century and
seventeenth century Protestantism, noted that the idea
that all religious institutions are "contractual in origin
and essence" is fundamental. In their relations to the
state, such religious societies conceived of themselves, in
extreme cases, "as an alternative to the political unit,
which likewise was regarded as contractual in nature."
The society would assume "responsibility for disciplin-
ing its members without appeal to the police powers of
the state," as well as for "settling intramural disputes in
its own courts." The society "forbade recourse to state
courts as well as participation in the military, judicial or
administrative functions of the state."[1] The structures
described by Niebuhr are recognizably those of some of
the American utopians.

An essential feature of the Anabaptist idea, held also
by others of the left wing of the sixteenth century Protestant Reformation, was that the true church is made up
of regenerate adults. One could not be born into a
church; one would, as an adult, choose it. In this regard,
the religious utopians can be seen as heirs of the radical

Reformation. Thus, Professor Franklin Littell suggested that many of the utopians stood in "the Free Church line, stemming directly from some point along the line of Anabaptist, radical Puritan, Pietist, voluntaryistic development."[2] A central feature of the Anabaptist idea was mutual aid, understood not only in theory but in practice as the sharing of goods and possessions. He notes that some of the utopians, like the Anabaptists, were "restitutionary" in orientation, that is, interested in the restitution of the true church of early Christianity. Separatist English Puritans also stressed that "a church must be a voluntary association of persons worthy to worship God," containing "only men who freely professed to believe, and tried to live according to, God's word."[3]

The idea of a voluntary church, a body of the faithful gathered out of the world, assumed legal form in the case of the four communistic societies. It is perhaps clearest in the case of the Shakers, who used the traditional church covenant and fused the legal and religious forms, so that the regenerate adult who joined the church was also the adult in civil law, the individual with legal capacity to contract. The merger of the two is a document called the Shaker covenant.

The theological aspect of the Shaker covenant is expressed clearly in the Shaker religious work, *The Testimony of Christ's Second Appearing*. The Shakers wrote that the covenant signed by the members was not the covenant itself. The contract was only evidence of what was crucial. "The internal spirit and substance of the Covenant is more than ever was, or ever will be, written with paper and ink, being the fulness of the law of Christ, written by the Spirit of God in the heart, and on the mind of every true member of his Church."[4] The spirit of the covenant was not contrary to the form, but was distinct from any written form. But it is also true that the "law of Christ written by the Spirit of God" had become a matter of civilly enforceable right, no longer dependent only on the churches or religion, but involving the state as well. Awareness of the legal aspects of the covenant is visible in the Shakers' "covenant hymn" (1813), which was published with this note: "This hymn was publicly used in the Church, both at Union Village and at Pleasant Hill, so that no room was left for any to say that the covenant was not well understood";[5] that is, understood by those who signed, or would sign, and would be then unable to say in court that they had been misled. Legal and religious themes are as evident in a much later description of the covenant published in *The Shaker* in February 1877.[6] The record of the covenant "is a written *Instrument*," carefully drawn "in behalf of sin-sick souls," the "heavily laden of the race, who have cast off their burdens of sin." The Shaker covenant "is a sure, temporal *Privilege*: so long as any acceptable member keeps this league inviolate," and a "spiritual *Protection*," the "*Conservatory* of the most sacred vows ever consecrated unto God or a godly life." Most pointedly, and invoking the state sanction, the Shakers note that the covenant is "strongly guarded from the aggressions of envious, jealous and vituperative backsliders."[7]

The religious motivation of the Shaker covenant and the merger of religious and legal forms is exceptionally clear. For other groups the formal contract was more a matter of expediency. "The real binding force" of the Harmony Society, Professor Arndt writes, "was, of course, not this agreement but the special message implicit in the faith of the Society," to the effect that the Harmony Society was "the embodiment of the Sunwoman in St. John's vision" (Rev. 12:1) and that "harmony would follow the Second Coming of Christ, when all things would be restored to their original harmony."[8] But probably even here, the joining of the society and the signing of the written document were to some degree a metaphoric indication of the entering into covenantal relations in religious terms.

The transfer of property and the contribution of labor were also understood in religious terms.[9] "What we wish to say," an Oneida leader wrote an applicant for admission, "is not that we want the deed to your farm or the money it will procure, but we want a proof of you that you will stand the test of trial. . . . We want your company but we want it only under circumstances which will secure to you with us the crown of unfading love."[10] Similarly, from the perspective of the Shakers, the point was not that property was required for admission; on the contrary, property as property was not required for admission. Rather, total consecration of everything—person and property—was to be made on joining the highest order. This "full dedication and consecration of person and property" was not a requirement but a privilege, granted only "to such as have been the most faithful to comply with the terms of probation."[11]

Although in fact some combination of charity and caution often led the four communistic societies to make settlements or to return property brought in, they came to the position that, in principle, no part of the property should be returned and the commitment ought to be irrevocable. They argued that to concede the right of withdrawal would have had several deleterious effects. Not only would it weaken the bond of the community, but it would tend to defeat the religious ideas of union and equality on which the community was built, for to permit withdrawal of property brought in would have had the effect of maintaining, in communities dedicated to the eradication of economic inequalities, the values and distinctions of the outside world.[12]

The consecrated religious life was demanding in all ways, and the societies insisted that such a life had to be freely chosen. Voluntary admission and voluntary withdrawal were fundamental and had as their corollary the idea of internal discipline with expulsion as the ultimate sanction. The Shakers made the point clearly: "As all who unite with this Society do it voluntarily, and can at any time withdraw, they are in duty bound to submit to its government."[13] Members were "required by the rules of the Society to do this, or withdraw."[14] Join voluntarily, obey voluntarily—obedience also is "a matter of free choice," the Shakers said[15]—or leave. Disobey, refuse to leave, and be expelled.

Internal governance, too, may be traced to the covenantal ideas of the Reformation. Professor Littell has described the internal discipline of the sixteenth century communities that arose out of the radical Reformation. The outer limit of governance was expulsion or excommunication. The idea of a "covenantal relation to God and one's fellows," Professor Littell writes, "is the foundation of the 'Anabaptist' community, and through it comes the use of the Ban (spiritual government)."[16] The Ban was derived from a reading of the New Testament:

> Moreover if thy brother shall trespass against thee, go and tell him his fault between thee and him alone: if he shall hear thee, thou hast gained thy brother.
>
> But if he will not hear thee, then take with thee one or two more, that in the mouth of two or three witnesses every word may be established.
>
> And if he shall neglect to hear them, tell it unto the church: but if he neglect to hear the church, let him be unto thee as an heathen man and a publican.[17]

It is commonplace that the most successful of the utopian communities were religious undertakings. Acting as religious groups, the successful utopians imposed the internal discipline, sanctioned finally by expulsion, that had been used in such groups from the beginning. But in these societies this threat was all the stronger because it might in extreme cases involve not only the loss of a spiritual home but forfeiture of a life's work, as agreed upon in the contract, which would be enforced by the state.

The American utopias were like the sects described by Ernst Troeltsch, often aspiring "after personal inward perfection" and aiming at "direct personal fellowship between the members of each group." The attitudes of the sects toward the world, society, and the state, Troeltsch said, might be indifference, or toleration, or hostility, since the sects do not want to control these forms but rather to avoid them. The Church, Troeltsch suggested, tends to a degree to "accept the secular order"; the sect either tolerates the state or wants to replace it.[18] But the well-known church/sect distinction tends to break down in the American context. As church historian Philip Schaff suggested in 1855, where there was no national church there could be no dissenter.[19] And in America, the religious communistic utopians, although part of a dissenting and separatist religious tradition, were groups that accepted and even relied on the protection of the secular state. The Shaker covenant hymn refers to the problem of the seceders:

What shall then be done with those who by
transgresion fall
When they wickedly propose, their off'rings to recal
Can you treat their high demands
As sacralegious false and vain?
Yea I can with both my hands, and justice says, Amen.[20]

But finally it was not the utopians who would decide what should be done with the seceders, but the state.

6

The Social Contract

The major importance of legal contract is to provide a frame-work for well-nigh every type of group organization and for well-nigh every type of passing or permanent relation between individuals and groups, up to and including states.

Karl N. Llewellyn

The utopian contracts were also, almost literally, contracts of government. Man being free and equal, John Locke had written, he cannot be "subjected to the political power of another, without his consent." Consent is given by "agreeing with other men to join and unite into a community for their comfortable, safe and peaceable living, one amongst another, in a secure enjoyment of their properties, and a greater security against any that are not of it."[1] In forming their communities, the utopians invoked the idea of social contract to create new forms congenial to their purposes. The preamble of the Shaker covenant or constitution of the church at Hancock, Massachusetts, says that the Shakers of Hancock felt "the importance not only of renewing and confirming our spiritual covenant with God and each other, but also of renewing and improving our social compact."[2] And the agreement used by the Shaker community at Pleasant Hill, Kentucky, in 1830, carried the title "A Revision and Confirmation of the Social Compact of the United Society Called Shakers" and the subtitle "Have respect unto the Covenant; for the dark places of the earth are full of the habitations of cruelty—David."[3] A theological perspective on the covenant and a reference to Locke's view of the original consensual nature of government are found here together, in a single document, which provided the legal form of the Shaker community. The Kentucky Shakers disclaimed dependence on the forms of men. "In forming our religious association," they said, "we have not consulted the civil authorities of men, further than to see that we did not trespass upon their premises." The Shaker faith and forms were "not chartered by any legislative power of a political nature."[4] Their main policy, the Kentucky Shakers said, "is to keep out of the reach of the municipal law, by strictly observing all its just requirements,"[5] and by "arranging our social concerns" so as not to "interfere with the rights and privileges of others."[6] But the social contract was not merely one of the forms of men. It was somehow primordial,[7] and free from the taint of the world's institutions.

The "idea that men can fix their rights and duties by agreement is in its early days an unruly, anarchical idea,"[8] wrote Pollock and Maitland. But it may be that this was, to some degree, true in its later days as well. The idea of contract that underlies the Mayflower Compact and the American Constitution could, for example, be used to support secessionist thinking of both the Northern and Southern style. Southern secessionists argued that the Constitution was a contract and that, like any contract, it could be dissolved. William Lloyd Garrison wrote of the Constitution on the masthead of *The Liberator*: "A covenant with Death . . . an agreement with Hell";[9] and finally, "No union with slaveholders." A sentence of Thoreau's suggests yet another form of secession: "Some are petitioning the state to dissolve the union," he wrote. "Why do they not dissolve it themselves—the union between them and the State."[10] On this view of compact, John Humphrey Noyes withdrew from his union with the American government in 1837. He wrote to Garrison: "I have subscribed my name to an instrument similar to the Declaration of '76, renouncing allegiance to the government of the United States, and asserting the title of Jesus Christ to the throne of the world."[11] In a meeting with Garrison, Noyes urged "revolt of the whole North from the unholy compact, in the interest not simply of Anti-Slavery, but of the whole regeneration of society."[12] Whatever their effects may or may not have been on Garrison,[13] these ideas led Noyes to communitarianism and the striking resolution adopted at a Perfectionist convention held shortly before the establishment of Oneida: "Resolved, That it is expedient immediately to take measures for forming a heavenly association in central New York."[14] Soon after, the Perfectionists adopted Principles of Association, which described the enterprise this way: It "embraces and provides for all interests of its members, religious, political, social and physical [and] is at once a church, a state, a family and a business association."[15]

Although Noyes can be seen as having withdrawn from one government compact and entered another, it should be noted that Noyes himself would probably have denied that any political theory—including the theory of the social contract—was involved in the formation of Oneida. Noyes was not engaging in political or social experiments. Those who "are seeking the true form of government," he wrote, should "turn away from 'American institutions,' French theories and British predictions, toward the nation that God has founded in the heavens."[16] Noyes believed that the "true plan of Association, about which many in these days are busily scheming," was not a matter yet to be discovered. On the contrary, the "church of the first-born has been for ages working out in theory and practice, all the problems of social science."[17]

Plainly, there was no way for Oneida or any other utopian community to withdraw completely from the state. Even the Mormons, who came closest to trying—

going to the valley of the Great Salt Lake when it was part of Mexico—were absorbed into the American structure as a territory by 1850. And Noyes's community of Perfectionists was to be located not, after all, in the deserts of Utah but in central New York State. Noyes's adjustment to the reality of the secular state is reflected in a statement published in *The Perfectionist* in 1843: "We are resident foreigners," he said, "citizens not of the United States, but of the kingdom of Christ; and as such we claim the protection of the government of the United States, while we disclaim allegiance to it, and participation in its evil deeds."[18]

Not all the nineteenth century utopians took this view. Where the Perfectionists were resident foreigners, the Shakers were citizens. "In every place we are subject to the laws of the country in which we live. Those laws claim the same control over our temporal interest as over the interest of other citizens."[19] The followers of Etienne Cabet at Icaria envisioned short- and long-range relationships. Icaria was "destined to become a City and a State obedient to the general laws of the United States," but "in the meantime, it is obedient to the laws of the State of Illinois."[20] The Zoar articles themselves recognized state authority, making explicit reference to "a court of justice beyond the limits of the society."[21]

As all of these expressions make plain, there was no question about sovereignty in any legal sense. The utopian communities existed inside other governments— local, state, and national. The images of sovereignty are only images, but they are there, and they are telling. "A Shaker village is not only a new church, but a new nation," wrote the English observer William Hepworth Dixon.[22] In the elaborate formulations of the Icarians there is, following the constitution, a set of regulations for the Icarian General Assembly: "In every country," the document said, "the law concerning the General Assembly is one of the most important; since it regulates the making of all other laws. In Icaria especially, it is one of the fundamental laws and nearly constitutional. . . ."[23] Icaria was "destined to become a City and a State," but the image is of a nation among nations.

Sovereignty was in the state. What the community did by way of contract it did because the state allowed it that freedom. The state recognized and supported private orderings and adjustments, and specifically the enforcement of contracts. The contract would be reviewed in the state courts in the same way that other contracts dealing with any number of problems and between a diverse group of parties would be reviewed—as legal documents subject to legal doctrines. Sovereignty was in the state, and the contract was the law of the parties.

Part 3

The Fall from Utopia

When a person has resolved to live in communism, and has made his demand for admission into Icaria, the greatest prudence, the most serious reflection, should be exercised in the accomplishment of the act, which, by its good or bad results, may be classed among the most important acts of his life. . . .

For, let us not forget, enthusiasm is ephemeral! When its inspiration has passed, deceptions, discouragement, succeed to the enchantment and a prompt return to individualism is often the sad consequence of it.

> Preamble, Law Upon Withdrawal and Expulsion
> from the Icarian Community (1879)

7

Turning Away

Icaria does not escape the rule of illusions!

Preamble, Law Upon Withdrawal and Expulsion
from the Icarian Community (1879)

From the point of view of Oneida's founder, John Humphrey Noyes, Nathaniel Hawthorne was an apostate Puritan and, perhaps worse, an apostate Socialist. Hawthorne, Noyes wrote, joined Brook Farm and then, after "a short experience, in which he discovered that he was unfit for the rough beginnings of a new form of society, he withdrew from Brook Farm and thenceforward gave the enemies of Association the benefit of his talent for sneering."[1] Hawthorne's *Blithedale Romance* has "probably done more than the New York *Herald* to dishearten all attempts at social reform in this country."[2]

As Noyes well knew, Hawthorne was not alone in finding a utopian life uncongenial. While disaffected utopians might then join other groups—the tendency of the utopians to migrate between communities was noted early, and is used by Professor Bestor as evidence of the strength and unity of the communitarian tradition[3]—still it is to be assumed that some left the movement as a whole and did not return.

That there might some day be former members of their associations, whether through weakness or apostasy, seems to have been contemplated by at least some of the utopians from the moment of the formation of their communities. "It is our faith never to bring Debt or blame against the Church," the early Shakers said in their first written covenant (1795).[4] The promise itself seems to contemplate a possible falling away. The 1805 Harmony constitution provided for the contingency that a member "could not stand to it" and "would within a few or more years break [his] promises and withdraw from the community."[5] The 1819 Zoar constitution outlined the rights of "backsliding members." And Oneida, in 1848, provided for the "subsequent withdrawal of the member."[6]

At one level of thought the association of the members with the community was conceived of as permanent, a commitment for life. Withdrawal from the community, Oneida's *Circular* explained, "is, in its nature, like withdrawal from marriage, or from church membership, or from the national Union, i.e., it is a withdrawal from a connection which, when it was entered into, was understood to be for life."[7] But at another level, it was entirely apparent that one might "fall from Utopia as we fell from Eden."[8]

The Shakers have had "thousands of secessions," Hinds noted.[9] The number may be uncertain, but clearly it is true that there were many who attempted the Shaker way of life and then abandoned it. When the Shaker life "came to giving up 'the world,' with its human instincts and relationships, its ambitions and its tempting rewards, for a life that seemed to offer little else than self-denial, many of them backed away from the prospect."[10] The Shakers recorded the departures in entries like these, from the records of the Shaker Society in Pleasant Hill, Kentucky: "Lydia and Mary Secrest went to the world from the center family. Silly lambs, you will wish you were in the fold when the wolves get you."[11] "April 24, 1864: Illinois Green absconded from the West family. What a spectacle! Nearly 40 years old and starting out in the wide world hunting flesh!"[12] And after that: "When a person leaves us, we disregard them," a New Hampshire Shaker said, "and do not shake hands with them."[13]

Oneida knew withdrawing members,[14] as did Zoar from the beginning of its history. Although Nixon reports that there is little detail available concerning the Zoar withdrawals, some records remain, revealing notations like "Left Zoar wilfully. . . . on account of dissatisfaction" or "Left without notice" or "Left by Mutual Agreement of both parties."[15] In the case of George Rapp's Harmony Society, some secessions were collective and constituted a split. The great schism of the Harmonists in 1832 resulted in 250 members withdrawing with $105,000 worth of property.[16]

There were those who left the societies peacefully, and who, as the Shakers said, "in parting with Society as their *Alma Mater*, have ever respected and honored her."[17] The comment of a nineteenth century scholar on the Icarians must have been true of other communitarians: There was many an old member, Albert Shaw said, "whose toil had helped to build up the establishment, and whose donation of his private possessions on joining the community had added to the wealth of the society."[18] Such a member might have, for personal reasons, "withdrawn from membership, taking next to nothing with him"; his consolation might then be "the thought that what he had left behind would perpetually promote the good cause of communism."[19]

There were others whose parting was less benign, and whose subsequent activity was sometimes polemical as well as legal. "It is well known," the Shakers observed, "that apostates from any religious society whatever, will naturally incline to seek the friendship of the world, and endeavor to justify themselves to the public for their apostasy; and the only reasonable prospect of success many such can have, depends on successfully slandering the society from which they have apostatized."[20] Seceders, wrote the Perfectionists, "with a few pleasant exceptions," have "gone out in the truculent spirit of the Southern states, reckless of the Constitution and covenant which they originally accepted, demanding the property they put in as a matter of legal right, sometimes adding the interest, sometimes with threats of legal hostilities, sometimes with actual summons from lawyers."[21] At Oneida these demands had a certain "power" because of the "unpopularity of some of our social principles; which, it was assumed, placed us in some sense at the mercy of the legal authorities and of anyone who might stir them up."[22]

The apostates brought out strong feelings in the community. "I loath thee from my very heart, Poor remnant of mortality,"[23] an Oneida poet wrote to William Mills. He is the "meanest human parasite we ever encountered," Noyes said of the former Perfectionist.[24] The Shakers referred to "malignant apostates, than whom Society has no more ignoble, unworthy foe."[25] Edward Deming Andrews quotes a Shaker hymn on apostasy: "I'll sense the awful situation / Of the souls that turn away; / They lose all hopes of their salvation, / For them Believers cannot pray."[26] Presumably the heat of the controversies is at least in part a result of a phenomenon noted by Chafee, that "the bitterness of a dispute is apt to be inversely proportionate to the area of conflict."[27] Family rows, Chafee notes, "are proverbial for their violence," and "similar acerbity pervades quarrels in clubs, trade unions, professional associations, secret societies, churches, and educational institutions."[28] Added to that, in the case of religious bodies, is the familiar response of believers to those who turn back from the light. Professor Arndt writes of the Harmonists that one of their leaders, in dealing with a seceder, was "completely blinded by a furious hatred which was all the

greater because his Bible told him that he was now dealing with the worst kind of enemies that the Bride of
Christ could possibly face, namely backsliders—men
who had belonged to the elect and had fallen from
grace."[29] And Melcher writes of the Shakers, "If they felt
bitterness for any, it was for the apostates: those who
had started on that hard trail, knowing all its hardships,
had promised to follow it to the end, and then had
changed their minds."[30]

By and large, the communities took the position that
their enterprises would be stronger without those who
dissented. Here is the Shaker view: "It is an established
maxim in the Society, that any member who is not reconciled to the faith, order, and government established
in it, is more injurious than beneficial to it."[31] A Zoarite
leader wrote to a Harmonist: "The spirit of worldliness
has torn away several of our young men, but from a
moral point of view, we have gained more than we have
lost."[32] Only occasionally is a voice of accommodation
heard. A former Icarian wrote of the Nauvoo period:
"[We lost] many of our most valuable members. The
most courageous, industrious. As soon as one showed
discontent he was suspected of making calculations to
leave and a sort of persecution was exerted. Life to him
was made unendurable and the position untenable. He
had to leave; instead of listening to their proposition and
making a few concessions to induce them to stay—no,
go they must."[33] For some of those who left, the issues of
apostasy and secession would arise early in the communal experience, and these might re-enter the world of
individualism with little lost. For others, the severing of
communal ties might occur after years or even decades
of communal service.

The communistic existence, Nordhoff commented,
"relieves the individual's life from a great mass of cark-
ing cares, from the necessity of over-severe and exhaust-

ing toil, from the dread of misfortune or exposure in old age." The communities provided "security against want and misfortune," and "provision for old age and inability."[34] No doubt, Nordhoff said, these were "an inducement with a great many to whom the struggle for existence appears difficult and beset by terrible chances."[35] A defender of the Shakers noted that those who signed the covenant stood in an "enviable situation," since they were "relieved from earthly care."[36]

But the communal life held dangers of its own, for the lazy or stubborn or difficult; for those who wanted children in celibate communities; for those tempted now by another doctrine or discipline, Owenism perhaps, or Mesmerism, as they had been earlier tempted by the first. Aristotle had noted that although one expected friendship and harmony to arise from the holding of things in common, there was often discord: "Indeed, we see that there is much more quarrelling among those who have all things in common, though there are not many of them when compared with the vast numbers who have private property."[37] Caution, the Icarians said, was necessary from the beginning. But even after every caution there might be errors or, more simply, changes of heart or mind. The severing of ties by some signers of the utopian contract threatened severe economic as well as emotional injury.[38]

The former communist was interested therefore not only in moral vindication but in support, or recompense in the form of wages or recovery of property contributed. The communities' responses to both the religious and the financial threat had the sound of holy war. A Shaker statement, published in 1872, notes that "some of those departing have, with unexampled ferocity, demanded large sums—a division of Society's substance, little of which was gathered by their efforts in her behalf but rather by the life-services of the saints departed, and the living faithful."[39] The Shaker publication recalls the "dark times" when "Society suffered the unjust allegations of living in secret impurity—hypocritically professing, but failing to demonstrate a pure life!" But, the Shaker article continued, "those times are past, and now the very reverse is believed; and we mean to take advantage of the change."[40] The note of militant engagement is clear. And at Oneida, it was argued that the "Mills war" was not a "useless calamity to us or to mankind." "We have long been expecting the order from headquarters 'PERFECTIONISTS TO THE FRONT!'" said Noyes. Through the wrath of Mills, the order had come. "We have reached the front, and are ready for battle."[41]

In response to the request of an individual for the intervention of the outside system, the communities would argue that the contract and the communities' rules should govern. "You can give us all the help we ask for without any *active* interference," Noyes wrote.[42] "Our regulation is sufficient if we are allowed to enforce it." The sentence itself acknowledges the dependence of the communities on the state.

8

The Bargain

When a member shall not wish to conform to the laws; when he shall refuse to fulfill his duties; when he shall conduct himself improperly toward his associates; when his general attitude shall constitute a real danger to the society, he can be expelled by a vote of two thirds of the members.

Section VIII, Article 22, "Expulsion," Law Upon Withdrawal and Expulsion from the Icarian Community (1879)

Some of the utopians attempted to reach that world in which no law was necessary. Thus the writing of Josiah Warren, even when descriptive of an actual society, reflects a desire to do without structure or organization. Warren, a former member of Owen's community at New Harmony, based the anarchist communities he later founded on the idea of individual sovereignty. He wrote: "Throughout our operations . . . everything has been conducted so nearly upon the Individualistic basis that not one meeting for legislation has taken place. No Organization, no indefinite delegated power, no "Constitutions," no "laws" or "Byelaws," "rules" or "Regulations," but such as each individual makes for himself and his own business."[1] And a resident of Modern Times said:

We do not believe in Association. . . . We believe in the sovereignty of the individual. We protest against all laws which interfere with INDIVIDUAL RIGHTS—hence we are Protestants. We believe in perfect liberty of will and action—hence we are Liberals. We have no compacts with each other, save the compact of individual happiness; and we hold that every man and every woman has a perfect and inalienable right to do and perform, all and singular just exactly as he or she may choose, now and hereafter.[2]

Passing the question whether there was nonetheless "law" at the communities called Equity, Modern Times, and Utopia, one notes only that such anarchist communities were unusual. More often, it was felt that some regulation was needed. The eighty-one-year-old Thomas Jefferson, responding to a letter from the communitarian William Ludlow in 1824, raised this problem clearly. A society of seventy families might possibly be governed as a single family, he suggested, but "some regulators of the family you still must have, and it remains to be seen at what point of your increasing population your simple regulations will cease to be sufficient to preserve order, peace and justice."[3]

This regulation might sometimes be the will of the leader. Some of the utopians functioned without formal law, but also without individual sovereignty. These were groups whose authority rested finally on an individual who was, in Max Weber's terms, a charismatic leader. In such a group there "is no system of formal rules, of abstract legal principles, and hence no process of judicial decision oriented to them."[4] Judgments are "newly created from case to case, and are originally regarded as divine judgments and revelations. From a substantive point of view, every charismatic authority would have to subscribe to the proposition, 'It is written . . . but I say unto you . . .'"[5]

Sometimes the regulations might take the forms of written rules. The regulation would be, expressly or implicitly, a part of the utopian contract. The communistic societies are literal illustrations of the theory that the law of contract involves a delegation of sovereign authority, a delegation to private individuals to legislate and then have their legislation—the contract—enforced through the power of the courts. Llewellyn and Hoebel observed that "the total picture of law-stuff in any society includes, along with the Great law-stuff of the Whole, the sublaw-stuff or bylaw-stuff of the lesser working units."[6] In this sense, the regulations of the utopians can be perceived as part of the "law" of nineteenth century America.

Sometimes the contract with members touching the issue of property was all the written "law" there was. Thus, in a letter to Samuel Worcester of Boston, Frederick Rapp (1822) described the principles of the Harmony Society: "We nither [sic] can refer to a Book nor send a pamphlet which could give any information of our principles and management," he wrote, "having nither a written nor a printed Constitution or form of Law for the organization of our Society." The society "merely found it necessary to make a sort of agreement with new Comers whereby they are insured, that in Case they should not stand the given time of probation, or if after being adopted into the Community they could not be made to lead a Christian life, and therefore withdraw, the[y] shall receive back the value of their property brought in." If they were "poor and layd in nothing, they shall receive a donation at their departure according to their Conduct and need."[7] Although the Harmony Society contract provided that the members of the society agreed to "submit faithfully to the law and regulations" of the community, there do not seem to have been any codifications. For Harmony Society, it may be that the absence of extensive written legislation served a theological purpose. Thus Professor Arndt writes of the 1805 Harmony contract: "The rules and regulations of the Society were not given because that would have been too much like the dogmaticism of the church they had left in Germany."[8] Further, the rules of the Harmony Society were considered the Word of God. It was not necessary to write them down, as they would be communicated to the Harmonists through Father Rapp's preaching.[9]

The Principles of Association (1848) of the Oneida Perfectionists said that the association had "not thus far resorted to constitutions and written compacts or rules, for the regulation of its members." Instead, the community relied on "inspiration, the care and admonition of those who approve themselves qualified to be overseers, and free criticism." These, the document says, "have been found sufficient."[10] After 1864, new members were asked to sign a paragraph speaking to the issue of wages and property, but Oneida seems never to have had a written code of rules and regulations, the institution of mutual criticism apparently serving it adequately.

The Amana Society had "Twenty-one Rules for Daily Life," beginning, "To obey, without reasoning, God, and through God our superiors."[11] This code was enforced through a peer sanction, described below (p. 96).

A detailed codified statutory law[12] regulated the life of the Shaker communities. The *Millennial Laws of 1821* begin with a statement that places the Shaker statutes and ordinances for conduct in an explicitly religious context. The Shakers

> possess one united and consecrated interest, and therefore must in all things and under all circumstances be led, governed and influenced by one spirit, which is the Spirit of God, and be subject to one general law, which is the law of Christ, in this day of his second appearing.
>
> But as this general law comprehends all that is necessary for the moral and religious government of Believers; so it is divided into a variety of statutes and ordinances which will apply to all general cases, and

teach us our duty in the various situations, circumstances and relations to which we may be called.

The first and great command enjoined upon all Believers is, "That we love the Lord our God with all our heart and with all our strength." And the second is like unto it, namely, that we love our Brethren and Sisters as ourselves.

Under the influence of the first we shall always be obedient to our Parents and Elders in the gospel; and under the influence of the second we shall always do to others as we wish others to do to us in like circumstances.

On these two important points depends [sic] all the statutes and ordinances contained in the following pages.[13]

A more secular orientation is revealed in the lengthy and elaborate Icarian constitution and laws, which apparently are modeled on the idea of the nation-state.[14] An Icarian quoted Etienne Cabet: "American laws . . . cannot be called upon by Icarians. For these People, between them, there are no other laws than Icarian Laws, no other Courts and no other Juges [sic] than their General Assembly, their Sovereign to all."[15] The Hopedale Community, which survived for seventeen years, was conceived of as something like a civil state "existing within, peacefully subject to, and tolerated by the governments of Massachusetts and the United States, but otherwise a Commonwealth complete within itself." Hopedale had its own

> constitution, laws, regulations, and municipal police; its own legislators, judiciary and executive authorities; its own educational system of operations; its own method of aid and relief; its own moral and religious safeguards; its own fire insurance and savings institutions; its own internal arrangements for the holding of property, the management of industry and the raising of revenue; in fact, all the elements and organic constituents of a Christian republic, on a miniature scale."[16]

But the community laws would have to be enforced, and if a community did not use the police and courts of the outside state, it would have to substitute something else.

It should be noted immediately that the issues raised in the Mormon context by the doctrine of blood atonement, and the image of the Danite bands, are hardly visible at all in accounts of the four utopian communities. Thus, Whitworth writes, "Some of the early [Shaker] apostates (several of whom were probably half-crazed by repeated exposure to revivalistic excitement and disappointed millennial expectations) claimed that recalcitrant members were cruelly punished and prevented from leaving the group, but there was probably little truth in these rumours." Shaker materials, Whitworth comments, stressed that "only faith and submission to the Spirit of God bound persons to the sect."[17] He quotes a Shaker hymn on the point:

> Now will you believe me? I'm really sincere.
> I'm not drag'd on, I'm a true volunteer.[18]

There is little in the literature on the utopians to suggest that concern with physical force being used to discipline members—let alone murder of apostates or outside enemies—was a serious issue in connection with the communistic societies.[19]

The question of the internal governance of the utopian communities has always been of interest to observers. When A. J. Macdonald began his research, he sent out a printed letter of inquiry (1851), which contained two related questions on the subject: "Was there a written or printed constitution or laws?" and "Were pledges, fines, oaths or any coercive means used?"[20] (Macdonald's inquiries did not reach the question of expulsion, which was the most serious sanction of the utopian communities, nor did it show any clear awareness of the peer sanctions that were sometimes used.)

Hinds analyzed the mechanisms of internal governance as they related to the central inspirations of community life: The communities, he wrote, must find means to keep their inspiration vital and strong.[21] Daily meetings served this function among the Shakers and the Perfectionists. At Zoar, Hinds felt, the mechanisms were inadequate. The Zoarites had few ordinances, nothing like Oneida's mutual criticism, and no meetings except on Sunday—and these were "not generally attended" and were "not of a kind to elicit special interest or enthusiasm."[22] Another commentator observed of Zoar that "punishment, except in the most serious offenses, can not be inflicted, and then only expulsion is provided." Thus, "lashings of conscience must take the place of the scourge of the law."[23]

The influence of conscience was not, however, left solely to the individual's sensibility and judgment. Peer pressure was strong. Nordhoff described the practices of Amana: "When any member offends against the rules or order of life of the society, he is admonished (*ermahnt*) by the elders; and if he does not mend his ways, expulsion follows; and here, as elsewhere in the communities I have visited, they seem vigilantly to purge the society of improper persons."[24] Nordhoff notes that, at Amana, at least once a year there was a "general and minute '*Untersuchung*' or inquisition of the whole community, including even the children—an examination of its spiritual condition." Each member of the community was expected to make confession of sins, and "any disputes which may have occurred are brought up and healed, and an effort is made to revive religious fervor in the hearts of all."[25]

The Perfectionist account of mutual criticism at Oneida notes that "Criticism . . . bears nearly the same relation to Communism as that which the system of judicature bears to ordinary society. As society cannot exist without government, and especially without a system of courts and police, so *Communism cannot* exist *without Free Criticism*" (emphasis in original).[26] There were two basic methods of governance at Oneida: First, there were daily evening meetings which members of the community attended, and at which matters of religion and business were discussed. Second, there was the system of mutual criticism. "This system," Noyes wrote, "takes the place of backbiting in ordinary society and is regarded as one of the greatest means of improvement and fellowship." All of the Perfectionists "were accustomed to voluntarily invite the benefit of this ordinance from time to time."[27] Nordhoff was present when some fifteen Perfectionists—including John Humphrey Noyes—criticized one of their group.[28] Nordhoff described the criticism in his book, and it was quoted as an "amusing account" by Hillquit, who reproduced a part of it.[29] But Henry James was not amused. In the unsigned review of the Nordhoff book in *The Nation*, James referred to Oneida's system as "hideous":

> ... the reader should glance at the account given by Mr. Nordhoff of the "criticism" he heard offered upon the young man Henry. In what was apparent here, and still more in what was implied, there seem to us to be fathomless depths of barbarism. The whole scene, and all that it rested on, is an attempt to organize and glorify the detestable tendency toward the complete effacement of privacy in life and thought everywhere so rampant with us nowadays.[30]

It was, James thought, the "worst fact chronicled" by Nordhoff.

The Shaker communities used a number of sanctions. These included remonstrance, reduction or removal of privileges, and finally expulsion. Thus one has the case of Augustus Grosvenor, "who drew the plans and built the Rural House with forty rooms in it, and . . . one day the Shakers ceased to call him Elder, and he was forced to tend the swine as a rebuke, and desperate with humiliation his heart stopped beating and he fell dead."[31] (Augustus Grosvenor apparently failed to adequately calculate the cost of his project and left the Shakers with a debt of $25,000.) An English observer described the discipline of the Harmonists: "When any one [*sic*] is remiss or irregular to an extent to become an object of attention, no coercive measures are resorted, [*sic*] to but the idle or offending person is treated with distance or neglect, which, together with verbal reproof, are found to be fully efficacious to reform."[32] But these sanctions might fail, and if they did, individuals would be expelled. The legal theorist Eugen Ehrlich noted that even in modern times "exclusion from the community . . . withdrawal of credit, loss of position or of custom, is the most efficacious means" of combating insubordination. "Even today," he said, "punishment and compulsory execution [meaning the compulsory seizure of property as part of the execution of a judgment], which the jurist is accustomed to look upon as the basis of all legal order, are merely the extreme means of combat against those who have been excluded from the associations."[33]

Excommunication was familiar as a sanction in religious groups, but was not limited to them. The principle of excommunication "applies not only to the Catholic Church, but to every human society where men are permanently organized for any rational purpose," wrote the Right Reverend James A. Corcoran in the *American Catholic Quarterly Review* in 1881. "Its ruling power, whether residing in the entire body or entrusted to its representatives, has a right to exclude members from a share in the benefits and privileges of which they have proved unworthy, and to cancel their membership by expulsion."[34]

Merely the threat of expulsion—short of expulsion itself—could sometimes be a powerful sanction. Levi Bimeler, a descendant of the founder of the community of German separatists at Zoar, came finally to believe that the conceded right of communists to withdraw from the community (although without a right to wages or property) should be supported by a right to receive a proper share of the community's wealth. In defense of this proposition he began to put out a newspaper, the only newspaper published at Zoar, in which he discussed the fear of expulsion. Thirty years ago, he said, members of the society at Zoar "were kept in ignorance of the true state of things," and "did not dare to think contrary to prevailing customs, not to speak of voicing them, for fear of expulsion from the Society." He also noted in one issue that the first response of some of the Zoarites of 1896 to his newspaper was to threaten to expel him. But this, he said, was more easily said than done. "The U.S. Constitution guarantees freedom of speech and press. We avail ourselves of this guarantee for a good purpose." But the threat worked, and Bimeler's newspaper died after only a few issues. The community itself dissolved shortly thereafter.[35]

The procedures for expulsion from the nineteenth century American utopias varied. Some were relatively informal, rooted in a notion of a spiritual incompatibility whose external manifestation, expulsion, was inevitable and in a sense automatic. A one-time member of the Oneida community, William Mills, was thus said to have been "expelled by the inexpungeable repulsion between him and the spirit of the community."[36] The Perfectionists threw him out of the Mansion House and into the snow in February 1864. "Mills found himself, one winter night, suddenly, inexplicably, unceremoniously, horizontally propelled through an open window, and shot, harmlessly but ignominiously, into the depths of a snow drift. It was the first and only compulsory expulsion in the history of the Community."[37]

The Shaker procedure also was notably lacking in formality and strict process, although informal hearings could be held. The Shaker Fayette Mace, discussing in 1838 the matter of excommunication, noted that the Shaker order "differs from all others in having no church meetings to excommunicate disorderly members." Fayette Mace's view of the process was that, finally, withdrawals were always, in a sense, voluntary. "When once a person departs from that rectitude, which the purity of the gospel requires, he consequently loses his confidence. A lack of union ensues; and unless the person make confession, and reform, he will soon find himself in a most uncomfortable situation. In the language of one of our friends, I would say, '*The fire becomes too hot for him*'; he 'clears out' to the world."[38]

An incident involving a Shaker convert to Owenism may be used to illustrate a more formal Shaker expulsion. The Shaker document, *The Investigator*, reprints a petition from John Whitby to the Kentucky legislature (1828) setting out, in effect, the case concerning his expulsion. The petition said, "We were told by them . . . that no coercive or arbitrary measures were ever taken in the government of this Society—that conscience was entirely free, that all required of each individual was always to act honestly according to that degree of faith which he or she should at any time possess: . . . that no member was ever expelled from the Society for any cause whatever." But for no other reason than a "private expression of certain opinions relative to moral sentiment, which we most conscientiously believed to be not only true but the strongest basis of pure morality," some of us were "publickly anathematized, grieviously misrepresented and most peremptorily ordered to leave the society or make a recantation of our sentiments."[39] The

Shakers responded: With regard to expelling members, they said, "no compulsion or arbitrary force has ever been used in that case."[40] What John Whitby stated could not, to begin with, be construed so as to "imply any act of violence." In his own book, the Shakers said, Whitby demonstrated that "he was the first who deviated from the terms of membership"; that he believed in the system of Robert Owen and "discarded the doctrine of *praise and blame, rewards and punishments*, &c." He was then "admonished by the Ministry and Elders not to propagate such doctrine—refused admonition—became contumacious and bold—rejected all authority, and was ordered to retract what the elders called *vile stuff* or leave the society.[41]

In fact, for the Shakers as well as other communities, it was probably largely unnecessary to invoke any sort of process, since the peer sanction would be entirely adequate. Professor Arndt describes its operation among the Harmonists. While celibacy was not a requirement explicitly stated in its constitution or in its bylaws, the state of celibacy was the holier state and "holiness was the goal of the Society." Marriage was not forbidden, nor was marital intercourse, "but those who succumbed to nature's temptation soon began to feel uncomfortable and were subjected to a feeling of inferiority, which usually resulted in their "voluntary" withdrawal from the Society."[42]

The "Law Upon Withdrawal and Expulsion from the Icarian Community" reflects a strikingly constitutional conception of the process to be followed, with serious consideration of the implications of expulsion for spouses and children.[43] At Zoar, a full-dress procedure was followed, involving a tribunal that made written findings and issued a written report. From these Zoar records Nixon concluded that it is apparent that nothing suggestive of Star Chamber procedure was ever employed by the offices of the Society. During the preliminary examination of the accused by the trustees, two other members were present as witnesses. The proceedings of the trial were open to all members who wished to be present, and the defendant was given full opportunity to testify in his own behalf. Before sentence was passed, the arraigned member was given an opportunity to recant. Trials were conducted with all the dignity and order of a regular court of justice, and all testimony was taken down verbatim.[44]

Nixon describes such a trial in detail. The counts included "irritable and rebellious conduct" in relations with other members and "detestable blasphemies and cursings."[45]

But expulsion was not the end of the question. There was still the question of adjustments for property and services contributed, which would have to be resolved as part of the process of separation. As a matter of right, these would be governed by the contract.

A member's rights on expulsion or withdrawal could, in some societies, be dependent on the particular class in which he had entered. Under the rules of the Shaker society there were three classes of membership.[46] The first or novitiate class was comprised of those who had some relation to the Shakers but lived in their own families and managed their own affairs. The second or junior class was for individuals "not having the charge of families,"[47] who contracted to work without wages but retain their property. Junior members "have the privilege, at their option of freely giving the improvement of any part, or all, of their property, to be used for the mutual benefit of the family to which they belong. The property itself may be resumed at any time, according to the contract, but no interest can be claimed for the use thereof."[48] The third or senior class or church order was composed of "such persons as have had sufficient time and opportunity practically to prove the faith and manner of life of the Society and who are prepared to enter freely, fully, and voluntarily into a united and consecrated interest."[49] Members of the highest class, the church order, agreed "to devote themselves and services, with all they possess, to the service of God, and the support of the Gospel forever, solemnly promising never to bring debt or damage, claim or demand, against the Society, or against any member thereof, for any property or service they may thus have devoted to the uses and purposes of the institution."[50] Entrance into this class was "considered a matter of the utmost importance to the parties concerned. . . . For, having made such a dedication, according to the laws of justice and equity, there can be no ground for retraction; nor can any one, by those laws, recover anything thus dedicated."[51]

The Shakers were asked whether "by some little alterations in the church covenant, permitting the withdrawing member to take back his property, and allowing him something for his labor, the institution might be more extensive and useful." They answered that if they themselves had been "set to contrive the plan, no doubt we should have adopted such views; but all we have had to do in the matter has been, to receive it as it has been originally constructed by a higher authority."[52]

At Zoar also there was a distinction between classes of membership. For members of the first class, money was deposited in the common fund and a receipt, payable on demand, was given. The second class of membership declared that members gave all property of every kind to the Society forever. Discretionary adjustments were referred to in the Zoar articles.[53]

Sometimes withdrawing members were entitled to refunds as a matter of right. Thus, the original Harmony Society contract provided for a refund "of all such property without interest, as he or they may have brought into the community."[54] If one brought nothing, there might be a donation from the society. The Amana constitution provided that members leaving the society, "either by their own choice or by expulsion, shall receive the amount paid into the common fund, without interest or allowance for services during the time of their membership."[55] Some utopian communities recognized wage claims. For example, New Harmony, in one of its constitutions, promised compensation for previous services, as much as "justice shall require," as well as the return of money deposited and "an equitable share of the value of any real estate acquired during the period of their membership."[56] However, among the communistic societies wage claims were generally rejected as a matter of right. But whatever the rules provided, it is clear that the practice of the communistic societies was often based on ideas of charity and justice, rather than strict legality.[57]

9

Settlements

For the running of affairs [the articles of association] say but little. The play of personality, the unrecorded adjustments from day to day, further factual agreement from time to time, informed by usage, and by initiative and acquiescence which do not even call for conscious agreeing—these are what fill the contract framework with a living content; these are what often so stretch and overlay it as to make the initial contract a wholly misleading guide as to what occurs.

Karl N. Llewellyn

In fact, the communities sometimes behaved toward seceders in a way quite different from what one might suspect, judging by the contract. Sometimes there is a hint of this in the contract itself, which would authorize discretionary gifts while barring refunds as a matter of right, as in the Zoar and Oneida contracts and the revised Harmony Society contract. But whether their contracts explicitly referred to discretionary refunds or not, it seems that the practice of the utopians was often charitable. But their practice, they insisted, should be entirely distinguished from their legal obligation. Thus, John Humphrey Noyes wrote, "On ground of liberality and expedience we pledge ourselves . . . in case of any member's withdrawal, to refund the amount he put in." This pledge, he said, "we have redeemed, and more than redeemed in our dealings with all who have deserted us."[1] However, the Perfectionists explicitly placed their practice on grounds of morality and not law. Even this pledge, Noyes insisted, "is expressly declared to be *not a legal obligation*. Whoever subscribes our terms of membership, as a man of honor relinquishes the right to *demand* repayment or to *enforce* it by legal action; and remits the whole question of refunding to the discretion of the Community."[2] The late Oneida covenant (1875) makes this clear by providing that the community "may also discontinue the custom of refunding at any time they see fit, or refuse in any case to refund all or any part" of property contributed.[3] Wage claims were unqualifiedly barred in the Oneida understanding.[4] The May 1864 Oneida *Circular* published a letter on the issue of return of property and wages, addressed to a former member who asked for twelve years' wages. The letter said first that the Oneida understanding would bar such a claim, and second that the wage claim "does not recognize any offset for services on the other side."[5] The community pointed out that if Oneida "were to reckon its labors and services for you, the balance would be very different from what you make it out, and not at all in your favor."[6] The practice at Oneida was in fact to refund to seceders all property brought in, or its equivalent in money, and to give those who had no property when they joined clothes and one hundred dollars in case of their "peaceable withdrawal."[7] The letter was, it was reported, accompanied by a check for the member's original investment.[8]

The practice of the Oneida community may be further illustrated by the case of Charles Guiteau, probably the most notorious of all utopian seceders, found sane and hanged in 1882 for the assassination of President James Garfield.[9]

Luther Guiteau, the father of Charles Guiteau, was an Oneida Perfectionist in spirit though not in fact, a devotee of Noyes's doctrines, and a loyal reader of Noyes's works. In 1860 his son Charles Guiteau (born 1841) joined the Oneida communists. Guiteau was not an effective or admired member of the Oneida group. Like the others, Guiteau was a subject of mutual criticism at Oneida, and was criticized largely for "egotism and conceit."[10] After a time, life at the community no longer satisfied him, and in April 1865 he left Oneida, intending to found a newspaper—"a theocratic daily." Three months after leaving Oneida he rejoined the community, but later left again.

Guiteau's conflict with Oneida is described at length in *Guiteau vs. Oneida Community*, the title not of a lawsuit but of a document submitted by John Humphrey Noyes at the trial of Guiteau in 1882.[11] Noyes did not appear at the Guiteau trial. He was then seventy years old and had "long been disabled by laryngitis and deafness, so as to be quite unfit for services as a witness." But he could "write a little yet," he said, and it was "no more than fair to the memory of the defunct Community" that the American public should understand the original purpose of an anti-Oneida circular (reprinted in the New York *Herald* of 1881) which Guiteau had prepared fourteen years earlier in the course of his campaign against Oneida. Noyes quoted a letter he had written to Guiteau's lawyer on December 5, 1867, in response to a demand for $9,000 in wages. Writing from Wallingford, Connecticut, Noyes had said: "Our case is briefly this. Your client was received into the O.C. at his own urgent solicitation. He well knew our fundamental mutual agreement was to consider the board and education of each member an equivalent for his services, and a bar to any claim of wages; and that we would not have accepted him as a hired laborer on any consideration."[12]

Noyes's letter reviewed Guiteau's two departures from Oneida and the two settlements. The first time Guiteau left, the community returned the $900 that he brought in, and he said that he was satisfied. (The community also gave Guiteau books and clothing.) When he came back, he made an "absolute donation of what remained of his $900" to the printing department. He left a second time, and again the community returned his donation. "He expected no more, and asked no more because he knew he was entitled to no more." Noyes defended the Oneida contract only briefly. "I will not stop here to argue the equity of our fundamental agreement," Noyes said. "It is sufficient to say it is as fair for one as it is for another; and that your client himself helped to impose and enforce it on others during the whole term of his membership." "The object of the Oneida contract," Noyes stressed, is "not to get services without remuneration, but to keep out knaves and speculators." But, Noyes continued, a case might be made out against the contract.* It might be argued that the "agreements" should be called "mere forms," and that an "equitable" (meaning apparently quasi-contractual) settlement should be reached, "on the principle that so much is due for so much services, form or no form." Even if this were true, Noyes insisted, "Guiteau must lose." The community "was willing to meet the case in this shape," Noyes said, and was "prepared to prove that your client was a very inefficient man and did not pay for his board and clothing while in the Community, but left us with a large balance on this score, due from him to us." Guiteau "during the whole period of his membership, was moody, self-conceited, unmanageable, and a great part of the time was not reckoned in the ranks of reliable labor." Thus, Noyes concluded, "forms are in our favor, and equity is in our favor."[13]

The practice among the Shakers was also sometimes different from the strict forfeiture provided by the terms of the covenant. Although Samuel Tilden disputed the point, a legislative report of the state of New York (1849) indicates that, despite the church covenant and

---

*Perhaps because Oneida's contract might be held to be against public policy? The Perfectionists were, of course, peculiarly vulnerable on that point.

the formal cutting off of claims, not only did the Shakers return property brought into the societies but also inheritances (presumably received after joining).[14] Shaker writings also make reference to the charitable practices of the group in relation to departing members. "Yet should any afterward withdraw, and be disappointed in their worldly prospects, the society may charitably supply their wants."[15] And again, "No person who withdraws peaceably is sent away empty."[16] Melcher writes that when "a young Shaker and Shakeress fell in love and wanted to leave and get married, if they went frankly to the elders and told them of their desire the elders put them on a kind of six-months probation to make sure that they really knew their own minds." Then, if they still wished to marry, "the Shakers let them go with their blessing, a sack of flour, a horse and a hundred dollars."[17]

Under the early Harmony Society contract, as already noted, refunds were a matter of right, but after 1836 they were discretionary. Hinds reported as to the Harmonists that although "claims on the part of seceders are cut off by the New Constitution, the Society is not prevented from dealing generously with those who leave; and I understand it is customary to make donations to them varying in amount according to time and value of services." Hinds met a Harmonist seceder at Zoar who told him that he had received a thousand dollars when he left the Harmony Society, but this, Hinds says, "was undoubtedly an exceptionally large donation."[18] It should be noted that though the record of contributions of individual members of the Harmony Society was publicly burned in 1818, nonetheless restoration of property brought in continued to be a contractual obligation of the society until the constitutional change of 1836. The Harmonists gave several reasons for the change in their contract. The provisions on refund, they said, "though assented to at the time, manifestly depart from the great principle of a Community of Goods." Refund "may tend to foster and perpetuate a feeling of inequality" at variance with the true spirit and objects of the association," and further, the principle of restoration of property was one that could not (since the destruction of the records) be "enforced with uniformity and fairness."[19]

At Zoar, if a member of the second class seceded, no property was given back, but if the member "made application for something, it would be considered how he had conducted himself and how valuable his services had been, and a gift made accordingly."[20] (A member who was expelled from Zoar was permitted to stay and work there for room and board.[21] The Zoar contracts give little hint of the availability of this option.)

The communities often asked departing members to sign releases expressing satisfaction with the donation received. The release was another contract and another rite of passage. The counterpart of rites of initiation, Van Gennep wrote, "are the rituals of banishment, expulsion, and excommunication—rituals of separation and de-sanctification."[22] Sometimes, he noted, these rites are identical.[23]

Hinds offered an imaginary colloquy concerning the law and practice of the Oneida community, which reflected the situation at several of the American communistic societies.

1. Are persons allowed to leave the Community? Certainly.

2. Can they take away property? Our practice has been to refund to seceders all the property they brought into the Community, or its equivalent in money, and to give to those who had no property when they joined a good outfit of clothing and one hundred dollars, in case of their peaceable withdrawal. But our present Covenant cuts off all claim on the part of seceders, and leaves the

matter of refunding any property entirely at the option
of the Community.

3. Why was this change made? To test more thoroughly the sincerity of applicants for admission, and to
avoid trouble in cases of secession.[24]

Nonetheless, trouble could not altogether be avoided.
The principle common to all the communities that had
contracts was that the rights of a withdrawing member
would be determined by the contract the member had
signed on joining the society. The conditions of membership had been clearly set down and defined, the Harmonists said in 1827, "so as to prevent mistake or
disappointment on the one hand, and Contention or disagreement on the other."[25] But sometimes agreement
could not be reached—or an agreement that had been
reached earlier was later challenged—and then there
might be lawsuits.

In defending the lawsuits the communistic utopians
were involved in a contradiction inherent in some related assertions of right, as where, for example, the attempt to preserve privacy through the law tends to
exposure on the records of the legal system. In seeking to
preserve their independent existence through the instrument of the civil courts, the utopias acknowledged limits
on their autonomy.

Part 4

Appeals to the State

Legal conflict rests on a broad basis of unities and agreements between the enemies. The reason is that both parties are equally subordinated to the law; they mutually recognize that the decision is to be made only according to the objective weight of their claims; they observe the forms which are unbreakably valid for both; and they are conscious that they are surrounded in their whole enterprise by a social power which alone gives meaning and certainty to their undertaking.

Georg Simmel

10

An Expensive Evil

I assume that . . . we hate lawsuits as we hate war.

John Humphrey Noyes

The thinking of the American communistic societies on the subject of lawyers and litigation should be viewed initially against the teaching of the New Testament, and particularly the letter of Paul to the Corinthians, stressing both that disputes should be settled within the group and that one should suffer wrong rather than litigate.

> . . . Is it so, that there is not a wise man among you? no, not one that shall be able to judge between his brethren?
>
> But brother goeth to law with brother, and that before the unbelievers.
>
> Now therefore there is utterly a fault among you, because ye go to law one with another. Why do ye not rather take wrong? why do ye not rather suffer yourselves to be defrauded?[1]

The language of Paul was echoed by the society of Shakers, who reported no case of "brother going to law with brother,"[2] and by the Perfectionists, who in relation to a seceder acted on the general principle that it was "better to suffer wrong than to quarrel."[3]

The Pauline teaching as it was carried through the sectarian tradition[4] was paralleled by the antilegal tradition of the literary utopias. Lawyers were banned from More's *Utopia* where "each man [was] expert in law," and where the most obvious interpretation of the few laws there were was considered the most fair.[5] Gerrard

Winstanley, the seventeenth century English Leveller, saw law generally as an instrument of oppression, the "declarative will of the conquerors, how they will have their subjects to be ruled."[6] Lawyers, like parsons, were subject to the death penalty in his utopia. In the picture of the future America presented by Edward Bellamy there was some need for judges but none for lawyers.[7]

The American communistic utopians believed that where disputes arose within the communities they should be settled within the group—perhaps, as at Zoar, by an arbitration mechanism.[8] They held, further, that litigation was, in general, a part of a system of private property. Oneida's William Alfred Hinds argued that "litigation and other expensive evils, necessary concomitants of individual property, disappear from Societies fully communistic."[9] And the Icarian leader Etienne Cabet made fundamentally the same point. "The simple fact of putting goods in common," Cabet wrote,

> entails necessarily the suppression: of inheritances and divisions; of selling and buying; of money for internal affairs; of lending at interest and usury; of banking, crediting and discounting; of internal trade and shops; of debts, of bills of exchange and bills payable at sight; of the Exchange and stock-jobbing; of competition, monopolies and obstruction in trade; of failures; of division, lawsuits, seizures, arrests for debt; of civil courts and courts of commerce; of judges, counsellors, attorneys, solicitors, bailiffs, notaries; stock-brokers, etc.[10]

The fundamental idea was that communism would eliminate not only the prize but the necessity of seeking it. The ideal corollary was that peace, harmony, and happiness would follow.

Thus, the idea of litigation, quite independently of the results of a particular lawsuit, might be troublesome for a community. With "all our respect for lawyers," Noyes wrote, "we are very averse to litigation and intended in framing [Oneida's] regulation to preclude the possibility of it."[11] A desire to avoid litigation is equally plain in the remarks of Shaker Elder David Meachum: One should try to settle with the claimants, rather than "try to overcome them by the laws of men," he said, for this was the "Law of Christ." And if "they still hold a demand against the Church, it may be necessary to make them a consideration, in order for a settlement—not as acknowledging or paying a debt on our part, or as justifying them in their demands, but as a settlement for peace sake, that the Church may be blameless; and they that do us wrong may be without excuse in the day of trial."[12]

But litigation between persons formerly brothers was a fact of life in the American utopias.[13] The litigation was the final step in a process of estrangement from the values of the group that might have had its origins in some trivial deviation or in some very large one. From the point of view of the societies the smallest might also be the largest, since if the large areas of loyalty and agreement made it possible for the group to withstand some deviation, that almost total unity could equally, as Simmel suggests, make it possible for the group to feel threatened by every internal conflict.[14] The litigation could be seen by a community as marking a failure fundamental to the conception of the enterprise. The Christian Commonwealth Community of Georgia in the late nineteenth century was confronted with the problem of a member who had written a book attempting to discredit the group. The member was expelled but came back

> vowing to effect the dissolution of the Commonwealth with the aid of an inside accomplice. . . . These two men, with the aid of about ten others sought to throw the colony into bankruptcy, hoping to benefit through the subsequent liquidation and distribution of the assets. The schism among the members of the colony over the principle of coercion and force implicit in the handling

of this affair created a crisis. At a meeting of all the members it was decided finally to fight the issue out in the courts. This was regarded by many as the final surrender of the principle of love, the acknowledgement after several compromises that the ethic of non-resistance was not an adequate standard for meeting the issues of a complex social situation.[15]

Other societies responded to the threat of litigation or to litigation itself with denunciations of apostates, backsliders, and parasites, and then closed ranks. There was no failure of the utopian conception; it was rather a question of a "trial" or of purging the evil in one's midst. A sociological perspective on the event would presumably raise issues concerning deviance as an imputed characteristic, one necessary for community self-definition. Deviance, Kai Erickson wrote, "is not a property *inherent* in any particular kind of behavior; it is a property *conferred upon* that behavior" by other people (emphasis in original).[16]

Their position could have been justified this way: The Pauline principle that one should settle within the group operated only for disputes between brothers. Seceders and apostates were in another category. The proposition that it was better to suffer wrong could not extend so far as destruction at the hands of the enemy. If litigation was a concomitant of private property, then the communistic utopians, collective owners of private property, would be forced to defend themselves in litigation against those who would take it from them.

The Shakers, for instance, were a "law unto themselves."[17] They did not invoke the civil law if it could be avoided. But when they were drawn into litigation, "they defended themselves by employing the ablest counsel that could be obtained."[18] The same point could be made for the other communistic societies.

John Humphrey Noyes, in "An Appeal of the Oneida

Community to all Lawyers, Justices, Judges and Courts of Law," published in the Oneida *Circular*, asked for what he saw as non-intervention: "We only ask you not to help the rascals, after signing [our contract] to break it." The courts should say to the seceders: "You have given your property to the Community for a good and sufficient consideration and you have placed the whole matter of repayment, in case of your withdrawal, at the discretion of the Community. We cannot interfere."[19] But when the courts assumed jurisdiction of the claims, they intervened. The public discussion and debate over the communities was carried to the courtroom. A lawyer for Zoar insisted that Zoar was a democratic institution, while a lawyer for the seceders described Zoar as a society of masters and slaves, the "only *plantation* in Ohio."[20] It was this question that the courts would finally decide.

The litigation brought by former utopians ("seceders") was of immense importance to the communistic societies, who perceived that their institutions were seriously threatened. If the seceders had been successful, a nineteenth century historian of the Harmonists wrote, the result would have been "the entire dissolution of the Society."[21] Repeated defeats in litigation brought by former members would have impaired their ability to meet their covenantal obligations and undermined their economic base. Noyes explained: We "cannot safely take men and their families and their property into our household and business, and give them an unlimited guaranty of maintenance, while they are at liberty to desert and wrench their property away from us at pleasure."[22] Oneida's James Towner made the point at greater length. Having joined a community, he said, members have no property to lose.

> And it is plain that on no other principle can a Community be sustained as a permanent institution. After such

social organization has existed for one or more generations its membership will consist of all classes and ages;
there will be a large proportion of children, aged persons
and invalids; persons unable from various causes to care
for themselves; and one of the principal objects of Community life is to secure reliable insurance against or-
phanage, old age and invalidism; and experience has
shown that the able bodied are most likely to become
factious and dissentient, and a few such persons would
have it in their power to greatly weaken and embarrass,
if not to destroy, the most successful Community, were it
admitted that they could at pleasure rescind their contract and take from the Community property contributed, or money under the guise of wages earned.[23]

The Shakers argued along the same lines. Their covenant had been tested at law and "pronounced a safe
document for the preservation of Society for the purposes it sets forth." To credit the demands of the apostates, the Shakers urged, "would bring society to an end
of practically fulfilling its sacred obligations to faithful
adherents, and obliterate the very purposes for which
Society was established."[24] Earlier, the Shakers had explained that an order like theirs could not be supported
"if its members, on withdrawing, should take whatever
they have given, and have the avails of their labors restored to them." If one should return their property, or
credit services, "it would be literally taking it from those
who remain faithful to their covenant" and giving it to
those who broke it.[25]

Additionally, the communities would see the litigation
as involving fundamental questions of their legitimacy,
as well as their capacity for survival. The Shaker writers
Anna White and Leila Taylor give an account of a case
in the courts of Cuyahoga County, Ohio, on the validity
of the Shaker covenant that created considerable interest
in the state. "Eminent counsel were employed on both

sides," and one of the Shaker attorneys, Judge Starkweather,

> in the ablest speech of his life, showed that the tree is known by its fruits, that these people called Shakers, by the simplicity and purity of their lives, by their exemption from the strife of worldly ambition and by the consecration of themselves and all they possessed to their religious faith, but imitated the example of the Christians in apostolic days more than any other people in Christendom, and that their views on the subject of matrimony were in no way variant from the teachings of the Apostle Paul. The result of this trial was a victory for the Shakers.[26]

Communistic societies wanted to win their lawsuits, but the legal details of the victory are sometimes less significant than the vindication of the work of the society, its customs, and its laws.

"How do you manage to keep communal property—but, nonetheless property?" Tolstoy asked Elder Frederick Evans. Evans's answer was, "We hold and defend our communial [sic] property under the Civil laws of the New Earth."[27] The results of the Shaker litigation and the litigation involving other groups was in general a triumph for community orthodoxy against individual apostasy. It could also be seen as a victory for communitarianism. For Hinds, the litigation involving Zoar, Harmony, and the Shakers was important as settling critical points in American law relevant to the communities; and the list of the points established by the cases, derived from Towner, is included in his work on the American communities. "In defending the rights of Communities as against seceders the Harmonists have done a great work for the general cause of Communism," Hinds wrote.[28] And "for their efforts in settling by resort to the highest tribunals, regardless of expense, some important principles," Zoar and Harmony would, he thought, "be gratefully remembered in the far future."[29] At the same time, as Hinds does not stress, the victories in the civil tribunals conceded that the communities were entirely dependent on the outside legal system for the enforcement of their rights and, indeed, for their existence.

11

Judgments on Utopia

Thereupon . . . [he] said that he did not rely on the society for protection, but would seek protection from the civil authority in the country.

Shain v. *Markham*, 27 Ky. 578, 581 (1830)

Lawsuits were brought on "almost all imaginable grounds," Towner wrote, and "by all sorts of claimants."[1] Seceders have sued "to collect wages for services rendered during their membership; and for a partition and distribution of the joint property accumulated. Heirs of members, dying as such, have sued to recover a distributive share of the common property; administrators of the estate of such members have done the same," and, he concluded, "in every case the party has failed to recover."[2]

One assumes that there were many disputes over the utopian contracts, particularly in the case of the very long-lived societies. Some of these were adjusted out of court.[3] Others may have been disposed of very quickly in legal proceedings. Some may never have been appealed, or may not have been reported.[4] The nine disputes treated below left a record in reported litigation. These cases provide a basis for the discussion of legal aspects of the utopian contracts offered in Part Five. The facts of the case reports are supplemented in this presentation by facts available in historical materials, and the discussion to this point is, in a sense, only an attempt to present the facts of these cases more fully.

Despite this emphasis on facts, it must be noted that appellate decisions themselves must be used with great caution as sources of historical fact. To begin with, there is the problem of "facts" as reported by appellate courts. Such facts, Llewellyn wrote, are found through this process:

> What is left in men's minds as to those raw events has been canvassed, more or less thoroughly, more or less skillfully, by two lawyers. But canvassed through the screen of what they considered *legally* relevant, and of what each considered legally relevant to win his case. It has then been screened again in the trial court through the rules about what evidence can be admitted. The jury has then reached its conclusion, which—for the purposes of the dispute—determines contested matters for one side. The two lawyers have again sifted—this time solely from the record of the trial—what seemed to bear on points upon appeal. Finally, with a decision already made, the judge has sifted through these "facts" again, and picked a few which he puts forward as essential—and whose legal bearing he then proceeds to expound.[5]

Thus, as Llewellyn indicates, the cases may not report events as they happened. Further, the cases may not represent a final historical result in factual terms. A lower court judgment could, for example, be affirmed or reversed, or a new trial might be ordered, but these rulings may or may not represent the actual solution to the problem the case presented. Some solution or settlement other than that ordered by the court may conclude the litigation. Such an extralegal accommodation ended one of the Zoar controversies, and it may have happened in other instances. In legal discussion, a case is a discrete event, defined on the page. In life, the court's judgment is one more legal relation which the parties may choose to redefine by contract. One moves cautiously therefore from "this is what the court said," or "this is what the court decided," to "this is what happened." The campaign in the courts was one part of a struggle that had begun in the communities and would finally end there. The courts' pronouncements are events in a series of events. This is particularly clear in the case of Zoar (cases 4 and 6), where we see a lawyer accompany a dissident faction into the community, lose there, take legal steps in the federal courts, lose there, issue a parting shot in a document directed at the court, and finally undertake yet another unsuccessful lawsuit on behalf of the dissidents in the state courts.

Some of the cases discussed below were brought in state courts and others in federal courts. Although in the broad sense the cases all involve utopian contracts, their detailed aspects, as Towner said, are different from each other. There are suits for wages, for the return of property brought in, for the return of property of an immediate ancestor, or for breach of contract of support. Some of the cases are formally brought "in equity" or "in chancery," referring to that system of remedial jurisprudence brought from England with the common law, which existed adjacent to the conventional legal system. The doctrines of equity were developed to avoid the harshness of some of the doctrines on the law side, and, indeed, Roscoe Pound describes the doctrines of equity as among the agencies in the legal system "for individualizing the application of law."[6] It was viewed conventionally as a "remedial system alongside of the law, taking the law for granted and giving legal rights greater efficacy in certain situations."[7]

Equity was empowered to order specific relief of various kinds, and would, for example, directly order parties to perform their contracts, where the courts of law could award, in general, only monetary compensation. But the courts of equity would not grant specific enforcement to an unconscionable bargain. Equity had a particular concern with the administration of trusts, and the beneficiary of a trust could specifically enforce his interest in a trust through proceedings at equity. The idea would be that the trustee who held legal title had acted falsely and fraudulently and the court should protect the beneficiaries.

The nine cases are first indexed in chronological order, then described at greater length below.

1. *Waite* v. *Merrill*, 4 Me. 102 (1826). Seceding Shaker brought suit for twelve years' wages. Held: for the defendant society.

2. *Gass and Bonta* v. *Wilhite*, 2 Dana [32 Ky.] 170 (1834). Seceding Shakers sued for partition of the communal property, either on the basis of property brought in or of equality. Held: for the defendant society.

3. *Schriber* v. *Rapp*, 5 Watts (Pa.) 351 (1836). Suit by seceding Harmonist as administrator, asking for accounting of property of his father, who had died in the society. Held: for the defendant society.

4. *Goesele* v. *Bimeler*, 10 Fed. Cas. 528 (D. Ohio) (1851); affd., 55 U.S. (14 How.) 589 (1852). Expelled from Zoar for good cause, a former Zoarite (with others) brought an action as heir to recover the property brought to Zoar by his father. Held: for the defendant society in the circuit court; affirmed on appeal to the Supreme Court of the United States.

5. *Baker* v. *Nachtrieb*, 60 U.S. (19 How.) 126 (1856); Case below: *Nachtrieb* v. *Harmony Settlement*, 17 Fed. Cas. 1139 (W.D. Pa. 1855). Former Harmonist, who signed a release indicating that he had withdrawn and was satisfied with his settlement, sued for wages for some thirty years of membership. The circuit court found that, despite the release, there had in fact been an unjust expulsion, and ordered a partition of the property of the society. Reversed on appeal in the Supreme Court, so that the defendant society prevailed.

6. *Gasely* v. *Separatists Society of Zoar*, 13 Ohio 144 (1862). Wife of expelled Zoarite, who left the society following the expulsion of her husband, claimed that she was still a member of the society and was entitled to a share of the communal property. Held: for the defendant society.

7. *Grosvenor* v. *United Society of Believers*, 118 Mass. 78 (1875). Shaker sisters expelled for doctrinal deviance sued, alleging an improper expulsion and asking the court to judge the issue of deviance. Held: for the defendant society.

8. *Speidel* v. *Henrici*, 120 U.S. 377 (1887). Former Harmonist sued in equity for partition of property of the Harmony Society, fifty years after his withdrawal. Held: after such a delay in assertion of rights before court of equity, equity would not act.

9. *Burt* v. *Oneida Community*, 137 N.Y. 346 (1893). Following the dissolution of the Oneida community, former member sued in equity claiming unjust expulsion and asking for an adjudication of membership and a new division of property. Held: for successor corporation of the society.

It would be reasonable to suspect—in regard to the Shakers and the other communities that asked, as a condition of a full covenant relation, the irrevocable contribution of all property—that the litigation would be brought mainly by those who contributed property and then withdrew. But some of the major cases on the subject of utopian contracts arose in quite another context. These cases involve second-generation utopians.[8] The plaintiffs were brought to the communities as children, were supported by the community, and worked for it for some time. Their parents may have contributed property, but they themselves contributed nothing but their labor, for they had nothing else to contribute. Their parents may have deprived them of their natural expectations of inheritance; they may have "found themselves beggars, because their parents had been saints";[9] but they were not themselves before the courts in the role of persons who had contributed substantial property[10] to religious communities and then changed their minds about the value of the enterprise.

1. *Waite* v. *Merrill*, 4 Me. 102 (1826), was described some fifty years after it came down as the case "regarded by all Shakers as the great bulwark protecting them from all liability to ex-members."[11] The decision by Prentiss Mellen,[12] Maine's first chief justice, is a catalogue of arguments for and against the contracts of the communistic societies. The Shakers were represented by a Mr. Orr and a Mr. Greenleaf. "Greenleaf" is likely to have been Simon Greenleaf, later Royall Professor of Harvard, who was at this time a lawyer in Maine, practicing before the Supreme Judicial Court of Maine while also serving as its reporter of judicial decisions.[13] The Greenleaf-Orr brief on behalf of the Shakers is exhaustive, and the opinion of Greenleaf's friend, Prentiss Mellen, hardly less so.

The general worth of the Shakers had already been passed upon judicially in Maine. The Supreme Judicial Court of Maine a year earlier, in a case (*Anderson* v. *Brock*, 3 Me. 243 (1825)) concerning not the Shaker covenant but the issue of competency of members of the Shaker Society as witnesses, had written: "The sect, with which the plaintiffs are connected, have been for some time known among us and their peculiar tenets and modes of discipline have been embodied and settled by their teachers in regular, and, among them, well established forms." The Shakers had once been persecuted "by the mistaken zeal of former days," but they were now "permitted, under more favorable auspices, to keep the peaceful tenor of their way, unmolested." And then the court described the Shakers themselves. "They are in general quiet, sober, and industrious; and the fruits of these commendable qualities are exhibited to the public eye, in their beautiful villages and cultivated grounds, and in the apparent comfort and abundance, with which they are surrounded." As part of its description of the Shakers, the court in *Anderson* v. *Brock* addressed the question whether the Shakers were to any degree independent of the state as a whole. They were not. "If the persons, who acquire authority and influence among them, should be found to abuse their power, they are answerable both civilly and criminally for their misconduct. Like all other citizens, they are amenable to the laws, by which they are protected; and from obedience to which their seclusions afford them no immunity or exemptions."[14]

The issue of *Waite* v. *Merrill* was raised by a seceder who had been brought to the Shakers as a child by his father, who was a Shaker and had bound him to the deacons as an apprentice from the age of fourteen. He stayed with the society, leaving and coming back twice. He finally left for good and sued for twelve years' wages, from the time of signing the contract. His argument was that the court should declare his actual (express) contract—the Shaker covenant, which barred wage claims—a nullity and find that there was a contract implied in law to pay wages for services.

The trial judge instructed the jury as follows: The Shaker witnesses were competent; the plaintiff seceder was competent, and there was no legal compulsion or undue influence. Further, if the signature were really the plaintiff's there was "nothing in the covenant itself inconsistent with law, or morally wrong, which could render it void" (p. 110).* However different from their own views the faith of the Shakers might be, if the jury found

---

*Quoted material in these nine cases is referenced by an initial page number, which governs all subsequently quoted material until the next number is given.

that the plaintiff had knowingly signed the contract, the verdict should be for the Shakers. The jury found for the Shakers. The appeal focused on a challenge to the jury instructions.

It is argued, Chief Justice Mellen said, that the covenant was void because it "deprived the plaintiff of the constitutional power of acquiring, possessing and protecting property" (p. 118). But the answer to this was clear: The covenant "only changed the mode in which he chose to exercise and enjoy this right or power."

As to the argument that the Shaker covenant was "contrary to the genius and principles of a free government, and therefore void" (p. 119), to this the court answered that "one of the blessings of a free government is, that under its mild influences, the citizens are at liberty to pursue that mode of life and species of employment best suited to their inclination and habits" (p. 119). In response to the argument that the covenant is a contract for "perpetual service" and "surrender of liberty," the court noted that by the contract itself, a secession was contemplated, and, in fact, the plaintiff had withdrawn. One could dissolve one's connection with the society at will, perhaps losing some property ("as the consideration of his dissolution of the contract"), but that was all. In this, the court said, "we see nothing like servitude and the sacrifice of liberty at the shrine of superstition or monastic despotism."

Then the argument on religious liberty: "It is said the covenant is void because it is in derogation of the inalienable right of liberty of conscience" (p. 119). To this, Chief Justice Mellen said, the reply is obvious. "The very formation and subscription of this covenant is an exercise of the inalienable right of liberty of conscience" (p. 120). And it is not easy, the court continued, "to discern why the society in question may not frame their creed and covenant as well as other societies of Christians; and worship God according to the dictates of their consciences." "We must remember," he said, "that in this land of liberty, civil and religious, conscience is subject to no human law; its rights are not to be invaded or even questioned, so long as its dictates are obeyed, consistently with the harmony, good order and peace of the community."

Finally, the court treated counsel's argument to the effect "that the covenant is void, because its consideration is illegal, that it is against good morals and the policy of the law." These objections, the court said, "cannot have any foundation in the covenant itself," since the covenant did not address "many particulars and peculiarities which the counsel for the plaintiff deems objectionable." The covenant only concerned such points as the admission of members, community of interest, mode of management and support, wage claims, "professions of a general nature as to the faith of the society," a solemn renewal of a former covenant, and the appointment of certain officers. It was a contract "never to make the present claim; and also as a complete bar to it." There was nothing here of illegal consideration and nothing against good morals or the policy of the law. The Shaker covenant, the court said, contained no principle that "an honest man ought to condemn," but on the contrary contained "some provisions which all men ought to approve."

But this was not the only view of the subject possible, and the court discussed other perspectives on the Shaker contract. It was certainly true that some Shaker doctrines "appear to the rest of the world as destitute of all scriptural foundation; and several of their consequent regulations unnatural [and] whimsical" (p. 121). The Shakers claimed "to exercise a perfect command over those passions, which others are disposed most cheerfully to obey."

In so doing, they might "chill some of the kindest affections of the heart," and perhaps gradually wound or endanger "the tender charities of father, son and brother." It was true, the court said, that the mode of education and government may be "too restrictive" and "the means used to preserve perfect submission to authority may be deemed artful, severe, and in some particulars highly reprehensible, especially in their pretended knowledge of the secrets of the heart." The Shaker faith "extends to unusual lengths; and leads to what others, at once pronounce to be absurdities," but this, Chief Justice Mellen said, "is not within our control; it is rightfully their own."

The court rejected the argument that the covenant amounts to a contract never to marry, which would be condemned as against public policy. The covenant was at most a contract not to marry while a member of the society. And "as it regards those members of the society who are married," Chief Justice Mellen wrote, "though they may live separate, without cherishing the gentle affections, still such conduct violates no human law" and "however lightly they may esteem the blessings of matrimony" (p. 122), the court said their opinions would not reduce the obligations the law attached to the marital state. As to the relation between father and son, the court said, Shaker principles "require the circle of benevolence and affection to be enlarged; but not that parental or filial tenderness should be destroyed or lessened." As to Shaker discipline, the court said, while "we may disapprove of many of the sentiments of this society in respect to the subject of education and discipline, yet as they steadily inculcate purity of morals, such a society has a perfect right to claim, receive and enjoy the full blessings of legal protection."

Finally, the court considered what the result might be if the contract were considered void. The plaintiff had voluntarily joined and for some time lived in the society, which he now claimed was reprehensible and devoted to purposes the law did not sanction. The parties (assuming the contract invalid as against public policy) were then equally culpable, and the law of contracts would leave them as it found them. Under the doctrine of *in pari delicto* [in equal fault] the suit could not be maintained (pp. 122–24).

2. *Gass and Bonta* v. *Wilhite*, 2 Dana [32 Ky.] 170 (1834). The seceders in *Gass and Bonta* were former Shakers about whom the case tells us very little. They sued in chancery for a division of the property of the community based either on equal shares or by contributions, and one assumes that they had in fact contributed property. The case is particularly interesting for its dissenting opinion attacking the covenant. The majority of the Kentucky court in *Gass and Bonta* (as summarized by a later Kentucky court) held that the Shaker society was a "charitable institution, or at any rate that it had charitable features, and that a seceding member could not upon withdrawal demand or recover from the society the property which he had put into it."[15] The court in *Gass and Bonta* concluded its opinion by saying that, "considering the objects and purposes of the trust under which the property of the Shaker society is held as legitimate and valid, and that the complainants never had any interest therein by the terms of the trust except as members and so long as they remained members, they have no right to the partition which they claim" (p. 185).

Justice Underwood,[16] in dissent, would not agree that "a voluntary abandonment, or expulsion from the society terminates the interest of a member in the joint estate" (p. 198). Judge Underwood raised the question whether a man would forfeit his interest if he changed faith and withdrew from the society. "If such be the

design of the covenant in regard to seceding members,"
he said, "it *ought* not to be enforced, because it is, to that
extent, without consideration, and in violation of the
policy and spirit of the constitutional principles" (p. 201,
emphasis added). "No man can sell his liberty and become a slave," he wrote, "nor can any one sell his liberty
of conscience, and make his temporal rights depend
upon a creed and its observances. There are inalienable
rights recognized by our constitution, and liberty of consciences is one of them" (p. 202).

> What is the effect of an agreement that if a man changes
> his creed and abandons his church, he shall forfeit his
> property, acquired by years of toil, and give up the
> means of his subsistence? Its direct tendency is, to bind
> down the conscience, and to suppress the "free commu-
> nication of thoughts and opinions," tolerated by the con-
> stitution, as "one of the invaluable rights of man." Who
> will speak out, when the publication of his opinions will
> cause him to be cast upon the world in a state of pauper-
> ism? (p. 203)

To the extent that the covenant imposed a forfeiture of
property contributed and the "proceeds of the labor" of
a seceder, to the benefit of those who remained, it was a
restraint upon the rights of conscience, and in violation
of the spirit and policy of the Constitution, and therefore
ought not to be allowed. "As a judge," dissenting Justice
Underwood concluded, "I have nothing to do with
creeds or their orthodoxy." But Justice Underwood believed that "no man's right to the enjoyment of property
owned by him, and earned by his own labor, can be
taken from him, in virtue of a contract which makes his
adherence to this or that religious creed and practice a
condition which, if violated, shall forfeit his right."

3. *Schriber* v. *Rapp*, 5 Watts (Pa.) 351 (1836). Jacob
Schriber came to the Harmonists as a child with the rest

of his family. A nineteenth century account of the Harmony Society notes that Jacob Schriber was a man of "somewhat visionary and enthusiastic character, an eager advocate for the removal of the Society to the Land of Palestine, there to await the Lord's coming."[17] In 1826, not finding many sympathetic to his views, and "having [come] under some unfavorable influences (among others probably, that of the tender passion)," [18] Schriber withdrew from the Harmony Society. Jacob sued as administrator of his father, Peter, who had died intestate as a member of the society, and asked the society for an accounting.

The documents involved in *Schriber* v. *Rapp* included articles of association dated 1805, 1821, and 1827, as well as a deed from Peter Schriber to George Rapp, dated 1826. There was testimony that this deed followed Jacob's withdrawal from the society and a rumor that he intended to bring suit. The articles of association involved in the case were the original Harmony Society articles, providing for a right of refund on the part of withdrawing members. Under the articles, therefore, if Peter, the father, had wanted to withdraw and claim his property he could have done so. This right was affected, however, by the deed and release, signed in 1826, in which, in consideration of support, maintenance, and five dollars, Peter granted to George Rapp and his associates "all the property, real, personal, and mixed, which I brought with me when I became a member of said society or at any time since may have put into their possession." For himself and his heirs the deed and release would "for ever discharge . . . George Rapp . . . from all manner of actions, causes of actions, suits, debts, dues, or sum of money, account, reckonings, damages, claim or demand . . . against the said George Rapp and his associates . . . I ever had, now have, or which I, my heirs, executors, or administrators hereafter shall or may have, for or by reason of any matter, cause or thing whatsoever, from the beginning of the world to the day of the date of these presents" (p. 354).

The decision was written by John Bannister Gibson,[19] a major figure among the state court judges of the nineteenth century. Gibson (b. 1780) was admitted to the Pennsylvania bar in 1803. In 1813 he was named president judge of the 11th Judicial Circuit of the Pennsylvania Court of Common Pleas, and in 1816 was named to the Pennsylvania Supreme Court. He became chief justice in 1827, and served in that capacity until 1851, when a system was introduced causing rotation of the office. He served the Pennsylvania court until his death in 1853.

There was no doubt, Chief Justice Gibson wrote, that the articles of association and the deed and release, "if fairly obtained" were conclusive (p. 360). The association itself was legal, and was not claimed to be detrimental to the public. Peter had a right to secede and withdraw property, but under the terms of the contract, his heir did not. Even if he did, the release would be a bar. The only real issue was, then, in the execution of the papers. Were the representations of Mr. Rapp to be labeled false and fraudulent? "To say nothing of our judicial incompetence to pass upon the truth," George Rapp "could not have been guilty of imposition if he actually believed what he uttered" (p. 362). Chief Justice Gibson wrote, "He who conscientiously declares an indifferent or absurd theory to be essential to salvation, may be a fanatic, but he is not a cheat." It had not been asserted that Rapp was "of superior intelligence or education, or less likely to harbour an extravagant opinion than the rest, or that those who are supposed to be his dupes, were under bodily or mental infirmity, or apprehensive of death," so as to give Rapp an advantage over them, or even that the "dogma predicated by him, was more than an ordinary and a standard doctrine of his church."

The plaintiff, Jacob Schriber, did show certain things, however. It was shown that in connection with the articles signed at Economy, "Rapp made a long speech; [he] said that every one who would sign, would have his name written in the Lamb's book of life; that if they did not, their names would be blotted out, and God would ask him about it; and that the members were induced to sign by what Rapp said" (p. 361). Peter Schriber was described as "a weak old man, who believed on the assurance of Mr. Rapp, that he would see the Lord in person within two years and a half from the time at which he spoke." "There is little doubt," the court concluded, that George Rapp "put in action all the springs of his influence, sustained by all his spiritual artillery." It was true, Justice Gibson wrote, that Peter Schriber had become old and weak. But it was also true that "he had been an orthodox member for more than twenty years," and had assented to, if not subscribed previously to, articles containing the same provisions and, further, had "delivered his money to the society as a free and absolute gift" while his mind was strong (p. 362).

In part on the basis of a commitment to the proposition that the civil law could not determine "that any point of doctrine is too absurd to be believed" (p. 363), Chief Justice Gibson found neither fraud on the part of George Rapp, nor undue influence, but only an attempt on the part of the Harmonist leader to "impress" his views on his followers in the "most striking terms" (p. 364). "The sum of the matter," Chief Justice Gibson said, "is, that a member of a religious society may not avoid a contract . . . on the basis of its peculiar faith, by setting up the supposed extravagance of its doctrines as proof that he was entrapped." There was a limitation on this doctrine. A contract "with a society whose principles would shock the moral or religious sense of the community, which is a legitimate subject of legal protection, would be void for illegality." But such, Justice Gibson said, "is not the society of George Rapp"; and besides, he added, "that ground of defense has not been taken."

4. *Goesele* v. *Bimeler*, 10 Fed. Cas. 528 (1851); 55 U.S. (14 How.) 589 (1852). The Zoar litigation, one phase of which was before the Supreme Court of the United States (and the next before the courts of Ohio, case no. 6 below) arose out of the expulsion of John Goesele from Zoar in 1845. Edgar Nixon provides an account of the facts surrounding the litigation,[20] which is the basis of the summary offered here. John Goesele, who had come to the society as a child with his father, one of the original members, was, with his wife Anna Maria Goesele, expelled from Zoar because they had mismanaged one of the Zoar enterprises, the Canal Tavern. The investigation at Zoar (January 15, 1845) revealed that the tavern "had been operated in a manner contrary to the rules of the Society, that drunkenness had been permitted on the premises, and that the society's funds had been misappropriated." The society then closed the tavern, and gave the Goeseles a home in the village. The Goeseles refused to vacate the tavern and ran it on their own. They were expelled from the society (p. 190). Before their case was filed in the circuit court, the Goeseles and their associates attempted to use extralegal means to get satisfaction from Zoar. On May 8, 1849, the dissident faction went to Zoar with their lawyer, David Quinn, posted circulars in the village, and took "forcible possession of the Meeting House." Their manifesto made the following points: "For a considerable time past," they said, "we have not been with you, having been banished

by the tyranny of one man, who serpent-like, full of deceit and cunning, wound himself around our Society, and . . . stripped it of all its liberties." They had not yet grown cold to the other Zoarites, however. While they knew "that mankind by continued suffering gets hardened and blunted, so that he is at length reconciled to even slavery itself, incapable of understanding his real situation," yet they also knew that many would "now step forward to assert their liberty and opinion," perhaps following the example of the American colonists in 1776.

They were cautious about litigation:

> To secure our rights by lawsuits, would not merely tend totally to break up the Society but also create an opening for the heirs of deceased members who then would take nearly half the property of the Society away, so that the actual members would have but the remaining half for partition and even this half would soon be squandered by [Bimeler's] schemes.

They proposed "a twofold way for the division of the estates"—one as a "practical partition of the real estate and movable property among the members," the other to estimate the value of the property and reduce it to $50 shares, and "then give to each member as many of these $50 shares in just proportion to the services rendered, and as compensation may require." This latter plan, they said, "would preserve the consistence of the Society and at the same time, take the right from one man, and give it to us all" (p. 195).

This appeal was signed by the Goeseles and others. The trustees of Zoar "immediately called a meeting of the Society in the schoolhouse, and called for a vote on the proposition." The proposals were discussed, Nixon reports, and rejected by unanimous vote, the Zoarites resolving "to make no concessions to the malcontents, but to leave the latter to seek what redress they could in the courts."[21]

The Goeseles' expulsion, considered an expulsion for cause, was not litigated. John Goesele and others stood before the circuit court and, later, on appeal, the Supreme Court of the United States, suing in equity for a partition of Zoar property as the heirs of Goesele's father, who had died in the society. The major points of David Quinn's argument for the Goesele party were that the members had made no valid contract with Bimeler, that they tried to transfer their property to an entity that had no legal existence and thus could not take the property, and that, in consequence, property rights remained in the members, subject to conventional rules of descent. Quinn characterized Zoar as a community of master and slaves. Goesele lost in both the circuit court and, on appeal, in the Supreme Court. There was a contract and it was valid. There were two opinions by Justice John McLean, first as circuit judge, then as a justice of the Supreme Court reviewing the case.

John McLean was nominated by President Jackson to the Supreme Court of the United States in 1829 and sat on the Court until 1861. He served as circuit judge for the seventh circuit (originally Tennessee, Kentucky, and Ohio, later Ohio, Indiana, Illinois, and Michigan). McLean was an active Methodist layman who held strong antislavery views. He was one of the dissenters in *Dred Scott* (60 U.S. (19 How.) 707 (1857)) and much earlier, as a judge of the Ohio Supreme Court, had written that "slavery . . . is an infringement upon the sacred rights of man."[22]

In the circuit court, Justice McLean held that while Zoar as an unincorporated association (before 1832) could not hold land, Bimeler, as an individual, could and did hold the property as trustee for the members of the society, who could contract with each other to give up individual rights in the trust property. The attempt made to "impeach the character of Bimeler, by taking the title to the real estate in his own name" as well as in the general mismanagement of the society, was not, in Justice McLean's opinion, justified.

McLean's opinion in the circuit court passed beyond a discussion of trustee and beneficiary to a discussion of the precise sort of association Zoar actually was: "If there be no principle of law opposed to such a community of property," McLean said, "it must be held valid," for there are "no moral considerations opposed to it" (10 Fed. Cas. 532). Zoar, in adopting communism, had followed the example found in the early history of the Apostles, and which received an awful sanction of heaven." There was no legal principle opposed to it, and the contract was upheld.

Justice McLean's discussion of Joseph Bimeler of Zoar demonstrates a refined understanding of the stresses and tensions in the religious communistic societies, perhaps resulting from McLean's own involvement in the affairs of the Methodists, or by contacts with the Shakers and the Harmonists.[23] His comments seem addressed to dissident members, and not to heirs. In communities like Zoar, McLean wrote as circuit judge, "dissatisfactions . . . arise from the contributions of labor required, or the distribution of the fruits of such labor" (10 Fed. Cas. 532-33). The "jealousy of the human heart often finds sources of discontent in the ordinary intercourse of life. Words are misconstrued, a look or an act is misunderstood, and many other things are considered as evidence of neglect or intentional offense, when the person charged is entirely innocent of the motive attributed to him." And then, "not unfrequently" these sentiments are "cherished by persons who are influenced by the base or unworthy motives which they attribute to others."

McLean returned to the defense of Bimeler in the opinion he wrote for the Supreme Court affirming the

circuit court decision: There are many depositions, he
said, on behalf of the Goeseles by "persons who have
been expelled from the Society, or, having left it, show a
strong hostility to Bimeler. They represent his conduct
as tyrannical and oppressive to the members of the association, and as controlling its actions absolutely" (14
How. 609). That Bimeler "is a man of great energy and
of high capacity for business, cannot be doubted,"
McLean wrote. "The present prosperity of Zoar is evidence of this." There are "few men to be found anywhere, who, under similar circumstances, would have
been equally successful." The people of his charge,
McLean wrote, "are proved to be moral and religious."
In addition, he noted, "It is said that, although the society has lived at Zoar for more than thirty years, no
criminal prosecution has been instituted against any one
of its members." And moreover, "the most respectable
men who live near the village say that the industry and
enterprise of the people of Zoar have advanced property
in the vicinity ten per cent." Bimeler himself, McLean
wrote, "has a difficult part to act. As the head and leader
of the Society, his conduct is narrowly watched, and often misconstrued. Narrow minds, in such an association,
will be influenced by petty jealousies and unjust sur-
mises. To insure success these must be overcome or
disregarded. The most exemplary conduct and conscientious discharge of duty may not protect an individual from censure."

Writing for the Supreme Court, Justice McLean repeatedly denied Quinn's version of the facts at Zoar,
from the character of Bimeler to the nature of the Separatist association. The evidence simply did not bear out
the arguments of complainants, Justice McLean insisted.
"The proofs and the statements in the bill are as remote
and inconsistent as can well be conceived" (14 How.
605). Complainants' counsel argued that their ancestors

had an interest "in the real and personal estate, owned by the association, and their counsel contends that the articles did not divest him of either, but both descended to his heirs at law at his death" (14 How. 606). This argument, Justice McLean responded, "does not seem to comprehend the principles of the association." As to the idea that John Goesele (who had died twenty-five years before) had once been wealthy and that his wealth had somehow been contributed to Zoar, "it is not shown that Goesele or any other member contributed to the general fund, with the exception of a small sum by Goesele which, probably, could not have exceeded five dollars." (The *Gasely* opinion, below, recites that John Goesele "had contributed to some extent to the general fund out of his private means.")

Justice McLean responded to the attack on the articles and addressed the issue of the possible "forfeiture" of rights upon excommunication of a member. But "what is the extent of this forfeiture? It is the right to a support from the society. And this is certainly reasonable. Can a member expect to be supported by the Society when he refuses to perform his part of the contract which entitles him to a support?" (14 How. 608). The term forfeiture was misapplied here, Justice McLean wrote: To begin with, no property was transferred to the association by John Goesele, but even if it had been, "would a court of chancery direct such property to be surrendered or paid for against the express contract of the owner? The surrender or giving up of the property was a part of the consideration on which the association stipulated to support him. It cannot be separated from that agreement."

The Zoar contracts, the Supreme Court said, were valid. Equity was not asked to enforce a forfeiture here. There was no forfeiture, against the will of the owner, but rather a contract in which any conveyance was part of the total exchange. There was no invalid perpetuity, because the organization existed at the will of a majority of the members, who could disband it when they chose to. And finally, there was no plantation at Zoar: "Many facts are proved wholly inconsistent with the charge of oppression."

The losing attorney, David Quinn, responded to the Goesele decisions in a "Review and Comparison" of the cases addressed to the Supreme Court. Quinn's review of the cases was not officially filed with the Supreme Court and was apparently not acted upon by that body. Its tone is more that of a protest than of a petition for re-hearing. Quinn regarded the Goesele decision as, in general, "McLean's decision only" because he could not believe that a "majority of the judges of the Supreme Court of the United States would willingly concur in as gross blunders of law, and misrepresentation of facts, as characterise it in nearly all its parts."

David Quinn denounced Justice McLean's decision at length: "It was known to his honour, that two parties existed at Zoar, one for, the other against Bimeler, and in addition to those who remained, others, who opposed him, had been driven off or compelled to leave by his tyranny and stripped of every farthing, which they had earned through thirty years of labor." Some of these former Zoarites "remained in the neighborhood of Zoar, others lay in the Poorhouse of Tuscarawas County, awaiting the decision of the court in this suit to determine whether or not they had any rights to the property, which they had earned." A "judge who is capable of making such a decision," Quinn wrote, "could do his country no better service than to DOUSE the ermine and leave the bench."[24]

5. *Baker* v. *Nachtrieb*, 60 U.S. (19 How.) 126 (1856). Case below: *Nachtrieb* v. *Harmony Settlement*, 17 Fed.

Cas. 1139 (W.D. Pa. 1855). Joshua Nachtrieb, on leaving the Harmony Society on June 18, 1846, had signed the following statement: "To-day I have withdrawn myself from the Harmony Society and ceased to be a member thereof. I have also received of George Rapp two hundred dollars as a donation, agreeably to the contract" (p. 128). At issue in the Nachtrieb case was the validity of this release, following a service of thirty years in the Harmony Society. A nineteenth century account of the Harmony Society discusses the Nachtrieb case and notes that "it was a hard case for the complainant. Public sympathy was very much in his favor, inasmuch as it appeared plainly in the course of the trial that his alleged *voluntary withdrawal* from the Society, which was plead as a bar to his claim, was virtually an *expulsion* by the authority of George Rapp." Nachtrieb was considered by the leaders to be a "disaffected and unsound member" and to be "in sympathy with those hostile seceders, who were still plotting against the Society and were reported as having threatened the destruction of the town."[25] The only offense charged against Nachtrieb was that he spoke for a few minutes with some friends outside the society.

The lower court opinion in the *Nachtrieb* case was written by Robert Grier. He was born in Pennsylvania in 1794 and was admitted to the bar in 1817. Grier was appointed a state judge in 1833 and served for thirteen years. The Senate confirmed Grier's appointment to the Supreme Court in 1846; he served until February 1870, when he retired, in failing health and under increasing mental disability.[26]

Justice Grier in his circuit court opinion discussed the provisions of the Harmony Society contract. It contained, he said, "no enumeration of offences by which a member should forfeit his rights and interest in their common property" (17 Fed. Cas. 1144). It "pointed out no tribunal which had a power to inflict the punishment of expulsion or forfeiture of all title to an immense property gained by their common contributions and labor." We can only look at the agreement of the parties, Grier said, but in this "we have found no power conferred on Rapp to expel, at his mere whim and caprice."

The court said that there was no proof of any act that would justify expulsion. If there was an expulsion, it was wrongful. That a party "wrongfully expelled would have a right to the interference of courts of justice," Grier noted, "has not been disputed." The point on which the case turns, Justice Grier said, was this: Did the complainant Nachtrieb "voluntarily and of his own accord abandon and forsake the society?" or "was he wrongfully and unjustly excluded or expelled?" Justice Grier discussed the release and discharge in some detail. In regard to the receipt, "when we consider the nature and extent of the authority exercised by Rapp over his followers—their reverence and fear of him, and their unbounded submission to his command—it must be evident that the signature of such a receipt would be but slender evidence that the complainant acted voluntarily in withdrawing himself from the society." It was plain, Justice Grier said, "that if Rapp commanded him to go, he would feel bound to go and that unless, after a servitude of thirty years, he was willing to go penniless, he must sign the receipt" (17 Fed. Cas. 1144-45). This was the "consideration for the means of departing without being reduced to beggary." If the complainant went from the society in obedience to the commands of Rapp, it might be said that he obeyed these commands voluntarily, since there was "no physical compulsion." Still, Justice Grier said, "we may easily conceive of a social or spiritual excommunication or a combination of both, which would leave as little choice to the party who feared them, as the rack or the inquisition."

On this perception of the case, Justice Grier decided in favor of Nachtrieb and ordered a division of the property of the Harmony Society with interest from that date. (Nachtrieb had asked for wages, which the court characterized as the "extreme and longest rate of compensation.")

The Harmony Society appealed the circuit court opinion, and the Supreme Court reversed. The defendant society's position, the Court said, was evidenced by a writing, signed by Nachtrieb, in which he acknowledged a voluntary secession from the society. This writing would have "much probative force" if treated simply as an admission of the statement it contained, but the Court felt the document was more than an admission (19 How. 129). "The writing must be treated as the contract of dissolution, between the plaintiff and the society, of their mutual obligations and engagements to each other" (19 How. 130). Considering the writing "as an instrument of evidence of this class, it is clear that the bill has not made a case in which its validity can be impeached." And, invoking general principles relating to the unassailability of written documents, the Court noted that "no evidence of prior declarations or antecedent conduct is admissible to contradict or to vary it."

It might have been possible to show, Justice Campbell wrote, that the Harmonist leader George Rapp, "instead of being patriarchal, was austere, oppressive, or tyrannical; his discipline vexatious and cruel"; that his instructions were "fanatical, and, upon occasions, impious"; that his system was "repugnant to public order, and the domestic happiness of its members"; that his financial management was "rapacious, selfish, or dishonest"; and finally, "that the condition of his subjects was servile, ignorant, and degraded, so that none of them were responsible for their contracts or engagements to him, from a defect of capacity and freedom." But to do this,

Justice Campbell concluded, "it was a necessary prerequisite that the bill should have been so framed as to exhibit such aspects of the internal arrangements and social and religious economy of the association." This was not done, and for this reason the evidence could not be considered. Nachtrieb's release was valid and binding.[27]

6. *Gasely** v. *Separatists Society of Zoar*, 13 Ohio 144 (1862). In 1862, the Goeseles, who had left Zoar in 1845, lost their battle against Zoar in the courts of Ohio, as they had lost earlier in the Supreme Court. David Quinn continued to attack the McLean opinion. The *Goesele* opinion, the Ohio court commented, "has been severely and somewhat rudely criticised by the counsel for the plaintiffs" (p. 157). Quinn again compared the Zoarites to slaves.[28]

The plaintiff in the action was Anna Maria Gasely and then, after she died, John Gasely as her heir. The plaintiff asserted membership in the society at Zoar and thus ownership of part of the property of the society. The bill asked for an accounting and partition of the Zoar property, which had passed to the society after the death of Joseph Bimeler in 1853.

The court's discussion of the Zoar articles noted that upon withdrawal or expulsion for cause the member's interests in the Zoar property ended. John Gasely, the court noted, was expelled, and Mrs. Gasely, who chose "rather to follow her husband than to remain, voluntarily departed and remained away until after the commencement of this suit, notwithstanding [that] the directors frequently notified her, that the society were still willing to receive and care for herself and her children if they would but return" (p. 152). This, the court

---

*Gasely = Goesele.

said, constituted withdrawal. She had, in 1824, signed the Zoar contract, which promised support out of the common fund while she was a member of the society. Her withdrawal must be regarded as voluntary insofar as continuing rights to the property were concerned.

"Mrs. Gasely may have been, and doubtless was, placed in a trying position; but this should not deprive the society of the right of self protection secured to it, and the most that can be said is, that it was her misfortune to be so connected by ties of affinity to one whom it became necessary for the society to expel" (pp. 153–54). She had received support while a member, which was all her contract entitled her to. Even if some argument were to prevail that might tend to void the covenant, she had no preexisting claim on the property (such as Gasely had as heir of his father), and her own claim, for support in exchange for services, had been fully met.

The Ohio court regarded the case as one "in which the equity powers of the court are invoked to decree an account and partition in favor of those who do not show any present legal or equitable right to the property . . . and found their right, principally if not altogether, upon the *legal incapacity* of the present possessors to hold it" (p. 156, emphasis in original). The court also noted that articles of 1824 had been upheld in the earlier Goesele case, and that it was not prepared to say that the decision was incorrect: "It is certainly sustained by several decisions closely resembling it" (p. 157, citing *Schriber, Nachtrieb, Waite,* and *Gass and Bonta*).

7. *Grosvenor* v. *United Society of Believers*, 118 Mass. 78 (1875). In May 1819, Maria F. and Roxalana Grosvenor went with their father, mother, and two brothers, Lorenzo and Augustus, to live with the Shakers. On June 11, 1834, they signed the covenant and became covenant members of the society. After forty-six years in

the Shaker community at Harvard, Massachusetts, Maria F. and Roxalana (who had become interested in mesmerism) were expelled on July 25, 1865, for doctrinal deviance.[29] They sued in the courts of Massachusetts, urging that their doctrines were not deviant. They lost. The civil courts have no standard by which to try doctrinal deviance. Their contract was an explicit agreement to leave all questions relating to expulsion to be decided by the Shakers, who had decided to expel them.

Judge Wells[30] delivered a short, straightforward opinion in the case, based first on the contract, and second on the proposition (from the field of church and state, though it is not identified this way) that the particular claim that Roxalana Grosvenor and her sister urged—to the effect that their beliefs were not nonconforming—could not be tried in a civil court. The Grosvenors did not attack the covenant; rather they argued that they had been denied rights under it. The Shaker covenant, Roxalana Grosvenor had written in her own publication of the Shaker document (1873) "must speak for itself." The covenant, "with all the power it gives, would be harmless," she said, "in the hands of such persons as were the Founders of the Institution." But, who, she asked, "shall vouch for 'their successors forever'?"[31] It was these successors, she argued before the courts of Massachusetts, who had violated her rights under the covenant by expelling her for religious nonconformity.

The Massachusetts appellate court heard the case in the spring of 1875. The case involved a wage claim to recover for services rendered the Shakers, a claim for damages for breach of contract (unjust expulsion), and a claim for expenses of the plaintiffs since their expulsion. The statement of facts in the case report contains an account of the expulsion.

> It appeared that a short time before [July 26, 1865] the ministers and elders charged them with entertaining

opinions and promulgating doctrines within the society, at variance with the established belief and subversive of the organization, and a hearing was had before the ministers and elders on that subject, and they were asked to state their views. There was much conversation on points of doctrine, and the discussion was confined to the question whether the plaintiffs were in conformity with the religious faith and doctrine of the society, the plaintiffs insisting that they were. The plaintiffs adhered to their views, and were told if they persisted they would have to leave. The next day they were again before the ministers and elders, and still adhering, they were told they must go to the office with their things, which was the equivalent to an expulsion. They did so and the next day left the community. No formal charges or charges in writing were made against them, and it was admitted by the defendant that there was no record of the proceedings. All the ministers and elders were present on the occasions mentioned (p. 85).

The Grosvenor sisters admitted at the trial that they were expelled for alleged nonconformity, but they denied that their views were in fact nonconforming. They offered proof on the issue, but the judge refused to admit the evidence and submit their question to the jury. The verdicts were for the defendant Shakers.

The opinion by Justice Wells for the Supreme Judicial Court of Massachusetts sustained the position of the Shakers. The rights of each of the Grosvenor sisters must be determined by provisions of the Shaker contract, and under this, first, each could not recover for her services because "all such right is expressly and explicitly renounced" (p. 90). She could not recover for the expenses of her support since her expulsion from the Shakers because "whatever support she was entitled to receive under the 'covenant' she was to enjoy as a member of the church so constituted," and only "while standing in Gospel union and maintaining the principles of this covenant." This, Justice Wells wrote, was "not an absolute right of support" but merely a qualified right, the "extent and manner of which can be measured and determined only by the constituted authorities of the organization thus created." Finally, neither sister was entitled to recover damages for expulsion from the church. By contract, she had accepted a particular authority and had been found by that authority[32] "to be not in conformity with the principles of the society" (p. 91). Upon receiving a warning she "refused to submit to the admonition." She was then "excluded for refusing to 'conform and subject' herself 'to the counsels and directions of the elders,' and, still persisting in and adhering to the objectionable opinions and doctrines, she proposes to try here the question whether they are in reality inconsistent with the established belief of the society." This could not be done, Justice Wells wrote. "We have no standard by which to try that question."

8. *Speidel* v. *Henrici*, 120 U.S. 377 (1887). Among the allegations of the complaint of Elias Speidel, an old man when he brought suit (he died before decision by the Supreme Court), are the following: He was born and raised in the Harmony Society, which Rapp fraudulently and corruptly created, taking advantage of the "ignorance and helplessness" of his followers and of their "blind reliance upon him as the prophet of the Lord, and the Lord's chosen mouthpiece in guiding them to salvation" (p. 379). He himself was "raised in and as a part of said community, and, in common with the younger members of the families forming the same, was taught from his earliest infancy by Rapp to believe, and by reason of said teachings did believe" (p. 381) in the doctrines of George Rapp. Until he left the community in 1831 to marry, "he was kept under such duress and restraint by the iron rule of said Rapp that he did not know, and had no means of ascertaining, the iniquity

and degradation thereof and the impious and blasphe-
mous character of the teachings of said Rapp" (p. 383).

The *Speidel* case was not a suit to avoid a contract.
The objective of the bill in equity was that the trust of
the Harmony Society should be rescinded, "as resting
upon fraud and iniquity and being contrary to public
policy and the laws of the land" and that the persons
interested in its assets, the plaintiff included, should "be
remitted to their original rights" (p. 384). The court did
not pass on the debate over the trust, finding only that
after a fifty-year delay, Speidel was not entitled to relief
in equity. A demurrer by the defendant society to the
effect that the complaint was stale had been sustained by
the circuit court, and this decree was affirmed by the
Supreme Court.

9. *Burt* v. *Oneida Community*, 137 N.Y. 346 (1893),
was an action in equity brought against the successor to
the Oneida community. The case was brought by a former member, the plaintiff urging that his expulsion
should be judged void, that he should be judged a member of the community, that a dissolution of the community should be considered void, that the community
should be held to hold the property in its possession in
trust for the plaintiff and other members of the community, and, finally, that a decree should be rendered for a
division and distribution of property. Justice Maynard
wrote the opinion for the New York Court of Appeals.
He reviewed the facts: The father of the plaintiff was
one of the founders of Oneida. Burt, then four years old,
had become provisionally a member of the community
during his minority. "Upon attaining his majority he formally assented to its article of covenant, and remained
in its communion until the year 1880, when the controversy arose" (p. 353). Judge Maynard, writing more than
a decade after the conversion of the utopian Oneida to a

joint stock company, was able to view the community strictly as a business enterprise. "It is not important to consider here the moral and religious teachings of the community, which were manifestly potent influences during the formative period of its existence. What principally concerns us now was its status as a business compact, and we must stop, when we have construed the contract relation of the parties and determined the rights acquired by virtue of a membership therein." In this respect, he writes, "the main purpose of its promoters was evidently the propagandism of certain communistic views as to the acquisition and enjoyment of property, and the endeavor to put into practical operation an economic and industrial scheme which should embody and illustrate the doctrines which they held and inculcated." Necessarily, "the basic proposition of such a community was the absolute and complete surrender of the separate and individual rights of property of the persons entering it." The court then summarized the Oneida compact: "the property of each subscriber immediately became an inseparable part of the community's capital, and, while no one was compelled to toil, yet labor was enjoined as a religious duty, and the earnings of all were mingled in the common treasury" (p. 354). Every member of the community was free "to withdraw at any time upon his own motion," but he "could not take with him or demand as a right any share of the joint property." Accounts were kept of the property contributed by a member upon his admission, and if a member withdrew "it was the practice to refund it or its equivalent in value without interest or increase." But this "was not regarded in the light of an obligation, but as a matter of good will and liberality." The refund would be given at a time and in a fashion decided by the community, which "might discontinue the custom at any time or refuse to refund in any case." The "education, subsistence, clothing and other necessaries of life furnished them and their children were to be received as just equivalents for all their labor and services, and no claim for wages was to be made by any withdrawing member." And there was "a mutual stipulation that no member or his heirs, executors, administrators or assigns would ever bring any action, either at law or in equity or other process or proceeding for wages or other compensation for services, nor for the recovery of any property contributed at any time, or make any claim or demand therefor of any kind or nature whatsoever." There was no fraud or duress in the signing of the contract and "viewing it solely as a business undertaking [the court thus avoids the difficult issue of the legal status of complex marriage], it was not prohibited by any statute or in contravention of any law regulating the possession, ownership or tenure of property" (pp. 354–55).

The court passed to a discussion of the particular history of the plaintiff. He had "contributed nothing in money or other property to the capital of the community" (p. 356), and was educated at Oneida's expense at the Scientific School of Yale College. From 1865, when he came of age, until 1879, he seemed to have been a devoted member of the community. "During the latter part of this period dissensions arose in the community apparently on account of some of its anomalous social practices." The court pursued Burt's history. In 1880 he decided to leave the community and enter the employment of the Erie Preserving Company, a rival manufacturer of canned goods. The court reviewed extensively Burt's engagements with the other company and the community's response to it, and finally concluded that if one accepted the plaintiff's version of his conduct and declarations, "we think it must be held that he renounced his obligations as a member of the community and severed his conventional relations with it" (p. 359).

It cannot help him, the court said, that he attempted to reserve to himself the privilege of returning and resuming his membership. "The constitution of the community did not admit the exercise of such an option" (p. 360). Burt had written to the administrative council of Oneida, telling them of his plan to be a traveling salesman of a rival company, and proposing to change his place of residence and keep his earnings. The administrative council adopted a resolution reciting that Burt had voluntarily withdrawn and saying that he "had, by this act, severed his connection with the community" (p. 358). This was referred to a meeting of the entire community, called a family meeting, where it was confirmed. Burt said he had been expelled; the community argued that he had withdrawn, and the court agreed. The court reviewed the nature of the contractual relationship:

> He could not withdraw when, in his judgment, such a course would be profitable and assert the right to come back and be received into the fellowship of the association when it suited his pleasure or convenience or self interest to do it. The community had not made a unilateral bargain of that kind with him. He had not so far surrendered his freedom of action that he might not go out at any time without notice and without their assent; but in so doing he terminated his right to share in the enjoyment of the use and possession of the property of the concern. It is not correct to say that by his withdrawal from membership he forfeited his interest in the lands and chattels of the community. He forfeited nothing. The contingency or event upon which the existence of his estate in the property depended had happened. By the terms of the contract under which that estate was acquired, its duration was only co-existent with the duration of his membership (p. 360).

The court noted that the plaintiff had staked his case entirely "upon the plea that he was illegally and unjustly expelled from membership" (p. 361). It is true that if Burt could have shown that, he would have had "a good cause of action," but the court found no proof in the record of an expulsion. Burt also attempted to argue that he was entitled to the conventional settlement from the Oneida community, but that the court found that a letter he had written in which he said he did not expect to make any settlement operated as an estoppel on this point.

Burt's lawyer argued, finally, that Burt had been expelled and that his expulsion was illegal, in part because "Burt never received any notice that the council or business board, or any body of members of the community intended to act upon the matter of his expulsion" (p. 348). He was, his counsel urged, entitled to notice and to be heard. "The omission to serve him with such notice is fatally defective, and of itself renders all proceedings null and void." He was unsuccessful on this point, as counsel for the Grosvenor sisters had been before him.

The critical point, for our purposes, is that *Burt* v. *Oneida Community* passed on the contract of the Perfectionists after they had abandoned complex marriage. The court did not so much approve the alternative domestic institution of the Perfectionists as declare it moot. In terms of the response of the legal system, Oneida presents an odd case. Unlike the Mormons, the community was not forced into submission. Although the possibility of state action was pervasive, in fact there was little state activity of any kind directed against Oneida in the thirty years of its existence in New York.[33] There was considerably more state concern with the celibate Shakers. But where the Shakers were often vindicated, and where the legal literature reveals clear statements concerning the worthiness of the Shaker sect and/or its right to exist in a free country, one finds little of the sort relating to Oneida. On the contrary, religious promiscuity is sometimes used as an example of a practice which will not be tolerated.[34] At best, it seems that Oneida was grudgingly accommodated. The outside society was often hostile, but the outside state was largely silent.

The largest legal proposition involved in these cases is hardly articulated in the legal syntheses on the law of the communistic societies—and was similarly not a direct issue in the litigation—not because it was too subtle for the commentators but because it was too obvious. The communities were to be judged by the positive law of the state. The point is stated emphatically in a headnote to *Nachtrieb*: "The law allows no communities, however independent in their structure of general society—or however long established—or however much in the habit of regulating, as a community in a community, their own concerns—to be above its constant and complete control" (17 Fed. Cas. 1139).[35] The communities as litigants did not debate the point. It was their existence that seemed to raise the issue.

The particular contracts that regulated the relationships between member and voluntary association were also the constitutional documents of churches and of tiny, semi-autonomous groups. The judgment of the courts must have been, in general, that the utopian communities considered as churches, or as associations, were deviant but not dangerous. The former utopians, as Towner so triumphantly noted, regularly lost, and they lost on the theory of freedom of contract. The history of the utopian communities presents in this respect an obvious contrast to the history of social and industrial reform in America. Where the labor movement and other movements for social reform were hindered by the doctrine of freedom of contract, the utopian movement was sustained by it. The Communist Manifesto of Marx and Engels referred to the utopians without enthusiasm. "They still dream of experimental realization of their social utopias, of founding isolated 'phalanstères,' of establishing 'home colonies,' or setting up a 'little Icaria' [footnote omitted]—duodecimo editions of the New Jerusalem—and to realize all these castles in the air, they are compelled to appeal to the feeling and purses of the bourgeois."[36] One might have added "law."

The attempt here is not to draw from this litigation conclusions relating to the utopian experience itself.[37] Rather, the point is that the litigation reveals one way in which contemporary law judged the communities. There was nothing absolutely inevitable about these judgments. If the courts had judged the communities differently, or had been presented with more compelling facts in favor of the plaintiffs, one might have seen quite different results. One can speculate on the results of a lawsuit over Oneida's contract, for example, had such a suit come to court during the years of complex marriage. A case involving a Mormon splinter group may serve to illustrate further.

After leaving Nauvoo, the Mormons under Brigham Young moved west to Utah. One splinter group that broke off and went its own way was led by Charles B. Thompson,[38] who arrived in Iowa in 1853 and soon built a community called Preparation. ("Preparation" because "it was to be but a brief biding place in which his followers were to so school and discipline themselves as to be fit partakers in that larger life that was to be the lot of these Latter-day Saints when their early careers were done."[39]) Thompson received gifts and tithings of personal property and land from his followers. With this property, he bought other land. Things did not go well. People living around Preparation began to suspect that Thompson was mistreating his flock. The residents of Preparation seem to have agreed, and by 1858 Thompson fled from the anger of his followers. After this, he conveyed to his wife, his brother, and one other the property claimed now to belong to the individual plaintiffs. He was sued by members of his group. They were actually farming a good deal of the land in controversy, and asked recognition of their legal claim to the property.

Justice Dillon of Iowa approached the facts of *Scott* v. *Thompson*[40] with something like astonishment: "The record in this case," the court said, "exhibits a transaction almost as marvelous as the pretended revelation of Thompson would have been if true" (p. 601), and the statement of the facts of the case "gives but a faint idea of the uncontrolled and absolute subjection of the members in body, mind and estate to him whom they for a time sincerely regarded and obeyed as the chief steward of the Lord and the first-born of the kingdom in these last days" (pp. 601–2). Thompson's wish was their law; the obedience they rendered was "cheerful, confiding and unquestioning." Thompson was their "guide, temporal and spiritual." This "boundless *confidence*" of the group in their leader must be borne in mind, the court said, in passing on the issue of fraud. The Iowa court ordered the case removed so that the trust might be closed "and the property divided if the parties desired it."

"We very much doubt that Thompson can be viewed as simply an enthusiast or a fanatic," the Iowa court said. "There is much evidence of a design from the beginning to draw to himself by various arts and devices the property of the society" (p. 603). He thought that he had done this, the court said, but "equity delights to brush away the barricades of formal documents, receipts, and papers." In *Thompson*, the special relationship between the leader and community was viewed as imposing a fiduciary duty. The property had not been conveyed to Thompson for his own individual benefit, but rather for the benefit of the group. Thompson held the property as a trustee for his followers and had violated his trust.

It is clear that the splinter group at Preparation was seen as a part of the larger movement of the Latter-day Saints. The evidence in the case, the court said, illustrated the extent of the "credulity which forms so curious a phase in certain proportions of the race," a "credulity which lies at the foundation of that wonderful spectacle of our own times, by which Mormonism, retreating from Nauvoo to the vastnesses of distant and then almost unexplored regions has, within twenty years, swelled its proportions, drawing its converts across the ocean and continents, from a mere handful to more than a quarter of a million of people."

The essence of the case is that Thompson was a prophet who had betrayed his followers. He appeared in court not only as a fanatic but as a fraud in the eyes of his own people. The court chose to protect the followers against an unscrupulous leader. Would the case have appeared differently if the claim was that Thompson had somehow betrayed not all of his followers but only some? Or one?

The next chapter reopens some of the issues of the utopian cases, examining them in light of a variety of policies and doctrines relating both to contracts and to religious liberty.

Part 5

A Framework for Pluralism

In enforcing contracts, the government does not merely allow two individuals to do what they have found pleasant in their eyes. Enforcement, in fact, puts the machinery of the law in the service of one party against the other. When that is worthwhile and how that should be done are important questions of public policy.

Morris Raphael Cohen

12

Law-Ways

Partly courts look directly at society. Partly they look at the deposit of their own work made in the past on similar occasions, that is, at the existing "ways" of law.

Karl N. Llewellyn

It is widely held that something basic in the legal system changed after the Civil War; that before the war judges were less rigid in their approach, responsive to the larger public issues, willing in their decisions to test propositions against considerations of policy.[1] Later, perhaps because of increased activity by the legislature, the role of judges became more formal. It was, Grant Gilmore noted, "during the post-Civil War period that the idea that courts never legislate—that the judicial function is merely to declare the law that already exists—became an article of faith, for lawyers and non-lawyers alike."[2] This is not a change in the available legal doctrine so much as a change in the thinking of the judges, among others, on the subject of appropriate judicial roles.

But other things in the legal system did not change so radically. "The years 1800 to 1875 were," J. Willard Hurst wrote, "above all else, the years of contract in our law."[3] The dominant conviction of nineteenth century industrial society, Kessler and Gilmore said, was the "deep-felt conviction that individual and cooperative action should be left unrestrained in family, church and market and that such a system of laissez-faire would not lessen the freedom and dignity of the individual, but would secure the highest possible social justice."[4]

The ideas of freedom of contract were the "judicial expression of the independence of the economic order from the overlordship of the state."[5] These ideas, operating in a system based on inequality of wealth, tended to validate the idea of inequality, in principle as well as in fact. This was recognized by the Supreme Court in *Coppage* v. *Kansas*[6] in 1914: "[W]herever the right of private property exists," the Court said, "there must be and will be inequalities of fortune; and thus it naturally happens that parties negotiating about a contract are not equally unhampered by circumstances."

> [W]herever the right of private property and the right of free contract co-exist, each party when contracting is inevitably more or less influenced by the question whether he has much property, or little, or none. . . . And, since it is self-evident that, unless all things are held in common, some persons must have more property than others, it is from the nature of things impossible to uphold freedom of contract and the right of private property without at the same time recognizing as legitimate those inequalities of fortune that are the necessary result of the exercise of those rights.[7]

In the case of the utopias, freedom of contract was being used to create institutions clearly opposed to the institutions of the outside world. At issue was whether these groups and this use of the law of contract would be tolerated.

In the case of the religious-communistic utopias, a legal question relating to church and state was added to the contracts issues, simply because the utopias were religious societies. They claimed exalted precedents, as clear even in the simple declaration that Oneida was created "for the purpose of religious fellowship and discipline."[8] In addition to freedom of contract, there was evident in the utopian contract cases a strong judicial commitment to both collective and individual religious freedom. One saw this commitment in *Waite* v. *Merrill*,[9] where it was argued that the Shaker covenant was invalid because it was in derogation of the "inalienable right of liberty of conscience." To this, Chief Justice Mellen said, the answer is obvious. "The very formation and subscription of this covenant is an exercise of the inalienable right of liberty of conscience." In addition, there was no reason "why the society in question may not frame their creed and covenant as well as other societies of Christians; and worship God according to the dictates of their consciences." We must remember that "in this land of liberty, civil and religious, conscience is subject to no human law; its rights are not to be invaded or even questioned, so long as its dictates are obeyed, consistently with the harmony, good order and peace of the community."[10] Tolerance, a modern biographer of Mellen has remarked, was the "hallmark of [his] religious faith."[11] But he was not unique. Justice Underwood of Kentucky (*Gass and Bonta* v. *Wilhite*) similarly insisted on religious freedom: "No man can sell his liberty and become a slave," he wrote, "nor can any one sell his liberty of conscience, and make his temporal rights depend upon a creed and its observances. There are inalienable rights recognized by our constitution, and liberty of conscience is one of them."[12]

Equally visible in the cases was the tradition of separation of church and state, in which courts have a limited role in church affairs. "As a judge," Justice Underwood said in *Gass and Bonta*, "I have nothing to do with creeds or their orthodoxy."[13] "Our laws," said Chief Justice Gibson in *Schriber* v. *Rapp*, "presume not to meddle with spiritualities."[14] Roxalana Grosvenor "proposes to try here the question whether [her beliefs] are in reality inconsistent with the established belief of the society," wrote Justice Wells in *Grosvenor.* "We have no standard by which to try that question."[15]

The separationist tradition was visible in the caution with which civil courts approached disputes within churches and disputes involving the covenants of churches—litigation involving the expulsion of members, for instance, or the disposition of church property. In dealing with such matters, the American tradition of separation of church and state combined statements of religious toleration with statements of the limitations on state and judicial action. The American constitutional position was that courts would not judge religious questions. "The law knows no heresy," the Supreme Court said, "and is committed to the support of no dogma."[16]

Thus, in the American system, religious organizations were granted considerable independence and autonomy in the running of the internal affairs of the group. Justice Brandeis, in 1929, stated the general proposition: "In the absence of fraud, collusion, or arbitrariness, the decisions of the proper church tribunals on matters purely ecclesiastical, although affecting civil rights, are accepted in litigation before the secular courts as conclusive, because the parties in interest made them so by contract or otherwise."[17] Respect for church autonomy and a concern for what is now termed "entanglement" dictated restraint.

It is also true that, through the nineteenth century, judges often spoke out of a legal tradition that had a deep respect not only for religion generally but for Christianity in particular. Chancellor Kent of New York in 1811 upheld a blasphemy conviction, on the theory that offense to Christianity was properly a crime in a Christian nation.[18] In 1844, Supreme Court Justice Joseph Story upheld the will of the philanthropist Stephen Girard, which had provided broadly that "no ecclesiastic, missionary, or minister of any sect whatsoever shall ever hold or exercise any station or duty whatever in the said college; nor shall any such person ever be admitted for any purpose."[19] The will was challenged by Girard's heirs, represented by Daniel Webster, on the grounds that the plan for the college for white orphans was in derogation of the Christian religion, as well as to law and policy, Christianity being part of the common law of the state of Pennsylvania. Justice Story agreed that Christianity was part of the common law—"in this qualified sense, that its divine origin and truth are admitted"—but not that the Girard will offended Christianity. It merely provided that the teaching of Christianity should be done by lay teachers. Girard had ordered that the "purest principles of morality" be taught, Story said, and these could not be learned so clearly from any source but the New Testament.[20] There was in the course of the century a weakening of religious commitment. "Religion," Henry James, Sr. wrote, "in the old virile sense has disappeared, and been replaced by a feeble Unitarian sentimentality."[21] Nevertheless, Christianity still provided the terms in which certain particularly heated questions were discussed. Polygamy, the Supreme Court said in 1890, was "contrary to the spirit of Christianity and of the civilization which Christianity has produced in the Western world."[22]

In the case of some judges, religious belief or religious affiliation is, in addition, a visible part of the judicial biography. Greenleaf wrote of Mellen that the "crowning trait of his character was his sterling integrity—his high moral principle—his religious and abiding sense of accountability to God; of whose omnipresence and holy attributes he was early imbued with a filial and profound reverence." Mellen "often and tenderly dwelt upon the hope of mercy and pardon through the merits of his Saviour Jesus Christ."[23] Grier, "down to his latest years," was a "daily reader and a very critical student, of the New Testament in its original Greek."[24] John McLean was an active Methodist layman.[25] John Wells of Massachusetts was president of the American Unitarian Association.[26]

It was a government of law, not of men; but the ideas and personalities of the men administering the law are a matter for inquiry. There are times when one is interested in the private opinions of judges on various questions because their views, seriously and conscientiously held, may conflict with the formal demands of the legal system.[27] Or we may be interested in the private views of judges because we suspect some hidden correlations between opinions privately held and the decisions publicly issued from the bench.[28] There are still other instances in which the formal and official demands of the legal system inevitably permit the judge considerable latitude in the application of the legal rules. Such a case may arise when a contract is denounced not as illegal but, more broadly, as against public policy. It may arise when the question is whether a contract is oppressive or unconscionable within the meaning of doctrines of the equity courts, or whether the means of securing consent—in a case involving single individuals whose state of mind at one moment in time is precisely the thing being examined—were legitimate. In the one example, public policy, the question addressed is so loose and large that often individual judgments will be introduced; in the other, the question is so sensitive and particularized that the values, capacities, and limitations of the individual passing on the question are inevitably involved.

Sometimes in the arguments of the lawyers in the utopian cases we can see lawyers directly appealing to a judge's sense of policy. Thus, a part of the defense of Zoar in the Supreme Court concentrated on the community's political and social aspects. "So far from being at all aristocratic," Zoar's counsel said, "this Society is a pure democracy." The officers were chosen by ballot, "every member, male and female, having an equal voice." "No single dogma in religion or politics is announced, no unusual restraint on marriage, nor subserviency to any doctrine out of the common way exist."[29] Henry Stanbery, who was the U.S. attorney general from 1866 to 1868 and counsel for Andrew Johnson in his impeachment proceedings, represented the Harmonists in the Supreme Court (with Loomis), as well as Zoar in its litigation. Stanbery's argument (*Goesele*) before the Supreme Court effectively distinguishes Zoar from other communities, particularly the Shakers and the Harmonists. In the opinion of John McLean, as judge in the circuit court proceeding involving Zoar, another policy consideration was evident. There was nothing wrong with the Zoar contract, Justice McLean wrote; the Separatist society followed the example of the Apostles.[30]

But respect for religion in general or Christianity in particular did not of itself dictate a high regard for the communistic utopians any more than it dictated regard for the Latter-day Saints. The citation of biblical authority did not end the legal question. To begin with, as Chief Justice Gibson noted, the community of goods described in the New Testament was not necessarily regarded as a universal objective.[31] Further, community of goods could be interpreted as an attack on property and was associated at times with attacks on marriage and the family. Thus, in seventeenth century England, there had been concern about the practices religious toleration might bring with it. "Liberty of conscience," it was said, "falsely so called, may in good time improve itself into liberty of estates and liberty of houses and liberty of wives."[32] In America, as the law developed, conscience was said to be free, but practices could be restrained.

Thus, in 1875, Justice William Strong of the Supreme Court wrote of the Mormons:

> It is well known one of the doctrines of that organization, is that polygamy is in harmony with the law of God and commendable. Revolting as such a doctrine is, and demoralizing in its influence, it has not been thought that either the common law or any statute of the United States can break up the organization or forbid its members from holding and avowing such a belief, or associating for its propagation. But, the practice of it, in other words, its outworking, is within the control of the civil law, and acts of Congress have been passed forbidding and punishing plural marriages. It would be idle for a Mormon indicted for bigamy to plead that his second marriage was recognized as lawful by his church, and sanctioned by his own religious convictions.[33]

Indeed, it was idle, and George Reynolds, whose appeal came before the Supreme Court only a few years later, was convicted of bigamy.

As Justice Strong had views on the Mormons, other judges had opinions on other utopians. "As a general thing, I have a very poor opinion of all common property communities. . . . Their objects may be benevolent, but their tendency is to degenerate and demoralize man. Against this particular community I have no prejudice. In their favor much may be said. . . ." The Court in the case of the Shaker Stephen Ball believed that certain aspects of Shaker life—industry, order, cleanliness— were "well worthy of imitation."[34] Descriptions of the Shakers in early Maine and New Hampshire cases seem to reflect a positive attitude. A description of the Shakers by the Supreme Court of Maine has already been quoted:

> They are in general quiet, sober, and industrious; and the fruits of these commendable qualities are exhibited

to the public eye, in their beautiful villages and cultivated grounds, and in the apparent comfort and abundance, with which they are surrounded.[35]

A case report of *Heath* v. *Draper* (New Hampshire, 1810) says that in that case, it had "been hinted, and *only* hinted, that this dedication of property and labour was to superstitious uses, to a false religion and so not binding." But, the report continues, "no one can see the improvements made in husbandry and manufactures by this sect, and at the same time believe the existence of the sect to be against the policy of the law."[36] Later, another court was less flattering about a utopian group: This is a "most extraordinary proceeding," based on a "unique and weird complaint," a New Mexico court said. "The most that can be gathered from the declaration is that the defendants had conceived some Utopian scheme for the amelioration of all the ills, both temporal and spiritual, to which human flesh and soul are heir."[37] Defendants had then "sent forth their siren notes, which, sweeter and more seductive than the music that led the intrepid Odysseus to the Isle of Calypso, reached the ears of the plaintiff at his far-off home in Georgia, and induced him to consecrate his life and labors, and all his worldly effects," to this new gospel.[38]

Even a sympathetic perspective on the utopian enterprise did not require, moreover, the proposition that religious exemptions from the civil law were appropriate. Perhaps a judge would believe that religious exemptions were fundamentally not ever appropriate. Chief Justice Morrison Waite said in *Reynolds* that a constitutional religious exemption would open the possibility that each man could create his own law. Justice Felix Frankfurter made the argument more elaborately: "It would never have occurred to Jefferson and others," Frankfurter said, "to write into the Constitution the subordination of the general civil authority of the state to sectarian scruples."[39] For Justice Frankfurter, religious exemption meant that "each individual could set up his own censor against obedience to laws conscientiously deemed for the public good by those whose business it is to make laws"; and rather than having separation of church and state, one would have "the subordination of the state on any matter deemed within the sovereignty of the religious conscience."[40]

But the course of the litigation has demonstrated that constitutionally protected religious liberty involves not only freedom to worship but freedom from certain aspects of state regulation. Sometimes, as in sabbatarian or religious pacifist exemptions, freedom from state regulation will be written into a statute. Sometimes, though infrequently, the exemption will be written in by a court. There seems to be some room in the constitutional system for the religiously motivated to seek exemption from generally applicable laws on First Amendment grounds. Such claims are often rejected (so that polygamy was not protected, nor child labor),[41] but sometimes upheld. Under constitutional principles of religious freedom and free exercise, the Amish, in 1972, were permitted what constituted in effect a religious exemption from the compulsory education law (*Wisconsin* v. *Yoder*), at least to the extent of two years of high school.[42] It is a necessary implication that there are instances in which exemptions will be allowed, and that the law sets for itself the determination, case by case, of those instances in which such exemptions will be permitted.

The utopian contract cases were resolved without breaking or even noticeably bending well-known doctrines in the field of contracts. But if we stress the relationship between policies relating to religious liberty and policies (particularly policing policies) relating to freedom of contract, these questions arise: Does one have a

First Amendment right to make (and have enforced against oneself later) an unconscionable contract? Has one a free exercise right to waive contract defenses which might otherwise be viewed as nonwaivable? Does one have a free exercise right, for example, to have a contract enforced that might be otherwise voidable for duress? And if the association cannot in the end remove itself from the authority of the state, can the individual remove himself, by finally and irrevocably subjecting himself to some other, intermediate authority through contract?

In the nineteenth century, as today, the body of legal rules and exceptions—or (worse) of rules and counter-rules—available to a court was large, large enough to support quite different results in a single case. The critical problem is thus, at times, not so much the finding of an applicable rule—let alone *the* applicable rule—as the choice between applicable rules.

The nineteenth century courts were accustomed to hearing contract cases and to dealing with a body of abstract contract doctrine as it applied to a variety of different situations. If we ignore for a moment the fact that the utopians established themselves in physically separate communities, we find that the religious-communistic societies were like conventional religious groups in the large system of voluntary churches, which, after the demise of the established state churches, characterized American religious organization. The contracts of the utopians can be seen as differing from the ordinary church covenant largely in degree, in their complexity, and, finally, in the comprehensiveness of the relationship that was created.[43] But the contracts had secular analogues as well. They had points of resemblance to two forms of contract well known to the law—the contract of employment and the marriage contract.

EMPLOYMENT CONTRACTS

From one perspective, the utopian contracts were contracts for labor and employment, fitting under economist Richard Ely's definition of contracts as "agreements of economic significance which are enforceable by public authority."[44] The contracts are in this sense exactly the kind of agreement generally protected under ideas of the right to contract for the disposition of one's own labor: "The general right to make a contract in relation to his business is part of the liberty of the individual protected by the 14th Amendment of the Federal Constitution" (*Lochner* v. *New York*).[45] In *Gasely*, the position of Anna Maria Gasely was explicitly compared to a worker for wages. Both had made an agreement that set compensation and both had been paid under that agreement—the laborer in wages, Mrs. Gasely in support. Why should she now be allowed to receive something more than the laborer by way of a claim to the property?

> Her labor contributed to its acquisition, it is true, and so did the labor of any outsider the company may have employed and paid his stipulated wages. Why should the rule hold good as to the one and fail as to the other? Both are now strangers to the property and both have received the entire compensation agreed to be paid to them.[46]

Although the communities were not bargaining for labor, or even for the able bodied (they did not seek particular labor attributes any more than they sought wealth in their new members), in fact, valuable skills might be offered a community as well as the money the member brought in. Thus Towner's approach to the Oneida community, for example, referred to his labor potential. The contracts of the communities and their members could thus legitimately be seen as labor contracts involving disparity of bargaining power, low wages, and either resignation or justified or unjustified termination of employment, all familiar to the outside society and to the courts.

MARRIAGE CONTRACTS

For all that some of the utopian doctrines were perceived as antagonistic to the conventional nineteenth century family, there was another sense in which the utopians had simply created another kind of family structure. The contract bore, in this respect, a resemblance to the particular form of legal contract by which individuals create a family unit. The obligation assumed by the society for the support of the member might reflect this sense of extended family and go explicitly beyond the individual. The maintenance provisions of the Harmony contract, for example, reached the case of children whose parents had either died or departed from the society.[47]

The image of the communities as families was used repeatedly by the communitarians and by those who observed them. Noyes himself insisted that the contract used by the Oneida Perfectionists created a family, and thus that the terms on which members could withdraw from the community, and the powers and obligations involved, would have to be sought in the field of family law "by inquiring on what terms members of a family—say a wife or minor children—can withdraw from the family organization."[48] T. W. Higginson, in an account of the Oneida community published in the *Woman's Journal*, referred to the sight of a "family of two hundred living in apparent harmony and among the comforts which associated life secures." Such a thing cannot be seen every day, Higginson remarks, but "this is what one at least convinces himself that he sees at Oneida."[49] The subdivisions in the Shaker societies were called families—North family, South family. The names of the leaders of the communities are sometimes familial—Mother Ann Lee, Father George Rapp.

There were several large themes in the nineteenth century treatment of marital contracts.[50] First, the marital contract, while very special, was still a civil contract. It was subject to certain conventional propositions of the law of contract including intent of the parties, their capacity to make a contract, and avoidance (annulment) for fraud or duress. But there was this large difference: The substance of the marital contract was determined on a formal basis not by the parties but by the law. Further, the contract having been undertaken and the family unit created, the state assumed a role in relation to the family different from its relation to other entities. The state preserved the family as a structure—the state was said to be the third party in a marriage contract—and did not permit variation from the conventional terms of the contract. One could not marry for a term of years or marry two spouses. One married subject to the law of the state concerning divorce, married women's property, and support obligations. A husband could not contract to pay his wife wages. If he did, the agreement would not be enforced. Such an agreement, though not inconsistent perhaps with the particular contract between these two parties, was seen as inconsistent with the fundamental status of a wife, whose services were performed for love and not for wages. Other terms, such as a pleasant disposition, could not be enforced because their enforcement would have reached too deeply into the intimacy of the family.

The family having been created, the state became exceedingly deferential toward the privacy of the family unit. Some antifeminist biases of the nineteenth century, and particularly the insistence on the unity of the family (that is, the primacy of the husband, seen to be threatened by political or economic independence of the wife), are, from another perspective, a recognition by the state of a limitation of its authority in favor of the autonomy of the family.

The force of the conception of the family unit was so strong that even where the contract itself failed, as when, for example, the marriage was invalid because bigamous, the "wife" (now a stranger to the estate) could not sue for wages as a servant. Her services had been performed in a marital role, and it would diminish her (although she was now quite willing to be so diminished) to reward her for her labors as if she had, all those years, been a servant. A New York court dealt with such a case in 1858. It sympathized with the situation of the non-wife, but would not grant her claim for wages. The law "would do injustice to the plaintiff herself, by implying a promise to pay for these services." It was the respect "for the plaintiff," as well as the law, which compelled the court to hold that the "services were performed not as a servant, with a view to pay, but from higher and holier motives."[51]

The use of different analogies by a court might result in different perspectives on the utopian contracts. If one used the employment contract analogy, one would see the utopian contracts as normal, minimizing questions of bargaining inequality, responsive perhaps to undue restrictions on the laborer's mobility, reluctant to reward plaintiffs who were themselves in default, but generally assuming that the worker would look after himself. By analogy to a labor contract, one knew that no member could be compelled to stay and work, since an order of specific performance would not have been made, and one knew also that the case of poor workers employed and then fired by wealthy employers presented, of itself, no particular claim on the court's sympathy. If one used the marital contract analogy (but could one possibly do this in regard to Oneida's complex marriage?) one would respect the internal privacy of the institution and be deeply sensitive to the limitations of judicial competence. Could a member, for example, have been called to court for a breach of the section of the Harmony Society contract that called for "cheerful" obedience? Using the marital analogy, there might have been feeling for the possible continued existence of a support obligation. Viewing the contracts primarily as the church covenants, one would have considerable respect for the autonomy of the churches but also a strong awareness of the proposition that courts had the power to review, cautiously, decisions of ecclesiastical courts where property rights were involved.

JUDICIAL REMEDIES

Pierrepont Noyes (b. 1870) was one of the fifty-eight children born at Oneida between 1868 and 1881. He was a son of John Humphrey Noyes, and was raised at the Perfectionist community. Pierrepont Noyes recalled a childhood nightmare:

> [We] . . . seemed about to be driven from home—pushed out into the world. . . . We were in a huge room. We . . . were standing together at one end, while facing us the entire membership of the community pointed at us (physically or metaphorically, I am not sure which), repeating some formula of excommunication. For several years thereafter, whenever I awakened in the night I

used to see that picture and hear those words which condemned us to exile.[52]

"Exile." It is separation from church, home, friends, family, property, business, everything. And this, for some of those who had committed themselves to the utopian life, is precisely what expulsion might involve. It might be that the expulsion was just under the contract and also procedurally correct. But persons expelled sometimes argued before the courts that their expulsions were neither just nor correct (e.g., *Nachtrieb*, *Grosvenor*). In short, they claimed a breach of contract.

The general rule was that remedy awarded by the courts in cases involving a breach of contract would be money damages. Thus, damages were awarded Nachtrieb in the lower court. In cases of expulsion from societies, other remedies are in theory possible. A court, finding that the expulsion had been invalid, might have ordered reinstatement, but here there would be difficulties. A person could be judicially restored to church membership, but "the church still could assert that such a coercive reversal of its decision had no effect on its spiritual validity, thereby denying the member in many cases the substance of the relief he desired."[53] Further, without the agreement of the group it is doubtful that the judicially ordered reinstatement of a member of a religious community would be valid. There would be an infringement of constitutional rights (in this case, the right of the religious groups), as wrong in its way as the improper expulsion might have been.

At a quite different level, the notion of reinstatement and restoration to membership raises the familiar problem of inadequacy of relief in personal terms. Forcible reinstatement, even if constitutional, would result here, as in other contexts, in untenable interpersonal situations. The Harmony Society insisted in *Nachtrieb* that the proper remedy in that case was restoration to membership.[54] Such a decree was not issued. Justice Grier saw clearly that this remedy might work additional hardship. It was possible, Justice Grier said, to remedy the wrong done to Nachtrieb in money, "without compelling him to leave his family, and spend his days among those who injured him."[55] Thus, the remedy ordered by Justice Grier was a division of the property of the society with an award to Nachtrieb of his share at the time of his expulsion.

Those who withdrew and those who did not challenge their expulsions (e.g., John Goesele) might seek a different remedy. Where the legal claim was not that of breach, but rather that there was no valid contract at all, other calculations for remedies might be appropriate, and particularly where the remedies were perceived as restitutionary, giving something back for that which was given. The claims for return of property brought in, or the claims for wages for services performed, were both, in this sense, restitutionary claims.

It seems clear, as a final point, that if (hypothetically) a society had sued a member for breach of a contract for personal services there would not have been specific performance.[56] An early case outlines some reasons for this.[57] Many covenants, the court said, the breaches of which are only compensated for in money damages, "might be specifically performed, either by a third person at a distance from the adversary, or in a short space of time. But a covenant for service, if performed at all, must be personally performed under the eye of the master; and might . . . require a number of years."[58] Specific performance, if legally enforced, "would produce a state of servitude as degrading and demoralizing in its consequences, as a state of absolute slavery; and if enforced under a government like ours, which acknowledges a personal equality, it would be productive of a state of feeling more discordant and irritating than slavery itself."[59]

It has already been noted that Noyes saw the problem as one of intervention versus nonintervention by the civil courts.[60] Formal nonintervention by the courts is a possibility. Courts may decline to hear cases for a variety of reasons. For example, a court could have found a lack of jurisdiction because there was no live controversy or because the wrong party was before the court. This would leave the parties where they were. Even here, however, in the sense that inaction is also action, the state would have influenced the outcome and "intervened." Because the state existed as the ultimate power, whatever it did or did not do would influence the outcome. But much more direct intervention was usually requested, and sometimes granted. Intervening through the lawsuits, the state might intrude in the privacy of the internal life of an association, penetrating not only the particular transactions but the general overall financial structure.

Professor Arndt refers to a letter (1854) from a Harmonist leader[61] stating that until *Nachtrieb* the Harmony Society had never been asked to give an accounting or inventory. The Harmonist added that they "almost refused to give an accounting but that the command of St. Paul to be obedient to the government combined with the exaggerated claims about the magnitude of their wealth persuaded them to comply." The result had shown, Professor Arndt writes, that "their property amounted to a little under a million dollars." But as with all things the Harmonist assured his Zoarite correspondent, "they lived by the principle expressed in the Bible that they possessed goods as though they possessed them not."[62]

The seceding or expelled member might be merely an individual acting alone or, as Lon Fuller suggested, he might be in fact a partisan as much as a victim, so that "what appears as a simple demand for the reinstatement of an expelled member may in fact represent a stratagem in an internal struggle for power between rival factions."[63] The struggle inside the organization is continued in the courtroom and the legislature. The state, in either acting or refusing to act, influences the course of the associational history. The legal complaint to the state, and the defense equally, are appeals to overriding state sovereignty. In this respect, the issues here touch directly on the problem that Chafee, in 1930, described as "one of the few fundamental problems of political science."[64] For at bottom, Chafee said, the problem of the member and the association is an aspect of the larger issue of the relation of state and the associations within it. Our reaction to a dispute between a member and an association is, Chafee suggests, influenced by one's view of the larger "undying controversy." We shall be somewhat more favorable to intervention, Chafee concludes, if we think that "the state is the sole ruler of all that goes on within its borders, and is the necessary safeguard of the individual against the closely pressed tyranny of associations." On the other hand, we will be more doubtful of the desirability of government intervention if we "think of the state itself as just one more kind of association, which, like the others, should keep to its own functions, and which must be judged according to the value and efficiency of the services it renders us in return for rather high annual dues."[65]

The controlling doctrine involved in the utopian contract cases was fairly straightforward. Contracts freely made will be enforced unless they are illegal, and religious liberty is not unlimited as to conduct. Difficulties lay not in the statement of the doctrines but in their application.

It is not at all impossible that under some circumstances a society might have lost a case. That alone would not necessarily have had too negative an impact on the community. One can imagine that particular defeats might, in the long run, have strengthened a society, forcing it to look again at its contract and redraft it in the interest of increased certainty in the courts. But too many defeats on the wrong grounds would have been damaging. Each case involved, from the point of view of the legal system, an opportunity to pass on the question of permissible deviance. Doctrinal applications were, in this sense, tests of political pluralism.

13

Who Can Choose?

Can we seriously say, that a poor peasant or artisan has a free choice to leave his country, when he knows no foreign language or manners, and lives from day to day, by the small wages which he acquires? We may as well assert that a man, by remaining in a vessel, freely consents to the dominion of the master; though he was carried on board while asleep, and must leap into the ocean and perish, the moment he leaves her.

David Hume

A former Harmonist, writing to Germany, denounced the Harmony Society in terms that emphasized the role of the courts. "Seven years I worked for nothing under the protection of this angel of revenge. . . . Money controls the world, and especially here in America where the court is all English and goes through the hands of lawyers, where a common man understands nothing. Thus Rapp has built a silver wall around his slave colony, and a person must be happy to get away with empty hands."[1] Still, there were legal doctrines which were available on the side of the member. At both law and equity it was possible to get out of a contract, to avoid it, if there were serious defects in the process by which the contract had originally been formed.

THE MEETING OF THE MINDS

"The minds of those who contract," Towner wrote, "must meet upon the same thing, in the same sense."[2] But what was that meeting like? If we tried to imagine a scene in which the first communistic society pooled its goods to create a model of the apostolic fellowship of Jerusalem, it might be, in terms of the state of mind of the participants, something entirely remote from the suspicious, self-protective, and even antagonistic posture that the common law assumes as normal for people whose position in the world is necessarily competitive.[3] The parties did not view themselves as standing at arms length. In the contracts of the communistic utopian societies, the getting and spending involved in the transaction was not, as is usually the case in the outside world, the point of the thing. Indeed, the tone of the transaction is one we might associate more with gift than with sale.

These two transactions—those of the market, of buying and selling, and those that are gift-making—are, as anthropologist Raymond Firth has noted, "sharply opposed" in conventional usage.[4] A sale is a market transaction, "impersonal, hoping for profit, competitive, contractual"; the tone of a gift is "friendly, personal, not seeking profit, contributory, free." Yet these are, finally, stereotypes, Firth writes, as "the opposition between these two spheres of transaction is by no means so clear-cut." In fact, buyer and seller in market transactions "do not always try to exact the last shred of profit," and, "conversely, the implications of a gift are rarely exhausted by a single transfer; the notion of reciprocity is often near the surface."[5] So here, although the legal form of the utopian transfer was contract, ideas of donation—albeit a reciprocated donation—are not entirely lacking.

It might also be that the state of mind of the participants was, in one sense, not altogether free and independent. As there is a contrast between a utopian image of man and a common law image, so also there is a contrast between certain religious ideas concerning individual autonomy and secular/legal ideas. In the legal context, the overborne will is the thing to be guarded against, so that a contract can be avoided if the act is not done freely. But in the religious area, the overborne will may be the thing desired. Thus, John Donne: "Take me to you, imprison me, for I / except y'enthral me, never shall be free."[6]

The religious context is not, however, the only one in which the problem arises. A legal scholar discussed this example: "A girl from the lower walks of life becomes engaged to a clerk. In order to enable him to go into business for himself, she turned her savings over to him."[7] When the business fails, and the engagement is ended, the girl sues for "her" money. He offers as a defense that the money was "expended in the business." The judge will now have to fit the behavior of the couple, and their intentions, into the categories of the legal system.

> The judge will have to determine whether the turning over of the money was a loan, or was the advancement of a marriage portion, or whether the business was to be owned by the girl with her fiancé acting merely as manager, or whether the business was a partnership, etc. The judge has to answer these questions although possibly, nay in all probability, the intention of the parties at the time the money was turned over was in no wise definitely fixed, and in any event left the legal aspects of their actions wholly out of account. What was in their minds was nothing more than that they loved each other, had perfect mutual confidence, were going to get married and that it made no difference whatever in whose pocket the money was kept.[8]

"In short," the writer concludes, "the thinking and willing of these two young people did not proceed according to the forms of the common law."[9]

That is the situation, perhaps, of those forming the first fellowship. But after a while, those in fellowship were not willing to leave it to a judge to guess, and so framed a contract that they understood. But the state of mind of the young couple still has some relevance to the situation of the individual entering the community.

CAPACITY

On the face of it, the plaintiffs in the utopian cases had contractual capacity. (The word *capacity* can be used in law in several senses. One can speak of a capacity for rights, for crimes, for torts, for undertaking legal transactions [contracts]. An individual may have legal rights, but be incapable of legal acts, or of responsibility for crimes.[10]) The plaintiffs were competent to make contracts. They were not infants (minors) when they signed their contracts, not visibly weak or infirm, or more lacking in understanding than was apparently considered common at the time. Thus the plaintiff in *Waite* v. *Merrill* was not incompetent. When he left the society he was "well acquainted with farming," although he knew very little of business transactions and was "totally ignorant of the comparative value of the common coins, not being able to distinguish one from another."[11]

Still, there might have been issues raised concerning the question of a contractual capacity. The Shakers insisted that the contracts were freely made by competent individuals. "No flattery, or any undue influence, is ever used to draw parties into a oneness of temporal interest," they said, "as this can be permanently satisfactory only when it is a voluntary act, understandingly performed."[12] And yet, W. D. Howells wrote in the *Atlantic Monthly*, "one has somehow the impression that the young people of the Shakers are held in compulsory allegiance." But "this is not at all the fact," he added immediately. "As soon as they are old enough to take care of themselves they are entirely free to go or to stay."[13]

But what would cause the impression? It was, one assumes, not so much that observers supposed that the young people of the Shakers or any other separatist group were physically coerced or psychologically broken down. It is more likely that the fear was that they had been inadequately exposed to the alternatives. Samuel Tilden, writing against the Shakers in 1837, had expressed the point clearly: "It is not sufficient to say that these individuals joined the Society voluntarily; . . . it may be frequently the case that the members of the Society, carried there during their minority, and educated in entire ignorance of the world, have had no real freedom of choice."[14] A description of an Oneida childhood suggests the point again. Pierrepont Noyes wrote: "I was born and brought up in a strange world—a world bounded on four sides by walls of isolation; a world wherein the customs, laws, religions and social formulas accumulated by civilization came to us only as the faint cries of philistine hordes outside our walls."[15] Even the disapproval of the outside world, which was considerable, was not known to the children. "I am not certain," he wrote, "at what age I first became conscious of the outside world's hostility toward the Community. Certainly throughout what I have called childhood there never entered my head any suspicion that we were regarded with unfriendly eyes, or that our isolation was other than a measure of protection for spiritual pearls-of-great-price. . . . It must have been when I was six or seven years old that the truth was forced upon me."[16] Noyes describes an Oneida communist upbringing: "The community must have exorcised the spirit of acquisitiveness very completely, since throughout my childhood the private ownership of anything seemed to me a crude artificiality to which an unenlightened Outside still clung . . . we were keen for our favorite sleds, but it never occurred to me at least, that I could possess a sled to the exclusion of the other boys."[17] Pierrepont Noyes tells the story of the breakup of the community and of his father's flight to Canada in 1879: "For myself, it was a first effective introduction to the idea of human instabilities. I felt bewildered. I do not recall any immediate fear over the possible loss of protection from the exigencies of a brutal Outside, chiefly because I did not then realize how protected our lives had been. . . . Nor do I remember dread of being plunged into the uncommunistic world with its struggle for existence. I was still but dimly aware that there existed any such struggle."[18]

The protections of Oneida involved more than money, and Pierrepont Noyes's state of mind, as he describes it, does not, it would seem, reflect the mental condition of the rich in a capitalistic world. On Bellamy's coach in *Looking Backward* (see above, pp. 3-4), the major preoccupation of the wealthy (early instilled, one assumes, in the next generation) was to retain their seats. Bellamy's rich cannot be said to be unaware of the struggle for existence.

What could it mean to say that an individual, raised in such a world as Oneida, had voluntarily and knowingly at the age of twenty-one signed a utopian contract? In a more general form, the question becomes, What is legal capacity for an individual socialized in a radically deviant environment? It is easy to see adverse consequences of saying that such individuals lack legal capacity. In the case of the utopian contracts, avoidance for lack of capacity in their makers would, one way or another, have injured the societies. But this would have been the least of it. The basis for such finding of incapacity—the authority of the patriarch, cultural isolation—would have opened the issue of capacity in cases involving not only all immigrant and religious groups but, finally, all socializing groups, including the family. And it might not be limited to contractual capacity. If people lack the ability to make decisions in their own interest, on what theory do they vote?

The tendency of the nineteenth century legal system was to enlarge the categories of those with legal capacity, rather than to contract them,[19] extending the legal capacity of married women and slaves. The object of society was to absorb immigrants and not to isolate them, to create freedom and economic opportunity for individuals and not restrict them in their endeavors. One is not surprised, therefore, to find that the courts in utopian cases failed to make a finding of incapacity in relation to the utopians, despite the fact that the allegations in a case like *Speidel* invite speculation on that possibility. In other cases in which the capacity issue might have been raised, the object of the lawsuits was to enforce the contract and not to avoid it (e.g., *Grosvenor* and *Burt*). Thus, findings of capacity were routinely made on the basis of petitions that rarely suggested the contrary.

DURESS AND UNDUE INFLUENCE

Some of the utopians did explicitly raise issues of duress and coercion. But there is only limited application by these nineteenth century courts—notably in Grier's decision in *Nachtrieb*—of the idea that coercion in the form of influence was a legitimate basis for contract avoidance on the facts presented.

Equity doctrines of undue influence, Professor Dawson said, "were aimed . . . at protection for the mentally or physically inadequate, whose inadequacy fell short of a total lack of legal capacity." The influence involved was not necessarily accompanied by a particular "wrong" under tort law or criminal law. "It was enough that the extraction of economic gain from persons mentally or physically handicapped was condemned by prevailing standards of ethics, defined and applied by equity courts through their own independent tests."[20] These doctrines, Dawson noted, were frequently reinforced by other equity doctrines relating to confidential and fiduciary relationships. Even when there was no actual blood or marital relationship, there might still be "a condition of dependence by the weaker party" which might operate to provide a reason to recast the contract.[21] The wrong came to be seen as the interference with free will. Dawson described a "basic contradiction" involved in some ideas concerning freedom in the contractual relationship. "On the one hand, doctrines of undue influence were attempting to 'free' the individual by regulating the pressures that restricted individual choice; on the other hand, theories of economic individualism aimed at an entirely different kind of freedom, a freedom of the 'market' from external regulation. It was not yet fully recognized that the freedom of the 'market' was essentially a freedom of individuals and groups to coerce one another, with the power to coerce, reinforced by agencies of the state itself."[22]

The issue of undue influence related to the question of duress but involves a milder presence. The idea here is not that the party signed the contract unwillingly. On the contrary, he was willing but he was led to be willing by his reliance on the judgment of someone sufficiently close to him that he was entitled to believe that that person would act in his interest. When the American Law Institute reformulated the common law of contracts in the *Restatement of Contracts* (1932), it stated the rule this way: "Where one party is under the domination of another, or by virtue of the relation between them is justified in assuming that the other party will not act in a manner inconsistent with his welfare, a transaction induced by unfair persuasion of the latter, is induced by undue influence and is voidable."[23]

Difficulties were apparent in the use of ordinary tests of undue influence in these cases. One related to conceptions of acting in a party's welfare. There was no showing, for example, that George Rapp did not believe his teachings. The leader of the Harmonists might "conscientiously think conformity to the lives of the primitive Christians to be essential to salvation," Chief Justice Gibson wrote, although a majority of Christians might think otherwise.[24] Another test of undue influence related to the peculiarity of the bargain, but the peculiarity of the bargain was, in these cases, taken as given. And there were other difficulties. George Rapp himself, for example, the party doing the influencing if anyone was, stood to gain nothing from the contracts, Chief Justice Gibson noted, since he had the same equal interest in the benefits of the property that the others in his fellowship had.[25] Conventional tests of interest and advantage were not adequate to the situation.

FRAUD

That is not to say, however, that one could never demonstrate fraud or what Chief Justice Gibson called "clerical hypocrisy."[26] Sometimes it was found that there had been a scheme from the start, and the combination of fiduciary relationship, dependence, credulity, and trust in a leader who then unmistakably violated the trust, would result in a finding for the members against the leader. This is what happened in *Scott* v. *Thompson*, involving the Mormon splinter group in Iowa. But without an obvious secular fraud (e.g., transfer of property of groups to third parties, as in *Scott* v. *Thompson*), the fraud may be difficult to prove.

W. D. Howells captured a part of the law's dilemma in his 1916 novel *The Leatherwood God*, dealing with

events in Ohio in 1828.[27] The prisoner Dylks is charged
with "claiming to be the Almighty." A spokesman for
the law responds that Dylks

> pleads guilty to that, and he could be fined and impris-
> oned if there was any law against a man's being God.
> There isn't, unless it's some law of the Bible, which isn't
> in force through reenactment in Ohio. He hasn't of-
> fended against any of our statutes, neither he nor his
> followers. In this State every man has a right to worship
> what God he pleases, under his own vine and figtree,
> none daring to molest him or make him afraid. With
> religious fanaticism our laws have nothing to do, unless
> it be pushed so far as to violate some public ordinance.
> This I find the prisoner has not done. Therefore, he
> stands acquitted.[28]

Dylks's explanation of his imposture suggests difficulties on the issue of fraud. "You're tempted by what's the
best thing in you," he says,

> by the hunger and thirst to know what's going to be after
> you die; to get near to the God that you've always heard
> about and read about. . . . That's what does it with *them*,
> and that's what does it in you. . . . When you begin to try
> for it, to give out that you're a prophet, an apostle, you
> don't have to argue, to persuade anybody, or convince
> anybody. They're only too glad to believe what you say
> from the first word.[29]

Finally, Dylks comes to believe his lie. "Their faith puts
faith into you. If they believe what you say you say to
yourself that there must be some truth in it."[30]

A modern case may also be used to demonstrate how
difficult the question of fraud may become in the religious context. In *United States* v. *Ballard* (1944)[31] the
Supreme Court reviewed the conviction of the leaders of
the I Am movement, who had been prosecuted criminally for mail fraud. The indictment charged that Guy

Ballard and others had secured money by misrepresentation, using the mails. The misrepresentations included claims of immortality and the power to cure disease. Justice Douglas, writing for the majority, remanded the case, saying that the truth of the beliefs could not be examined, but sincerity might be. (The convictions ultimately were upset on the ground of systematic exclusion of women from the jury.)

Justices Stone, Roberts, and Frankfurter dissented. They would have sustained the conviction on the theory that the question submitted to the jury was only whether the petitioners honestly believed that the particular facts had occurred. "The state of one's mind is a fact," they said, and as a fact, it is as "capable of fraudulent misrepresentation as is one's physical condition or the state of his bodily health."[32]

There was another dissent. Justice Jackson wrote: "I do not see how we separate an issue as to what is believed from considerations as to what is believable. The most convincing proof that one believes his statements is to show that they have been true in his experience."[33] Likewise, he continued, "what is knowingly falsified is best proved by showing that what he said happened never did happen." These were things the government could not prove. "How can the Government prove these persons knew something to be false which it cannot prove to be false?" Further, Justice Jackson wrote, "any inquiry into intellectual honesty in religion raises profound psychological problems." "If religious liberty includes, as it must, the right to communicate such experiences to others, it seems to me an impossible task for juries to separate fancied ones from real ones, dreams from happenings, and hallucinations from true clairvoyance." It is difficult "in matters so mystical to say how literally one is bound to believe the doctrine he teaches and even more difficult to say how far it is reliance upon a teacher's literal belief which induces followers to give him money." "Prosecutions of this character easily could degenerate into a religious persecution."[34]

INSANITY

Edward Deming Andrews describes the unsuccessful attempt of relatives to upset the deed of Malcolm Worley to the Shakers on what appears to be claim of insanity.[35] The famous nineteenth century lawyer and politician Tom Corwin is said to have argued in defense of the deed that "George Fox wore leather breeches and did many eccentric things; Martin Luther threw his inkstand at the devil; but the Quakers will not admit that George Fox was crazy, and Protestants will not admit that Martin Luther was crazy; neither can it be allowed that Malcolm Worley was crazy, because by deed drawn by himself he chose to give his property to this peculiar people!"[36] The question suggested is this: If one could not use the substance of his religious belief to show, for example, that George Rapp did not believe his doctrines, could one have shown that Peter Schriber was insane because he *did* believe them, and thus that his contract should be avoided?

A central proposition of the law of church and state, at least from the time of *Reynolds* v. *United States*, has been that religious opinion in America is free. The theory is that an act can be both religiously motivated and unacceptable, and that it is the act, not the belief, that is before the court. "Congress was deprived of all legislative power over mere opinion, but was left free to reach actions which were in violation of social duties or subversive of good order,"[37] Chief Justice Morrison Waite wrote in *Reynolds* v. *United States*. And also from *Cantwell* v. *Connecticut*: The first amendment "embraces two concepts,—freedom to believe and freedom to act. The first is absolute but, in the nature of things, the second cannot be. Conduct remains subject to regulation for the protection of society."[38]

This distinction concerning the protections available to "action" and "belief," classical though it is, overstates the case on both sides. Some "actions" (e.g., religious services) cannot be forbidden by the state.[39] And some "beliefs" may cause difficulties.[40] As a practical matter, for example, freedom to believe is limited by the law of insanity to the extent that beliefs are classified by state agencies (e.g., courts) as insane. There may be free exercise questions involved in the determination of mental competence. In most cases, there presumably will be some action on the basis of which the determination of insanity can be made, so that it will not be necessary to judge belief. But where there is only highly ambiguous action, it is exceedingly difficult to deal with the fact that certain categories of religious belief overlap certain categories of mental illness. William James suggested that, in general, religious leaders "have been subject to abnormal psychical visitations"; they have been "creatures of exalted emotional sensibility" and often have led a "discordant inner life."[41] Such leaders have been "liable to obsessions and fixed ideas" and have "fallen into trances, heard voices, seen visions,"[42] presenting "all sorts of peculiarities which are *ordinarily* classed as pathological" (emphasis added).[43]

Here again, it is the caution of the nineteenth century courts in making judgment on the mental state of the utopians that is striking. The Shakers, for example, were spiritualists some ten years before the spiritualist activities of the Fox sisters began in 1848.[44] They wrote poetry in unknown tongues and did spirit paintings. Yet there is no suggestion in the cases over the Shaker covenant that the Shaker plaintiffs were for these reasons insane. Nor did the courts find insanity or other mental incapacity because of the peculiarities of the bargain. The view of these nineteenth century courts was that the bargains were, to be sure, quite strange, but nothing that one could not intellectually comprehend and nothing that one could not imagine people in a certain state of religious belief freely agreeing to. That state of religious belief might finally be deplorable, but it was not insanity.

14

What Can Be Chosen?

Sometimes a hard-working and poverty-stricken drudge of another country voluntarily chooses slavery in Utopia.

Thomas More, *Utopia*

A contract freely made will not be enforced if the
substance is unconscionable or against public policy.
But what is the substance of the contract? What does the
contract mean? This question, that of the interpretation
and construction of contracts, was before a court dealing
with any contract. One possibility was that a court could
deal with the contract in such a way that the utopian
contract was not in litigation, but some other sort of
agreement entirely. Could one say, for example, that the
utopian contract should not be enforced because it was,
legally speaking, not a contract, that it was understood
by all concerned to be not worth the paper it was written
on?[1] Could one suggest that the donation by the communities to the individual had the force of contractual obligation? In *Burt* v. *Oneida Community* it was argued that
a "custom which had acquired the force of an obligation
existed," under which a "withdrawing member was ac-
corded the privilege of returning and resuming his relations with the community," or perhaps to receive a
settlement and allowance.[2] The argument failed.

The most objectionable features of a contract can
sometimes be mitigated, or even eliminated, through interpretation. Sometimes, however, as in the case of the
utopian contracts, the intent of the agreement is so insis-

tently stated that it is difficult to deny. The harshness of the utopian contract did not arise out of ambiguity or obscurity, but precisely out of the uncompromising clarity of the contractual purpose. In the course of the debate over the policies of reconstruction, Senator Trumbull said that it was "idle to say that a man is free who cannot go and come at pleasure, who cannot buy and sell, who cannot enforce his rights."[3] He addressed the situation of the former slaves, but he described the situation of some who had chosen to live in the religious common-property utopias of nineteenth century America.

Voluntary slavery is the classical case in which limits on freedom of contract must be imposed so that more general freedom of contract can be sustained. "Voluntary contract must then sometimes be forbidden in order to avoid slavery,"[4] said Richard Ely in 1914. To "put no restrictions on the freedom to contract would logically lead not to a maximum of individual liberty but to contracts of slavery,"[5] wrote Morris Raphael Cohen. There "is a perpetual danger," Dicey said, "that unlimited contractual capacity, which is looked upon as an extension of individual freedom, may yet be so used by some individual as to deprive him of the very freedom of which it assumed to be the exercise."[6] The evil, the perceived danger in these observations, is commonly that the poor will enslave themselves out of necessity. The utopian contracts raise the question whether the religious may enslave themselves out of devotion.[7]

The image of slavery and bondage is used surprisingly often in connection with the American utopias. William Faux, an Englishman who visited the Rappites, observed that "the spell, or secret, by which these people are held in voluntary slavery, is not to be known or fathomed by inquiry."[8] The product of insanity or not, Charles Guiteau's description of his Oneida experi-

ence—"I felt like a slave all the time I was there"[9]—
finds resonances in the accounts of others writing on the
utopias.

David Quinn's arguments in connection with the Zoar
cases make the slavery point repeatedly. Zoar is not an
association or community, but "an institution of a master and his slaves."[10] If the Zoarites "escaped from the
community, they could be returned under the fugitive
slave law."[11] Zoar's members of the highest class, he
said, promised to serve the community for life.[12] The
Zoar contract—if there was a contract at all—was an
agreement "under which a man obligated himself to
serve somebody, no matter whom, forever and ever, and
never to own anything present or future." Such a contract "is against the first principles of our polity and
unconditionally void." On the "inalienability of rights
our whole polity is built," Quinn said, but "Zoar's polity
rests on an alienation of them all."[13] Bimeler "has, no
doubt, impressed them with a superstitious awe which
makes them humble and submissive." They are, he said,
"mere passive creatures, with scarcely any aspirations
above that of a mere plant, which vegetates and rots."
The Zoarites are "excluded from all information except
that which pertains to their labors" or that which is
"dealt out to them by a master in his sermons." No
newspapers reached them, and "the great volume of the
age is closed upon them," he continued. As a consequence, "*not one of them has ever risen nor ever can rise
above the level of a mere drudge*."[14]

So, too, it had been argued that the Shaker contract
had a "tendency to fetter and enslave the mind and person," and that it was therefore "contrary to the genius
and principles of a free government" (*Waite* v. *Merrill*).[15]
In effect, it is a "contract for unlimited servitude, without any other compensation than bare support; and is

therefore unconscionable, and void, being in derogation of the right of personal liberty."[16]

The image of slavery would be found in the decisions of some judges. Judge Underwood of Kentucky had said in his argument against the Shaker covenant that one could not sell one's liberty and become a slave,[17] and Justice Grier had written of slavery in *Nachtrieb*:

> As yet the complainant was not free from the shackles of the spiritual and temporal slavery to which he had been all his life subject; a power which forbade him to learn English, to marry, or if married, denied him intercourse with his wife. Free will can hardly be predicated of actions, performed at the command of a ruler believed to possess the keys both in this world and the next, and who taught that disobedience to his orders was a sin against the Holy Ghost, not to be forgiven here or hereafter.[18]

But the courts as a whole rejected the comparison to contracts of voluntary slavery. While it might be that someone at some time would contract away too much—particularly, for example, the right to leave the community[19]—it was not voluntary slavery that bothered the courts in relation to the utopians. They had the problems of African slavery too deeply before them, and life among the Harmonists and Perfectionists and Shakers, no matter how restricted or confined, was, in material terms, no worse than life in a nineteenth century factory, for example. (The farms and factories of the outside world were before Nordhoff's eyes when he reviewed the communities, and if one accepts his judgment, there can be little doubt that, as to the material world, the utopians were better off.)[20]

The oppression that concerned the courts lay in the issue of forfeiture. One was free to leave, but could it be acceptable that to leave one had to pay such a price? If so, was one after all free to leave? As to this, the courts were clear. Rights of property meant the right to dispose of one's property as one saw fit. The grants of property to the society were legitimate exercises of a property right. Similarly, the agreement of support for work done was valid, and one had no claim for anything else by way of remuneration.

The protection of the individual is seen in his right to sue a society for breach of its contract of support—that is, in the extreme, for unjust expulsion. The courts agreed that there was a cause of action for damages for unjust expulsion, but, except for Justice Grier, failed to find an unjust expulsion on the facts of any case presented.

One of the large problems of these cases is the difficulty in distinguishing between withdrawal and expulsion at all.[21] The failure of the communities (except, arguably, Oneida[22]) to sharply distinguish between the remedies available to those who withdrew and those who were expelled may have had roots in their perception of the psychological confusion between the two events. Further, it might have been difficult to decide which category was more deserving of the donation given to some on their departure. A community could reward diligence and virtue, and provide a donation to those who had withdrawn peaceably, while giving nothing to those who were expelled for cause. A contract might therefore have authorized donations in the case of one who withdrew, while denying them to those expelled. But there were those expelled whose fault seems to be not that they were lazy or refused to try, but rather that their efforts were perceived as directed toward the wrong ends (e.g., Roxalana Grosvenor). With such a case in mind, one might say that there is a stronger case for refund in the case of expulsion than in the case of withdrawal. The one who withdrew voluntarily gave up all rights, including refund, which he waived along with his membership. One who was expelled for a change in religious belief—that is, the community chose to withdraw support over the objection of the member—is entitled to a refund.

This is the argument that Oneida lawyer James Towner suggested in his treatment of *Grosvenor*, a case, he noted, that has been "somewhat criticized."[23] The general principles governing withdrawal and forfeiture, Towner wrote, might be acceptable in cases of voluntary withdrawal, yet questioned when applied to cases like that of the Grosvenor sisters, who were expelled from the society for doctrine deviance.

Towner's answer to the point is emphatic:

> If a community is established, wholly or in part, upon the basis of a certain religious belief, that belief becomes part of the contract or covenant between the members, and in fact a part of the Home, just as much as conduct would be in case they had agreed upon a certain standard of purity of life; and in either case he who changes his belief or life withdraws from the organization and abandons the home just as really and effectually as he can, though he may remain within its outward walls.[24]

Towner suggests members might draft their own provisions. They may "provide themselves with further safeguards against possible arbitrary or other wrongful exercise of power, by prescribing in their covenant for right of arbitration, or appeal to some other tribunal which may promise to be impartial; or to make their contract less stringent in its terms and conditions as to membership."[25] This was for some communities perhaps a live possibility. An Icarian group suggested that "special contracts"[26] might be negotiated. Still, it seems likely that most of the utopian contracts could not be adapted this way. While it might happen that the contractual form would be changed from time to time by the society, it is exceedingly unlikely that any individual member could negotiate terms more favorable to himself on any particular point. Noyes, for example, said that the community would receive as an "insult" a proposal that a member join on condition that he receive wages or that property would be refunded with interest.[27] The contracts were clearly conceived as contracts of adhesion, offered on a take-it-or-leave-it basis to individuals who were under no obligation whatever to undertake such formidable commitments and, in principle, would do so only as a matter of faith in the enterprise.

What of a clause providing for expulsion at the sole decision of the leader, without trial, process, opportunity for rebuttal, written charges, notice? The lawyer for Roxalana and Maria F. Grosvenor attacked the covenant on these sorts of grounds and argued that a formal written charge was "so essential to justice and fairness it might never be dispensed with."[28] Joshua Nachtrieb, Edwin Stanton argued, was entitled to a fair trial and defense.[29] Counsel for Charles Burt argued that he was entitled to notice and hearing.[30] Could a court find this lack of process acceptable in the case of a group that religiously believed that this procedure, or lack of it, was religiously mandated? On this point, Mark DeWolf Howe's question seems relevant: "Is it possible, perhaps, that a church is denied its constitutional liberty in a state which compels it to adopt a form of government which its tradition repudiates?"[31] The nature of certain associations, Chafee comments, "is such that the person who joins them is clearly aware of the autocratic control which they possess over the continuance of his relation. For example, when a prophet like [John Alexander] Dowie establishes a religious community, his absolute power is an integral feature of the enterprise, and any person who joins it knows exactly what he is in for."[32] Roscoe Pound observed in 1902 that "we must remember that it is not our province to impose our views as to such matters [as notice and hearings] upon religious denominations."[33]

One issue of procedure is assumed, however. One could not absolutely waive one's right to a hearing in a civil court. A court may decide that by contract the individual has limited the court's ability to resolve the issue (*Grosvenor*), but there is no holding that the promises not to bring claims or debts constitute a jurisdictional bar. Such promises might, after all, have been made by persons under age, or under duress. Here, as in other contexts, the courts would not permit the ouster of their jurisdiction. Even comparing these contracts to, for example, agreements to submit to arbitration or releases, we would have to say that it was initially for the courts, in such cases, to determine whether in fact an agreement had been made. In fact, the utopians were not civilly dead. They had voluntarily joined communities under peculiarly rigorous contracts. They had done this in the exercise of rights under the legal system, and that legal system remained available to scrutinize the contracts and to determine what rights were left to the parties.

Conclusion

Violence shall be no more heard in thy land,
Desolation nor destruction within thy borders;
But thou shalt call thy walls Salvation,
and thy gates Praise.

Isaiah 60:18

The vision of Isaiah may be viewed as the object of the American religious utopias.[1] Their boundaries were to protect them as enclaves of peace and harmony within a larger political state; their gates opened out onto a spiritual universe. Perhaps because the utopians set out to be separate from the political world, they are often perceived as existing in isolation from it, largely free of the laws and institutions of the surrounding society. In fact, the communities functioned inside the American system, visibly sanctioned by its laws. Oneida was a heavenly association in the state of New York.

The legal experience of the American utopias reveals that whatever the reasons for the dissolution of the various groups, suppression by the state through its legal system was not among them. The state did not condemn the practice of the utopians through the criminal law (though it did condemn the practices of the Mormons), and when the issue of acceptability arose on the civil side in the case of the strongest of the utopian groups, the communistic societies, the state preserved the utopias from slow execution at the hands of former members.

Unlike the Mormons, the major utopian groups were

not perceived as raising serious threats to the sovereignty of the state. Rather, the question in relation to the utopians was focused on the welfare of individual adherents and their dependents. The decision of the state was taken carefully, on a number of different occasions, and the response of the nineteenth century legal system to the utopian societies was highly particularized. Each community, each set of facts, was considered separately by the courts and the legislatures. The legal system that passed on the utopians understood that their objectives were fundamentally different from, and even antagonistic to, the ideas of nineteenth century America. This of itself did not cause difficulty. "It may be true," Chief Justice Gibson wrote in connection with the Harmonists, that "the business and pursuits of the present day are incompatible with the customs of the primitive Christians; but that is a matter for the consideration of those who propose to live in conformity to them."[2]

The history of the utopians and the law is largely illuminated by the principles of voluntarism; largely, but not entirely. Choices were sometimes inoperative and, indeed, punished because they were in contravention of the criminal law. So the Mormons could not choose to live in polygamy, and the Perfectionists might ultimately have been forced by the state to abandon complex marriage. Other choices were governed by the law of contracts, which is definitionally concerned with the choices of consenting adults. Here too, on the civil side of the law, there are limits on the principle of voluntarism. Perhaps one can choose for oneself, but not for one's children. Since adults form communities into which children are born, and since the state has an unquestioned interest in the welfare of children, the state will consider whether a society, legal in itself, should be denied the right to serve as a socializing agency for those too young to be said to have chosen. Contracts must be freely made by consenting adults. The state will decide which adults are as children, incapable of choice. Contracts against public policy will not be enforced by the courts of the state. In this sense, there is a state-imposed limit on the things to which even fully capable consenting adults may freely bind themselves: The state will refuse to assist the enterprise.

One limit on free choice is suggested by the legal discussions of the utopian contracts: The contract could not deny the individual the right to rejoin the larger society. The public policy implicitly affirmed was this: There had to be freedom to assert the residual status "non-member of the utopian community." That status might, the courts said, be resumed at considerable cost, the loss perhaps of a life's work, but it had to be possible to regain it. David Quinn, arguing for the dissident Zoarites, might refer to them as slaves, but in fact they were not, since they were free to rejoin the larger society, at least in principle. Were they free in fact to rejoin the larger society? The many seceders, by their existence, provide evidence. We know that it was possible to withdraw from utopia because so many did. We do not know—but then we never know—what choices might have been made if things had been different. But what things? And how different? If, for example, the state had supplied, or required that the group supply, economic security to seceders equivalent to the security available to loyal members of the group, some might have chosen not to stay. Presumably, people whose choices related not to utopia but to work and marriage might also, then, have had a different kind of freedom of contract. If the state had insisted on exclusively secular education outside the community for fifteen years, some might, at 21, have chosen differently. But if the state had claimed the exclusive right to socialize the child, it would have affected the choices not only of the children of the utopians but of all children.[3]

Freedom of contract in the nineteenth century ignored and perhaps even assumed a substantial inequality of economic condition.[4] The doctrine provided a framework for the radical economic egalitarianism of the communistic utopias. It was in the formation of these communities that the freedom of the individual was expressed, and in the recognition of the rights of these communities in relation to their members that a limitation on state power was acknowledged.[5]

We tend to think that individual liberty and political pluralism are preserved in America through the checks and balances of our governmental structures, and through our constitutional limitations on the power of government. In the nineteenth century these goals were also served by the private law of contract, used by individuals not only for economic transactions but also for the creation of new social orders, in the continuing attempt to form more perfect unions.

Appendix

Four Communities

Because the cases which were the starting point of this discussion involved particularly four major utopian communities, it seems useful to set out for reference brief conventional accounts of the four communities. The descriptions below are reprinted from the 1910 edition of Morris Hillquit's *History of Socialism in the United States*, originally published in 1903. Hillquit was not an eye-witness observer of the American utopias; he arrived in America in 1886 and worked from the earlier accounts of Noyes, Nordhoff, and Hinds.

The Shakers [pp. 29-31]

Among the sectarian communities of the United States, the Society of the Shakers is one of the oldest. The first Shaker settlement was established at Watervliet, New York, in 1776. The founder of the movement, and first "leader" of the society, was "Mother" Ann Lee, an illiterate Englishwoman, who, with a handful of followers, came to this country in 1774 to escape religious persecution at home.

Ann Lee died in 1784, and was succeeded by James Whitaker, Joseph Meacham, and Lucy Wright, under whose administration the society made great gains in members and wealth, and branched out into a number of communities. What strengthened the movement most was the epidemic revivals of the close of the eighteenth and the beginning of the nineteenth centuries, and especially the unparalleled religious excitement which developed in Kentucky in 1800 and lasted several years.

The Shaker societies seem to have reached their zenith in the second quarter of the last century, when their combined membership exceeded 5,000. In 1874 Nordhoff reports the total Shaker population of this country as 2,415; this figure was reduced to 1,728 in 1890, according to census returns. Scarcely more than 500 survive at present.

The Shakers are divided into three classes or orders:

1. THE NOVITIATE.—These are communicants of the Shaker church, officially styled the "Millennial Church" or "United Society of Believers," but they live outside of the society and manage their own temporal affairs.

2. THE JUNIORS.—These are members on probation. They reside within the society and temporarily relinquish their individual property, but they may return to the world and resume their property at any time.

3. THE SENIORS, OR CHURCH ORDER.—This order consists of persons who have absolutely parted with their property and irrevocably devoted themselves to the service of the Shaker church.

The unit of organization of the Shaker society is the "family." This consists of men and women living together, and ranging in numbers from a very few to a hundred and more. They maintain common households, and as a rule conduct one or more industries in addition to agricultural pursuits.

The spiritual interests of the family are administered by "elders," and the temporal affairs by "deacons."

Several families, usually four, constitute a "society."

The central government is vested in an executive board styled the "ministry" or "bishopric," and consisting of two elder brothers and two elder sisters; the head of the ministry is called the "leading elder" or "leading character." The ministry appoints the deacons, and in conjunction with them the "caretakers," or foremen, of the various branches of industry.

The leading elder fills vacancies in the ministry, and designates his own successor. Each officer of the society, spiritual or temporal, takes orders from his immediate superior, and women are represented on all administrative bodies in the same manner as men.

The principal tenet of their peculiar creed is, that God is a dual being, male and female, Jesus representing the male element, and Ann Lee the female element. Man, created in the image of God, was originally also dual. The separation of sexes took place when Adam asked for a companion, and God, yielding to the request, cut out Eve from his body. This was the first sin committed by man. The Shakers, therefore, regard marriage as appertaining to a lower order of existence, and are strict celibatarians.

The religious history of mankind they divide into four cycles, each having a separate heaven and hell. The first includes the period from Adam to Noah, the second embraces the Jews until the advent of Jesus, the third extends to the period of Ann Lee. The fourth, or "heaven of last dispensation," is now in process of formation and will include all Shakers.

They profess to hold communion with the spirit world, and the revelations received by them from the spirits are generally heralded by violent contortions of their bodies. It is this peculiar feature which earned for them first the appellation of "Shaking Quakers," and then of "Shakers."

The Shakers lead a well-ordered and healthful mode of life. They retire at about nine o'clock and rise at five. They breakfast at six, dine at twelve, and sup at six. Their diet is simple but sufficient. Their favorite dishes are vegetables and fruit, and many discard meat altogether. They eat in a general dining-hall, the men and women sitting at separate tables.

Their dormitories, dining-halls, and shops are scrupulously clean, and the strictest order prevails everywhere.

Their amusements are few and of a very quiet order. Instrumental music is looked upon with disfavor, reading is restricted to useful and instructive topics. Singing of hymns and discourses in the assembly-room are frequent, and lately they have begun quiet outdoor sports, such as picnics, croquet, and tennis.

The communism of the Shakers is part of their religious system, but it extends to the family only. There is no community of property in the Shaker society as a whole; one family may possess great wealth, while the other may be comparatively poor.

The Shakers are at present divided into fourteen societies, located in the states of Maine, New Hampshire, Massachusetts, Connecticut, New York, Ohio, Kentucky and Florida, and their aggregate wealth is estimated in millions, their landed possessions alone amounting to over 100,000 acres.

Harmony Society [pp. 32–34]

Within a few miles of Pittsburg, in the State of Pennsylvania, lies a little village, consisting of about 100 dwelling-houses. Until a few years ago it was owned jointly by a few old men of puritanical habits, who exercised a rigid supervision over the mode of life of the inhabitants.

The name of the place was Economy, and the few village autocrats were the last survivors of an erstwhile hustling and prosperous community.

The community, officially called the "Harmony Society," was more popularly known as the "Rappist Community," and had an eventful history, covering a period of almost a full century.

Its founder, George Rapp, was the leader of a religious sect in Würtemberg denominated "Separatists." The peculiar beliefs of the sect provoked the persecution of the clergy and government, and in 1804 Rapp, with about 600 sturdy adherents, left Germany and came to this country by way of Baltimore and Philadelphia. The main body of immigrants were farmers and mechanics, but there were also among them men of liberal education, and one of them, Frederick Reichert, an adopted son of George Rapp, possest considerable artistic taste and great administrative talent.

The first community established by them was "Harmony," in Lycoming County, Pennsylvania, and within a few years they erected a number of dwelling-houses, a church, a school-house, some mills and workshops, and cleared several hundred acres of land.

But despite their apparent prosperity, they came to the conclusion that the site of the settlement had not been well chosen. In 1814 they sold their land with all on it for $100,000, and removed to Posey County, Indiana, where they purchased a tract of 30,000 acres.

Their new home was soon improved and built up, and became an important business center for the surrounding country. They grew in wealth and power, and received large accessions of members from Germany, until in 1824 their community was said to comprise about 1,000 persons.

In that year they removed again. Malarial fevers infesting their settlement had caused them to look for a purchaser for some time, and when at last they found one in the person of Robert Owen, they bought the property at Economy, and took possession of it at once.

How rapidly they developed their new village, appears from an account of the Duke of Saxe-Weimar, who visited them in 1826. He was full of praise of the neatness and good order of the village, of the beauty of the houses, the excellent arrangement of the shops and factories, and the apparent happiness of the settlers.

The peaceful course of their lives was only once seriously disturbed. In 1831 a "Count Maximilian de Leon" arrived at Economy in gorgeous attire and surrounded by a suite of followers. He pretended to be in accord with the religious views of the settlers, and announced his desire to join them.

The simple-minded people welcomed him most cordially, and admitted him to their society without any investigation. "Count de Leon," whose real name was Bernhard Müller, and who was an adventurer, soon commenced to undermine the beliefs of the Harmonists, and to advocate worldly pleasures. By smooth and insinuating manners he gained the support of many members, and when a separation became inevitable, and the adherents of each faction were counted, it was found that 500 members had remained true to "Father Rapp," while 250 declared for the "Count." The minority party received the sum of $105,000 for their share in the common property, and, with De Leon at their head, removed to Phillipsburg, where they attempted to establish a community of their own. But their leader forsook them, escaping with their funds to Alexandria, on the Red River, where he died of cholera in 1833; the seceders then disbanded.

The Economists meanwhile had recovered their prosperity very rapidly. At the outbreak of the civil war they had about half a million dollars in cash, which, for better safety, they buried in their yards until the war was over.

The Harmonists had not been celibatarians at the outset of their career, but in 1807, during a strong "revival of religion," the men and women of one accord determined to dissolve their marriage ties, and henceforward "no more marriages were contracted in Harmony, and no more children were born."

Outside of their celibacy, the Harmonists were by no means ascetics: they enjoyed a good meal and a glass of good beer, and in the earlier stages of their history, when the members were more numerous and youthful, they led a gay and cheerful life.

Their communism, like that of the Shakers, was part of their religious system, and was limited to the members of their own community and church. When their own population was large and their pursuits were few, they employed no hired labor, but as their numbers dwindled down and their industries developed, the wage-workers at times outnumbered their members ten to one.

In the beginning of the present century the community had practically evolved into a limited partnership of capitalists owning lands, oil-wells, and stocks in railroad, banking and mining corporations. They admitted no new members and had no children, and as the original members gradually died out, the community disintegrated. In 1904 it was formally dissolved, and its property divided among its few survivors.

Zoar [pp. 34–37]

The community of Zoar, like that of Economy, was founded by Separatist emigrants from Würtemberg.

For a number of years the founders of the sect carried on an obstinate feud with the government of their country, whose enmity they had provoked by their dissenting religious doctrines, but principally by their refusal to serve in the army and to educate their children in the public schools. They were fined and sent to prison, and driven from village to village, until they determined to look to the hospitable shores of the United States for a refuge from the persecutions of their intolerant fatherland. The generous assistance of some wealthy English Quakers enabled them to pay their passage, and in 1817 the first detachment of the society, about 200 in number, arrived in Philadelphia, headed by their chosen leader, Joseph Bäumeler.

Immediately upon their arrival they purchased several thousand acres of land in Tuscarawas County, Ohio, and went to work clearing much of the land and erecting a number of log houses for the members of the community, many of whom had remained behind working for neighboring farmers. This village thus founded by them they called Zoar.

The land, for which only a small cash payment had been made, was purchased in the name of Joseph Bäumeler, with the understanding that a parcel was to be assigned to each member, to be worked and the cost paid off by him individually.

They had no intention of forming a communistic society. But they had a number of old and feeble members among them who found it difficult to make their farms pay by their own efforts, and it soon became apparent that their members would be compelled to scatter, and that the enterprise would fail unless it was reorganized on a different foundation.

In April, 1819, after a thorough discussion of the situation, they resolved accordingly to establish a community of goods and efforts, and from that time on they prospered. They organized a blacksmith's, carpenter's and joiner's shop, kept cattle, and earned a little money from work done for neighboring farmers.

The building of a canal through their land in 1827 was a piece of rare good fortune to them. They obtained a contract to do part of the work for the sum of $21,000, and secured a market for many of their products. Within a short time they lifted the mortgage on their property, and purchased additional lands.

Much of their early success the Zoarites undoubtedly owed to the wise administration of their leader, Joseph Bäumeler. Bäumeler, who in later years spelled his name Bimeler, was a man of little education, but of great natural gifts. He was the temporal as well as the spiritual head of the community. He had the general supervision of its affairs, attended to all its dealings with the outside world, and on Sundays delivered discourses to the Zoarites on religion and all other conceivable topics. Many of these discourses were collected and printed after his death. They make three ponderous octavo volumes, and were highly treasured by his followers.

The Zoarites prohibited marriage at first, but after ten or twelve years of celibate life they came to the conclusion that it was not good for man to be alone, and revoked the prohibition.

It is related that this change of sentiment on the question of marriage was caused by the fact that Joseph Bimeler, at a rather advanced age, fell in love with a pretty maiden who had been assigned by the community to wait on him. But be this as it may, the fact is that the leader of Zoar was one of the first to make use of the new privilege.

In 1832 the society was incorporated under the laws of Ohio, adopting the name of "The Society of Separatists of Zoar."

Under their constitution the government of the society's affairs was vested in three trustees, who appointed the superintendents of their different industries, and assigned each member to a certain kind of work, always taking into consideration the inclinations and aptitudes of the member.

They had a standing arbitration committee of five, to whom all disputes within the community were referred, and annual village meetings at which all members of legal age, female as well as male, had a vote.

The highest point in their development they seem to have reached shortly after their incorporation, when their membership exceeded 500. In 1874, according to Nordhoff, they still had about 300 members, and were worth over a million dollars.

As long as the community was poor and struggling hard for its existence, perfect harmony prevailed among the members, but when it had acquired considerable wealth, the temptation came in, and efforts were made from time to time by discontented members to bring about a dissolution of the community and a division of its property. Thus in 1851, and again in 1862, suits for partition were brought in the Ohio courts by former members, but the courts upheld the community, and dismissed the suits.

The movement for a dissolution of the community continued, however, and in 1895 it acquired much strength from the support of Levi Bimeler, a descendant of the venerated founder of Zoar, and himself an influential member of the community. The discussion continued for three years, and at times waxed very warm and acrimonious, until, at the annual village meeting of 1898, the motion to dissolve was finally carried.

Three members were by general agreement elected commissioners to effect an equitable division. The amount awarded to each member was about $1,500.

The Oneida Community [pp. 42-47]

The first historian of communism in the United States was himself the founder of one of the most noteworthy of communistic societies. The Oneida Community was the creation of John Humphrey Noyes.

Noyes was born in Brattleboro, Vt., in 1811. He was graduated from Dartmouth College and took up the study of law, but soon turned to theology, taking courses at Andover and Yale. While pursuing his theological studies he evolved the religious doctrines which later received the name of Perfectionism.

In 1834 he returned to Putney, Vt., the residence of his parents, and gradually gathered around him a little circle of followers. His first permanent adherents were his mother, two sisters, and a brother; then came the wives of himself and his brother and the husbands of his sisters; then came several others, until in 1847 he had about forty followers.

The movement was at first purely religious, but the evolution of its doctrines, coupled with the reading of the *Harbinger* and other Fourieristic publications, gradually led it to communism, and in 1848 Mr. Noyes established a communistic settlement at Oneida, in the State of New York.

During the first years of the experiment they had to cope with great difficulties, and succeeded but poorly. Noyes and his followers, most of whom seem to have been men of means, had invested over $107,000 in the enterprise up to January 1, 1857. The first inventory of the community taken on that day showed a total of assets amounting to little more than $67,000, a clear loss of about $40,000.

But during that time they had gained valuable experience, and had organized their industries on an efficient and profitable basis. They manufactured steel traps, traveling bags and satchels; they preserved fruit, and engaged in the manufacture of silk. Whatever they undertook, they did carefully and thoroughly, and their products soon acquired a high reputation in the market.

Their inventory for the year 1857 showed a small net gain, but during the ten years following, their profit exceeded the sum of $180,000.

In the mean time they bought more land and gained new members, and in 1874 they owned about 900 acres of land and their membership consisted of about 300 persons.

They had had several communities originally, but by 1857 they concentrated all their members in Oneida and Wallingford, Conn.

The Oneida Community was the only important sectarian community in the country of purely American origin. The bulk of its members consisted of New England farmers and mechanics, but they also had among them a large number of professional men—physicians, lawyers, clergymen, teachers, etc. Their standard of culture and education was considerably above the average.

Their affairs were administered by twenty-one standing committees, and they had forty-eight heads of industrial departments. Notwithstanding the apparent complexity of the system, their government was purely democratic and worked well.

The most striking features of the Perfectionists were their religious doctrines, their views on marriage, their literature, and the institution of "mutual criticism." They held that the second advent of Christ had taken place at the period of the destruction of Jerusalem, and that at that time there was a primary resurrection and judgment in the spirit world; that the final kingdom of God then began in the heavens, and that the manifestation of that kingdom in the visible world is now approaching; that a church on earth is rising to meet the approaching kingdom in the heavens; that the element of connection between these two churches is inspiration or communion with God, which leads to perfect holiness—complete salvation from sin—hence their name of Perfectionists. The following definition of Perfectionism is quoted by Nordhoff as coming from one of the believers:

"As the doctrine of temperance is total abstinence from alcoholic drinks, and the doctrine of antislavery is immediate abolition of human bondage, so the doctrine of Perfectionism is immediate and total cessation of sin."

Their communistic theories extended to persons as well as to property, and they rejected monogamous marriage just as vigorously as they rejected individual ownership of property. Their marriage system was a combination of polygamy and polyandry. They pretended to conduct the propagation of children on a scientific basis, preferably pairing the young of one sex with the aged of the other. This system they styled the "complex marriage" system. They strongly resented the charge of licentiousness, and exacted "holiness of heart" before permitting "liberty of love."

The children were left in the custody of their mothers until they were weaned, when they were placed in the general nursery under the care of special nurses. Outside observers attested that they were a healthy-looking, merry set of children.

They maintained an excellent system of schools, and sent many of their young men to college to fit them for such professional callings as were needed within the community.

For the propaganda of their ideas, they published a number of books and periodicals, the most popular among which was the *Oneida Circular*. This was a weekly magazine, well edited and printed, and was published on these singular terms, printed at the head of its columns:

"The Circular is sent to all applicants, whether they pay or not. It costs and is worth at least two dollars per volume. Those who want it and ought to have it are divisible into three classes, viz.: 1, those who can not afford to pay two dollars; 2, those who can afford to pay only two dollars; and 3, those who can afford to pay more than two dollars. The first ought to have it free; the second ought to pay the cost of it; and the third ought to pay enough more than the cost to make up the deficiencies of the first. This is the law of Communism."

"Mutual Criticism" was said to have been invented by Noyes in his college days, and became a most important institution in the Oneida Community from the very beginning of its existence. It took the place of trials and punishments, and was regarded by the Perfectionists not only as a potent corrective of all moral delinquencies, but also as a cure for a number of physical ailments.

Criticism was administered in some cases without the solicitation of the subject, but more often at his own request. A member would sometimes be criticized by the entire society, and sometimes by a committee selected from among those best acquainted with him.

Plainly speaking, the procedure consisted in each member of the committee giving to the subject criticized a piece of his or her mind—a pretty large one as a rule—and the salutary effect of this "mutual criticism" was supposed to show itself in revealing and thereby curing the hidden vices of the subject.

Nordhoff, who had the good fortune of attending one of these criticisms, gives an amusing account of it, which we reproduce in substance.

On one Sunday afternoon a young man, whom we will call Charles, offered himself for criticism. A committee of fifteen,

Mr. Noyes among them, assembled in a room, and the procedure began by Mr. Noyes inquiring whether Charles had anything to say. Charles said that he had recently been troubled by doubts, that his faith was weakening, and that he was having a hard struggle to combat the evil spirit within him. Thereupon the men and women present spoke up in turn. One man remarked that Charles had been spoiled by his good fortune, that he was somewhat conceited; another added that Charles had no regard for social proprieties, that he had recently heard him condemn a beefsteak as tough, and that he was getting into the habit of using slang. Then the women took a hand in the criticism, one remarking that Charles was haughty and supercilious, another adding that he was a "respecter of persons," and that he showed his liking for certain individuals too plainly, calling them pet names before the people, and a third criticizing his table manners. And as the criticism progressed the charges accumulated. Charles was declared to have manifested signs of irreligiousness and insincerity, and a general hope was exprest that he would come to see the error of his ways and reform. During this ordeal, which lasted over half an hour, Charles sat speechless, but as the accusations multiplied, his face grew paler and big drops of perspiration stood on his forehead. The criticisms of his comrades had evidently made a strong impression on him.

These frank talks seem not to have provoked any ill-feeling among the members. The history of the Oneida Community discloses no discords of any kind; perfect harmony reigned at all times, and only one member was ever expelled.

The community existed and thrived over thirty years, but public opinion, aroused by the clergy of the neighborhood, finally became so pronounced against the "complex marriage" system, that the Perfectionists deemed it advisable to abandon that custom.

This was the signal for the dissolution of the Oneida Community as a communistic society. Noyes himself, accompanied by a few faithful followers, removed to Canada, where he died in 1886, and the remainder of the community was incorporated in 1880 as a joint stock company under the name of "Oneida Community, Limited."

The company is now very wealthy. The industries have all been preserved. The interests of the members in the property of the corporation are represented by the stock held by them. A common library, reading-room, laundry, and lawns are the only surviving features of the old communistic regime.

NOTES

NOTE: This discussion has been based on printed materials, primary and secondary. These are for the most part available in research libraries or in law libraries. In only a few instances has it seemed advisable to include a library reference in a footnote. Citations have been given in a form intended to be intelligible to the general reader. Where citations are given to paperbacks or reprint editions, original dates of publication are usually indicated.

Introduction

Henry Sumner Maine, *Ancient Law: Its Connection with the Early History of Society and Its Relation to Modern Ideas* (New York: Holt, 1861, 1885), pp. 163-65.

Benjamin Cardozo, *The Nature of the Judicial Process* (1921) in *Selected Writings of Benjamin Nathan Cardozo*, ed. M. Hall (New York: Matthew Bender, 1947), pp. 118-19.

1. These four will be called "communistic," i.e., holding to the idea and practice of complete community property. Only a part of the movement called "utopian" or "communitarian" was communistic in this sense. See Arthur Bestor, *Backwoods Utopias: The Sectarian Origins and the Owenite Phase of Communitarian Socialism in America, 1663-1829*, 2nd enlarged ed. (Philadelphia: University of Pennsylvania Press, 1950, 1970), p. vii.

On factors relating to longevity and success among the nineteenth century utopians, see Rosabeth Moss Kanter, *Commitment and Community: Communes and Utopias in Sociological Perspective* (Cambridge, Mass.: Harvard University Press, 1972), Part Two, "Lessons of the Past." On domestic institutions among the Mormons and the utopians, see Raymond Lee Muncy, *Sex and Marriage in Utopian Communities: Nineteenth-Century America* (Baltimore: Penguin, 1974).

2. See Professor Bestor's discussion of voluntary associations (*Backwoods Utopias*, pp. 16–18) and his comments regarding parallels between communitarianism and federalism (p. 18). Professor Bestor quotes a dissenting opinion of Oliver Wendell Holmes: The Supreme Court ought not "to prevent the making of social experiments that an important part of the community desires, in the isolated chambers afforded by the several states, even though the experiments may seem futile or even noxious." *Truax v. Corrigan*, 257 U.S. 312 (1921), p. 344. See also Laurence H. Tribe, *American Constitutional Law* (Mineola, N.Y.: Foundation Press, 1978), pp. 988–90.

3. There was a right under the legal system to a remedy for unjust expulsion.

4. On the development of contract doctrine in the nineteenth century, see Grant Gilmore, *The Death of Contract* (Columbus: Ohio State University Press, 1974); Lawrence M. Friedman, *Contract Law in America: A Social and Economic Case Study* (Madison: University of Wisconsin Press, 1965); Morton J. Horwitz, *The Transformation of American Law, 1780–1860* (Cambridge, Mass.: Harvard University Press, 1977), ch. 6, "The Triumph of Contract."

5. Friedrich Kessler, "Contracts of Adhesion—Some Thoughts About Freedom of Contract," *Columbia Law Review* 43 (1943): 629, 640.

6. *St. Benedict Order v. Steinhauser*, 234 U.S. 640 (1914), p. 649. See *Law Notes*, August 1914, p. 81; compare *Virginia Law Register* 19 (April 1914): 949.

7. J. H. N. [John Humphrey Noyes], "Law Questions," *The Circular*, December 19, 1864. *The Circular* was the newspaper of the Oneida community. It was renamed the *American Socialist* in 1876.

8. Professor Karl J. R. Arndt offers an extended treatment of litigation involving the Harmony Society. See *George Rapp's Harmony Society: 1785–1847*, rev. ed., vol. 1 (Rutherford, N.J.: Fairleigh Dickinson University Press, 1972) (hereafter cited as Arndt 1); and *George Rapp's Successors and*

Material Heirs: 1847-1916, vol. 2 (Rutherford, N.J.: Fairleigh Dickinson University Press, 1971) (hereafter cited as Arndt 2).

On Shaker litigation, see Gerard C. Wertkin, ed. and comp., "An Annotated Bibliography of the Reported Decisions of the Courts . . . Relating to the Shakers," in *Shaker Literature: A Bibliography*, 2 vols., ed. Mary L. Richmond (Hanover, N.H.: University Press of New England, 1977), 2:247-53.

Some Shaker cases are treated briefly in Edward D. Andrews, *The People Called Shakers: A Search for the Perfect Society* (New York: Dover, 1953; new enlarged ed., Magnolia, Mass.: Peter Smith, 1963), and Edward D. Andrews and Faith Andrews, *Work and Worship: The Economic Order of the Shakers* (Greenwich: New York Graphic Society, 1974). See also discussion of litigation ("legal squabbling," p. 200) in Henri Desroche, *The American Shakers: From Neo-Christianity to Presocialism*, tr. John K. Savacool (Amherst: University of Massachusetts Press, 1971).

Two historical monographs on Zoar, published at about the same time, offer discussions of Zoar litigation: E. O. Randall, *The Separatist Society of Zoar: An Experiment in Communism—From Its Commencement to Its Conclusion*, first published in *Ohio Archaeological and Historical Quarterly* 8, no. 2 (1899); George B. Landis, "The Society of Separatists of Zoar, Ohio," *American Historical Association Annual Report* (1898), pp. 163-220. Zoar litigation is also treated in Edgar B. Nixon, "The Society of Separatists of Zoar" (unpublished dissertation, Ohio State University, 1933).

Litigation is referred to in all three of the contemporary works on the American utopians: John Humphrey Noyes, *Strange Cults and Utopias of the Nineteenth Century* (Philadelphia: Lippincott, 1870 [original title: *History of American Socialisms*]; reprint ed., New York: Dover, 1966); Charles Nordhoff, *The Communistic Societies of the United States: From Personal Visit and Observation* (1875; rev. reprint ed., New York: Schocken, 1966); and William A. Hinds, *American Communities* (1878; reprint ed., Secaucus, N.J.: Citadel, 1973) (hereafter cited as Hinds 1878). William A. Hinds, possibly because of his association with the lawyer James Towner, revealed the sharpest awareness of the meaning of the seceder litigation for the societies. Hinds also provided some texts of utopian contracts as an appendix to his 1878 work on the American communities.

9. Morris Hillquit, *History of Socialism in the United States*, 5th ed. (1910 [1st ed. 1903]; reprint ed., New York: Dover, 1971), p. 127.

10. Hinds 1878, p. 108, quoting points "as epitomized by Judge Towner." These had been published by Towner in *The Circular*, December 21, 1874, as part of his first series of articles. These articles discussed the cases indexed below (pp. 126–27) as 1–7. In Hinds's 1908 edition of *American Communities* the Towner summary (with the omission of point 5) was attributed to "Judge Towner of Santa Ana, California" (William A. Hinds, *American Communities and Cooperative Colonies*, 3rd ed. [1908; reprint ed., Philadelphia: Porcupine, 1975] [hereafter cited as Hinds 1908]), p. 61. In 1879, when Towner published a somewhat expanded discussion of utopian contract cases, he added a seventh point to his statement: "That where by such contract continuance in membership in the Community depends upon conformity to a certain religious faith, which is to be determined in some prescribed mode and by some constituted authority in the Society, the decision of such authority on the question of conformity or nonconformity is final, and the rightfulness or the wrongfulness of an expulsion for nonconformity, by such authority, will not be adjudicated by the civil courts. The parties to such a contract form and choose their own tribunal (an ecclesiastical one) for the decision of such questions, and by its decisions they are bound." J. W. T. [James Towner], "Community Contracts 10," *American Socialist*, December 25, 1879. Both the 1874 and the 1879 series of articles are hereafter cited as Towner 1, Towner 2, etc., followed by the date on which the article appeared.

Towner wrote that he had reviewed all the reported cases, and had not heard of any unreported cases in any lower court in which "a dissatisfied or recalcitrant member of any Community," or a party claiming through him, had been able to invalidate his contract with a community. Towner 10, December 25, 1879.

See also Towner's letter on the general subject of seceders' claims (December 12, 1867), published in *The Circular*, December 23, 1867.

On James Towner see generally Robert S. Fogarty, "Nineteenth Century Utopian," *Pacific Historian* 16 (Fall 1972): 70-76, which is the source of the following biographical material.

On April 4, 1866, attorney James Towner wrote to John Humphrey Noyes from Jackson, Michigan. He wanted to leave the military and, before choosing a home, thought it sensible to visit Oneida. "I wish to visit you for the purpose of observing the working of communism as illustrated by you," he said. "I'm not decided whether in endeavoring to 'work out our own salvation' and to spread the gospel, it is best now to join in organized effort such as yours or to work as we can in our present relations to each other and the world." He believed that he and his wife were measurably "free from the bondage of the marriage spirit." His wife had "worn the short dress most of the time since our marriage." Towner indicated that he had "some money and other properties, in all about $2400," and could bring some $1700 to be used, or not as might seem best. "I'm used to most kinds of manual labor," he concluded, "with a good knowledge of law and business generally." (Towner had been admitted to the bar in Iowa in June 1859, and practiced there until August 1861.)

Towner was not then admitted to Oneida and so lived with the free love community at Berlin Heights, Ohio. He finally joined the community at Oneida in 1874, and ultimately became the leader of the anti-Noyes faction ("Townerites") at the Perfectionist community. Following the breakup of Oneida, Towner and some others went to Southern California, where Towner became a superior court judge. Towner's neighbors in Santa Ana "never knew of his past activities," since the "move from central New York to Southern California was enough to bury old sins" (Fogarty, p. 74).

11. Towner 1, October 23, 1879.

12. Carl Zollman, *American Civil Church Law* (1917; reprint ed., New York: AMS, 1969), p. 315.

13. See generally Roscoe Pound, "Liberty of Contract," *Yale Law Journal* 18 (1909): 454; also Walton H. Hamilton, "Freedom of Contract," *Encyclopaedia of the Social Sciences* (1931), p. 450.

14. Grant Gilmore, *The Ages of American Law* (New Haven: Yale University Press, 1977), p. 63.

15. See Karl N. Llewellyn, "What Price Contract? An Essay in Perspective," *Yale Law Journal* 40 (1931): 704. The "power of contract is not pent within economic confines" (p. 727).

16. "There are two social conceptions which can be expressed only in terms of myth. One is the social contract, which presents an account of the origins of society. The other is the utopia, which presents an imaginative vision of the *telos* or end at which social life aims." Northrop Frye, "Varieties of Literary Utopias," in *Utopias and Utopian Thought*, ed. Frank E. Manuel (Boston: Beacon, 1967), p. 25.

" . . . what was myth in one world might always be fact in some other." C. S. Lewis, *Perelandra* (1944; New York: Collier, 1962), p. 102.

Chapter 1

Experiments and Institutions

Nathaniel Hawthorne, *Blithedale Romance* (New York: Dell, 1975), p. 41.

Quoted in George B. Lockwood, *The New Harmony Movement* (1905; reprint ed., New York: Dover, 1971), p. 85.

1. Richard T. Ely, *Recent American Socialism* (1885; reprint ed., New York: AMS, 1977), p. 13. On Ely, see James Dombrowski, *The Early Days of Christian Socialism in America* (New York: Columbia University Press, 1936), ch. 4; see

also Henry F. May, *Protestant Churches and Industrial America* (1949; reprint ed., New York: Octagon, 1963).

2. Edward Bellamy, *Looking Backward, 2000-1887* (1888; New York: Modern Library, 1951), p. 3. For a discussion of influences on Bellamy, see Henri Desroche, *The American Shakers: From Neo-Christianity to Presocialism*, tr. John K. Savacool (Amherst: University of Massachusetts Press, 1971), p. 374.

3. Bellamy, *Looking Backward*, p. 3.

4. James Kent, *Commentaries on American Law*, 13th ed. (Boston: Little, Brown, 1884), ch. 4, p. 18, contrasting monarchies and landed aristocracies with republican forms of government.

5. J. H. N. [John Humphrey Noyes], "An Appeal of the Oneida Community to all Lawyers, Justices, Judges and Courts of Law," *The Circular*, December 9, 1867.

6. Member of Oneida Community, quoted in Pierrepont Noyes, *My Father's House: An Oneida Boyhood* (New York: Farrar & Rinehart, 1937), pp. 17-18.

7. The society "was to be a church consecrated to total Christianity, a group of individuals who would survive the wrath preceding the Millennium and who would live and rule with Christ a thousand years." Arndt 1:96; also 1:604. On Harmonist religious beliefs, see also Arndt 2, ch. 8.

8. Macdonald's materials provided the basis for John Humphrey Noyes, *Strange Cults and Utopias of the Nineteenth Century* (Philadelphia: Lippincott, 1870 [original title: *History of American Socialisms*]; reprint ed., New York: Dover, 1966) (hereafter cited as Noyes, *Strange Cults* [*American Socialisms*]), and his questionnaire is reprinted there (pp. 4-6). Macdonald died before being able to complete the book he had contemplated.

9. Noyes, *Strange Cults* [*American Socialisms*], p. 6.

10. Hinds 1908, p. 119. Hinds (b. 1833) left Putney, Vermont, with John Humphrey Noyes in 1847. He died in 1910.

11. Richard T. Ely, "Amana: A Study of Religious Communism," *Harper's Monthly*, October 1902, pp. 659-68.

12. Ralph Albertson, "Survey of Mutualistic Communities in America," *Iowa Journal of History and Politics* (1936), p. 376.

13. Ambrose Bierce on the California colony Altruria, quoted in Robert V. Hine, *California's Utopian Colonies* (1953; New York: Norton, 1973), p. 113.

14. Morris Hillquit, *History of Socialism in the United States,* 5th ed. (1910 [1st ed. 1903]; reprint ed., New York: Dover, 1971), p. 25.

15. Arthur Bestor, *Backwoods Utopias: The Sectarian Origins and the Owenite Phase of Communitarian Socialism in America, 1663-1829,* 2nd enlarged ed. (Philadelphia: University of Pennsylvania Press, 1950, 1970), ch. 3.

16. Bestor, *Backwoods Utopias*, p. 50. Nordhoff's book on the utopias itself produced several membership applications to Zoar. See Edgar B. Nixon, "The Zoar Society, Applicants for Membership," *Ohio State Archaeological and Historical Quarterly* 45 (1936): 341, 347.

17. Bestor, *Backwoods Utopias*, p. 50, citing John A. Bole, *The Harmony Society: A Chapter in German American Culture History* (1904; reprint ed., New York: AMS, 1973), pp. 126-27. See also Karl J. R. Arndt, *Documentary History of the Indiana Decade of the Harmony Society, 1814-1824,* vol. 1: 1814-1819 (Indianapolis: Indiana Historical Society, 1975), p. 228.

18. Bestor, *Backwoods Utopias*, p. 7.

19. Edmund Wilson, *To the Finland Station: A Study in the Writing and Acting of History* (1940; Garden City, N.Y.: Doubleday Anchor, 1953), p. 102.

20. Charles Nordhoff, *The Communistic Societies of the United States: From Personal Visit and Observation* (1875; rev. reprint ed., New York: Schocken, 1966), p. 387.

21. W. D. Howells, *A Traveller from Altruria* (1894; New York: Hill & Wang, 1957), p. 141.

22. Quoted in Eric Foner, *Free Soil, Free Labor, Free Men: The Ideology of the Republican Party Before the Civil War* (New York: Oxford University Press, 1970), p. 27.

23. Howells, *A Traveller from Altruria*, p. 141.

24. See James M. Upton, "The Shakers as Pacifists in the Period Between 1812 and the Civil War," *Filson Club History Quarterly* 47 (1973): 267; Edward D. Andrews, *The People Called Shakers: A Search for the Perfect Society*, new enlarged

ed. (New York: Dover, 1963), p. 216; Anna White and Leila S. Taylor, *Shakerism: Its Meaning and Message* (1904; reprint ed., New York: AMS, 1972), particularly ch. 10, "In War Time."

25. Nordhoff, *Communistic Societies*, p. 348.

26. Constitution of the Brook Farm Association for Industry and Education, West Roxbury, Mass., Introductory Statement (Boston: Butts Printer, 1844; University Microfilms International Facsimile, 1977), p. 7; Noyes, *Strange Cults [American Socialisms]*, p. 524; see generally Bestor, *Backwoods Utopias*, p. 235.

27. Noyes, *Strange Cults [American Socialisms]*, p. 646.

28. Wilson, *To the Finland Station,* p. 104.

29. Russell Conwell, quoted in *God's New Israel: Religious Interpretations of American Destiny*, ed. Conrad Cherry (Englewood Cliffs, N.J.: Prentice-Hall, 1971), p. 215.

30. Jeremy Bentham, "The Theory of Legislation," in Jerome Hall, *Readings in Jurisprudence* (Indianapolis: Bobbs-Merrill, 1938), p. 168.

31. See Andrews, *The People Called Shakers*, pp. 291-92. Alice Felt Tyler noted in 1944 that it was "impossible to find two accounts giving the same number of Shaker settlements." Alice F. Tyler, *Freedom's Ferment: Phases of American Social History from the Colonial Period to the Outbreak of the Civil War* (1944; New York: Harper Torchbooks, 1962), p. 140.

There is considerable current interest in the Shakers and their history. In 1976 the Canterbury Shakers in a foreword to Charles E. Robinson's *The Shakers and Their Homes* (1893; Somersworth: New Hampshire Publishing Co., 1976) noted that "never before has the Shaker story received more attention than in the last decade."

32. See *Schwartz v. Duss*, 187 U.S. 8 (1902): "This is not the first time that the Harmony Society has been before the Courts" (p. 16).

33. Francis Lieber, *On Civil Liberty and Self Government*, 3rd ed. (Philadelphia: Lippincott, 1881), p. 146.

34. For Lieber on the Mormons and Oneida see [Lieber], "The Mormons: Shall Utah Be Admitted to the Union?" *Putnam's Monthly* 5 (1855): 225. Attribution: Francis Lieber,

Miscellaneous Writings, vol. 2. (Philadelphia: Lippincott, 1881), p. 534; Frank Freidel, *Francis Lieber: Nineteenth Century Liberal* (Baton Rouge: Louisiana State University Press, 1947), p. 262.

35. Alexis de Tocqueville, *Democracy in America*, 2 vols. (New York: Vintage, 1960), 2:114.

36. David Reisman, "Some Observations on Community Plans," *Yale Law Journal* 57 (1947): 173.

Religious toleration may have sometimes existed more in theory than in fact. See Ray Allen Billington, *The Protestant Crusade, 1800-1860: A Study of the Origins of American Nativism* (Chicago: Quadrangle Paperbacks, 1964). Also, Robley Whitson, "American Pluralism: Toleration and Persecution," *Thought* 37 (Winter 1962): 492-526.

One must also acknowledge the force of Professor Bestor's point that while religious liberty and cheap land may have attracted the communitarians initially, these factors tend to favor assimilation of groups into the greater society in the long run. " . . . religious toleration and cheap land were not allies but enemies of the sectarian ideal." Bestor, *Backwoods Utopias*, p. 262.

37. *Waite v. Merrill*, 4 Me. 102 (1826), p. 120; see, generally, Irving Zaretsky and Mark Leone, *Religious Movements in Contemporary America* (Princeton, N.J.: Princeton University Press, 1974), pp. 3-50.

38. Shaker hymn, quoted in John McKelvie Whitworth, *God's Blueprints: A Sociological Study of Three Utopian Sects* (Boston: Routledge & Kegan Paul, 1975), p. 46.

39. Noyes, *Strange Cults [American Socialisms]*, p. 669.

40. Ibid. Noyes may have overestimated the influence of the Shakers (Bestor, *Backwoods Utopias*, p. 54). "Rappites" refers to Harmonists. The Ebenezers were a name for the Amana Society of Inspirationists, originally founded as the Ebenezer Society, in New York. See Bertha Shambaugh, *Amana That Was and Amana That Is* (1932; reprint ed., New York: Arno, 1976).

41. Frederick W. Evans, *Shakers: Compendium of the Origin, History, Principles, Rules and Regulations, Government and Doctrines of the United Society of Believers in Christ's Second*

Appearing, 4th ed. (1867; reprint ed., New York: AMS, 1975), p. 34. Born in England and emigrating to America in 1810, Frederick Evans became a convert to Shakerism in 1830. Before joining the Shakers, Evans worked with his brother, George Henry Evans, in the promotion of social reform, and he remained interested in Shaker ideas throughout his life. See *Dictionary of American Biography*; also, Frederick W. Evans, *Autobiography of a Shaker and Revelation of the Apocalypse* (1888; reprint ed., New York: AMS, 1973).

42. Frederick W. Evans, *Two Orders: Shakerism and Republicanism* (Pittsfield, Mass.: Sun Printing Co., 1890), p. 4.

43. Quoted in Arndt 1:84. The petition resulted in a bill empowering George Rapp to buy land in the Indiana territory. The bill was defeated (February 18, 1805). Arndt 1:90. Compare the later experience of the Mennonites (pp. 42-44).

44. Ibid., p. 84.

45. Ibid., p. 62.

46. Noyes, *Strange Cults [American Socialisms]*, p. 267.

Chapter 2

"A Painfully Interesting Problem": The Case of the Mormons

Johan Huizinga: *America: A Dutch Historian's Vision, From Afar and Near*, tr. Herbert H. Rowan (New York: Harper & Row, 1972), p. 187.

1. *The Times* (London), September 4, 1855, quoted in Frederick H. Piercy, *Route from Liverpool to the Great Salt Lake Valley*, ed. Fawn M. Brodie (Cambridge, Mass.: Harvard University Press, 1962), p. xv. See generally Leonard J. Arrington and Davis Bitton, *The Mormon Experience: A History of the Latter Day Saints* (New York: Knopf, 1979), and Thomas O'Dea, *The Mormons* (Chicago: University of Chicago Press, 1957).

2. "The Reformation in Utah," *Harpers New Monthly Magazine* 43 (1871): 602.

3. Bernard DeVoto, "The Centennial of Mormonism: A Study in Utopia and Dictatorship," in *Forays and Rebuttals* (Boston: Little, Brown, 1936), p. 77.

4. Quoted in Heman C. Smith, "Mormon Troubles in Missouri," *Missouri Historical Review* 4 (1910): 239-40.

5. Ibid., p. 247.

6. New York *Herald*, June 17, 1842. Quoted in Fawn M. Brodie, *No Man Knows My History: The Life of Joseph Smith*, 2nd ed. (New York: Knopf, 1972), p. 273.

7. Ibid., ch. 27, "Carthage."

8. Leonard J. Arrington, *Great Basin Kingdom: Economic History of the Latter-day Saints, 1830-1900* (1958; Lincoln: University of Nebraska Press, 1966), p. 352.

9. Ibid., p. 7; see generally Leonard J. Arrington, "Early Mormon Communitarianism: The Law of Consecration and Stewardship," *Western Humanities Review* 7, no. 4 (Winter 1953): 341-69.

10. Arrington, *Great Basin Kingdom*, pp. 7-9.

11. Ibid., p. 9.

12. Ibid., p. 9. See also on this point Hamilton Gardner, "Communism Among the Mormons," *Quarterly Journal of Economics* 37 (1922): 154-55. Gardner reprints documents relating to the consecration of Titus Billings.

13. Arrington, *Great Basin Kingdom*, p. 11.

14. Brodie, *Joseph Smith,* pp. 108, 112.

15. *Evening and Morning Star*, July 1838, p. 219. See Brodie, *Joseph Smith,* p. 122, noting contrast to the Shakers.

16. Arrington, *Great Basin Kingdom,* p. 27.

17. Ibid.

18. O. Linford, "The Mormons and the Law: The Polygamy Cases," *Utah Law Review* 9 (Pts. 1 and 2, 1964-1965): 308, 543.

19. Henry Blackwell (husband of Lucy Stone) writing in *Woman's Journal*, June 21, 1879, p. 196.

20. Andrew Sinclair, *The Emancipation of the American Woman (The Better Half)* (New York: Harper Colophon, 1965), p. 214. On polygamy, see Kimball Young, *Isn't One Wife Enough?* (New York: Holt, 1954); Stanley S. Ivins, "Notes on Mormon Polygamy," *Western Humanities Review* 10 (Summer 1956): 229-39; Davis Bitton, "Mormon Polyg-

amy: A Review Article," *Journal of Mormon History* 4 (1977): 101-18.

21. *Davis v. Beason*, 133 U.S. 333 (1890), p. 341.

22. Ibid., p. 342.

23. *Harper's* 15 (1857): 129.

24. Amanda Dickinson in *Woman's Journal*, March 28, 1879.

25. "The Mormon Question," *Albany Law Journal*, November 4, 1871, and December 30, 1871, p. 231. See also T. W. Curtis, *The Mormon Problem: The Nation's Dilemma* (New Haven: Hoggson & Robinson, 1885).

26. George Tichnor Curtis, *A Plea for Religious Liberty* (1886), p. 16; argument in *Snow v. United States*, 118 U.S. 346 (1886).

27. D. C. Haskell, *Mormonism: An Address* (New York: American Home Missionary Society, 1881), p. 19.

28. *Utah* III, 1: Polygamous or plural marriages prohibited; the provision not to be changed without consent of the United States. *Arizona* XX and *New Mexico* XXI, 1: Polygamous or plural marriages and polygamous cohabitation forever prohibited; the provision not to be changed without consent of the United States. *Idaho* I, 4: Bigamy and polygamy prohibited and the legislature is to provide for punishment. *Idaho* VI, 3: Bigamists or polygamists may not serve on jury or hold civil office. *Oklahoma* I, 2: Polygamous or plural marriages prohibited.

29. Brodie, *Joseph Smith*, p. 380.

30. Ibid.

31. Peter Cartwright (1785-1872) quoted in Anson Phelps Stokes, *Church and State in the United States*, vol. 2 (New York: Harper, 1950), p. 45.

32. Josiah Strong, *Our Country* (1885), quoted in Stokes, *Church and State*, 2:281.

33. Angelina Newman, "Woman Suffrage in Utah," Petition to Senate and House of Representatives, 1886, 49th Cong., 1st Sess. Misc. Doc. 122, p. 4.

34. J. G. Shea, "Vagaries of Protestant Religious Belief," *American Catholic Quarterly Review* 10 (January-October 1885): 436-37.

35. On the Mormons in fiction, see Neal Lambert, "Saints, Sinners and Scribes," *Utah Historical Quarterly* 36 (Winter 1968): 64-72.

36. J. H. Beadle, *Life in Utah; or, the Mysteries and Crimes of Mormonism. Being an Exposé of the Secret Rites and Ceremonies of the Latter-Day Saints, with a Full and Authentic History of Polygamy and the Mormon Sect from its Origin to the Present Time* (Philadelphia and Chicago: National Publishing Co., 1870), pp. 212-13. Beadle was editor of the only Gentile paper in Utah, 1868-69. (The phrase "a painfully interesting problem," used in the title of this chapter, is a quotation from Beadle, p. 9.)

37. Ibid., pp. 400-1.

38. O'Dea, *The Mormons*, p. 101.

39. Senator Bayard of Delaware, quoted in Linford, *The Mormons and the Law*, 1:319.

40. *Mormon Church v. United States*, 136 U.S. 1 (1889), p. 49.

41. Ibid., pp. 63, 64.

42. *Davis v. Beason*, 133 U.S. 333 (1889), pp. 342-43.

43. On *Reynolds*, see R. J. Davis, "Plural Marriage and Religious Freedom: The Impact of *Reynolds v. United States*," *Arizona Law Review* 15 (1973): 287; R. J. Davis, "The Polygamous Prelude," *American Journal of Legal History* 6 (1962): 1; Linford, "The Mormons and the Law" (see also Thomas G. Alexander's discussion of the Linford articles in "The Church and the Law," *Dialogue* 1 [1966]: 123); Weisbrod and Sheingorn, "*Reynolds v. United States*: Nineteenth Century Forms of Marriage and the Status of Women," *Connecticut Law Review* 10, no. 4 (Summer 1978): 828. See also *Cleveland v. United States*, 329 U.S. 14 (1946). Compare *Cleveland* at p. 20 (Douglas, J.) with Justice Douglas's opinion in *Wisconsin v. Yoder*, 406 U.S. 205, 247 (1972) (concurring and dissenting in part).

44. *Reynolds v. United States*, 98 U.S. 145 (1879), pp. 165-66. On Morrison Waite, see Bruce R. Trimble, *Chief Justice Waite: Defender of the Public Interest* (Princeton, N.J.: Princeton University Press, 1938); C. Peter Magrath, *Morrison R. Waite: The Triumph of Character* (New York: Macmillan, 1963); C. Peter Magrath, "Chief Justice Waite and the 'Twin

Relic': Reynolds v. United States," *Vanderbilt Law Review* 18 (1965): 507.

45. *Mormon Church v. United States*, p. 49.

46. *Mormon Church v. United States*, p. 46. See Kauper and Ellis, "Religious Corporations and the Law," *Michigan Law Review* 71 (1973): 1500.

47. Richard T. Ely, *Property and Contract in Their Relations to the Distribution of Wealth*, 2 vols. (1914; reprint ed., Port Washington, N.Y.: Kennikat, 1971), 1:455. See also Ernst Freund, *The Police Power: Public Policy and Constitutional Rights* (Chicago: Callaghan & Co., 1904), pp. 375-76, 495. It may be noted that holding too much land might create difficulties for the communities in quite another way, since hired workers would be necessary to work the land, and care of the extra land would drain the energy of the communities. Land limitation was one of the reforms that interested the Shaker Elder Frederick Evans. See also Noyes, *Strange Cults [American Socialisms]*, p. 19.

48. David Brion Davis, "Some Themes of Counter-Subversion: An Analysis of Anti-Masonic, Anti-Catholic and Anti-Mormon Literature," *Mississippi Valley Historical Review* 47 (1960): 205.

49. Ibid., p. 211.

50. Ibid.

51. Beadle, *Life in Utah*, p. 8.

52. *American Socialist*, March 13, 1879, p. 84.

53. *Harper's* 15 (1857): 129.

54. Ibid.

55. Arrington and Bitton, *The Mormon Experience*, pp. 22, 348 (n. 5).

56. DeVoto, *Forays and Rebuttals*, p. 122.

Chapter 3

The Dark Side

Alexis de Tocqueville, *Democracy in America*, 2 vols. (New York: Vintage, 1960), 2:142, continuing: "Religious insanity is very common in the United States."

1. Henry J. Raymond, editor of *The Courier and Enquirer* in debate (1847) with Horace Greeley, excerpted in Albert Fried, *Socialism in America: From the Shakers to the Third International: A Documentary History* (Garden City, N.Y.: Doubleday Anchor, 1970), p. 159.

2. *White v. Miller*, 71 N.Y. 118 (1877). See James White and Robert Summers, *Handbook of the Law Under the Uniform Commercial Code* (St. Paul, Minn.: West, 1972), p. 308 (a case involving legal issues—e.g., the powers of trustees, capacity of the society to be sued—that are not considered here).

On the economic life of the Shakers, see particularly Edward D. Andrews, *The Community Industries of the Shakers* (1932; reprint ed., Philadelphia: Porcupine, 1972). It may be noted here that the section called "The Shakers and the Law" in Edward D. Andrews and Faith Andrews, *Work and Worship: The Economic Order of the Shakers* (Greenwich: New York Graphic Society, 1974) is not a full discussion of that subject. (See review, Gerard C. Wertkin, in *Shaker Quarterly* 14, no. 3 [1974]: 110.) Serious investigation of the totality of legal relationships in even one community would require not only detailed examination of community materials but a sense of the legal contexts in which those materials were generated. A discussion of even one group (in one state? at one period of time?) would cut across many fields of law. The present work does not, of course, make this attempt.

See Dallin H. Oaks and Joseph I. Bentley, "Joseph Smith and the Legal Process: In the Wake of the Steamboat *Nauvoo*," *Brigham Young University Law Review,* no. 3 (1976), pp. 735-82, for an example of the kind of archival research that largely remains to be done as to the utopians.

3. *Kreisinger v. The Icarian Community*, 16 Iowa (Withrow) 586 (1864).

4. For a discussion of the dark side of the literary utopias ("that dream often had its dark places") see Marie Louise Berneri, *Journey Through Utopia* (1951; New York: Schocken, 1971); see also Rosabeth Moss Kanter, *Commitment and Community* (Cambridge, Mass.: Harvard University Press, 1972), ch. 9, "The Limits of Utopia."

5. [Henry James], unsigned review of Nordhoff's *Communistic Societies of the United States*, *The Nation*, January 14, 1875, p. 27. Attribution: The Nation Index, 1865-1917; Haskell, vol. 2 (New York, 1953), p. 256; Leon Edel and Dan H. Laurence, *Bibliography of Henry James* (London: Rupert Hart-Davis, 1957), p. 297. Still, there was a "wholesome conservatism" in the Shaker philosophy, as described by Nordhoff, which James liked: "It is grotesque and perverted in many ways, but at its best points it is both the source and the fruit of a considerable personal self-respect."

6. Ibid.

7. Ibid.

8. "Muddled Ministers," *Manifesto*, March 1879; see also the letter from F. W. Evans (Mt. Lebanon, February 21, 1879) to the *American Socialist*, published February 27, 1879, p. 67; also correspondence in *Manifesto*, August 1879.

9. "Positivism Versus Woman Suffrage," *Woman's Journal*; see also John Mears, "Utah and the Oneida Community," in *The Independent*, April 10, 1879.

10. Ely Van de Warker, "A Gynecological Study of the Oneida Community," *American Journal of Obstetrics and Diseases of Women and Children* 17 (August 1884): 785.

11. Hinds 1908, p. 191.

12. "Oneida Communism," *The Nation*, September 4, 1879.

13. "The Oneida Community," T. H. Higginson in *Woman's Journal*, March 2, 1872, p. 65; reprinted in the Oneida publication *Male Continence* (Oneida, N.Y.: Office of the Oneida Circular, 1872), pp. 22-24.

14. "Utah and the Oneida Community," John Mears in *The Independent*, April 10, 1879.

15. Acts of Ohio (1811), ch. 8, pp. 13-15.

16. The concern was not essentially that children might be mistreated, although that was occasionally also suggested. See the charges against the Shakers brought before the New Hampshire legislature in 1848, reprinted in "Report of the Minority of the House Committee on the Judiciary," in Richard F. Upton, "Franklin Pierce and the Shakers: A Subchap-

ter in the Struggle for Religious Liberty," *Historical New Hampshire* 23 (1968): 13.

17. Ferdinand Toennies, *Ferdinand Toennies on Sociology: Pure, Applied, and Empirical*, ed. Cahnman and Heberle (Chicago: University of Chicago Press, 1971), pp 160-61. For a discussion of Gemeinschaft and Gesellschaft aspects of utopian life see Kanter, *Commitment and Community*, pp. 148ff.

18. Acts 2:44, 45; Acts 4:32: "And the multitude of them that believed were of one heart and of one soul; neither said any of them that ought of the things which he possessed was his own; but they had all things in common." Chief Justice Gibson referred to Shakers and Moravians. A later list included Zionists. See *State v. Amana Society*, 132 Iowa 304 (1906), p. 312.

19. Morris A. Hillquit, *History of Socialism in the United States*, 5th ed. (1910 [1st ed. 1903]; reprint ed., New York: Dover, 1971), p. 34.

20. Ibid.

21. Max Weber, *The Sociology of Religion*, tr. Ephraim Fischoff (1922; paperback ed., Boston: Beacon, 1964), pp. 252-53.

22. "Troubles in Shakerdom," *New York Times*, December 31, 1875, pp. 4-5 (regarding beards).

23. Hinds 1878, p. 160. In the 1870s there were riots in the coal mines. The Railway Strike of 1877 resulted in hundreds killed. "Not since slaveholders had ceased to be haunted by dreams of a slave uprising had the propertied elements been so terrified." Joseph G. Rayback, *A History of American Labor* (1959; expanded and updated ed., New York: Free Press, 1966), p. 135.

Henry F. May, in *Protestant Churches and Industrial America* (1949; reprint ed., New York: Octagon, 1963), suggests that attacks on socialism were not frequent among the Protestant clergy.

24. Mears, *The Independent*, April 10, 1879. The nineteenth century anarchist D. D. Lum believed, however, that the attacks on the Mormons had a great deal to do with their collective economic system. See John McCormick, "An Anar-

chist Defends the Mormons: The Case of Dyer D. Lum," *Utah Historical Quarterly* 44 (1976): 156-69.

In denying any identification between the Perfectionists and the communists of Europe, Hinds continued a conventional Oneida strategy. The Perfectionists had always been careful to distinguish their ideas from the apparently similar ideas of others, repeatedly dissociating themselves from the Mormons, from Free Lovers, and from antinomians. See John McKelvie Whitworth, *God's Blueprints* (Boston: Routledge & Kegan Paul, 1975), pp. 104, 111.

25. Quoted in Hinds 1878, p. 31.

26. See Richard Hofstadter, *The Idea of a Party System: The Rise of Legitimate Opposition in the United States, 1780-1840* (Berkeley: University of California Press, 1969), pp. 91ff, on Washington's annual message to Congress, November 1794.

27. See Dorothy Ann Lipson, *Freemasonry in Federalist Connecticut, 1789-1835* (Princeton, N.J.: Princeton University Press, 1977), pp. 110-11.

28. David Brion Davis, "Some Themes of Counter-Subversion: An Analysis of Anti-Masonic, Anti-Catholic and Anti-Mormon Literature, *Mississippi Valley Historical Review* 47 (1960): 211.

See generally L. Coser, "Greedy Organizations," *European Journal of Sociology* 8 (October 1967): 196-215.

29. Davis, "Themes of Counter-Subversion," p. 211.

30. Quoted in Constance N. Robertson, *Oneida Community Profiles* (Syracuse, N.Y.: Syracuse University Press, 1977), pp. 112-13.

31. Ibid.

32. Arndt 1:400.

33. Quoted in Eric Foner, *Free Soil, Free Labor, Free Men: The Ideology of the Republican Party Before the Civil War* (New York: Oxford University Press, 1970), p. 229.

34. Maldwyn A. Jones, *American Immigration* (Chicago: University of Chicago Press, 1960), p. 123.

35. Ibid., p. 124.

36. See C. H. Smith, *The Coming of the Russian Mennonites: An Episode in the Settling of the Last Frontier,*

1874–1884 (Berne, Indiana: Mennonite Book Concern, 1927), p. 58. The Canadian government met the demands.

37. *"The Congressional Debates on the Mennonite Immigration From Russia, 1873–1874,"* ed. Ernst Corell, *Mennonite Quarterly Review* 20 (1946): 185ff.; also Smith, *Coming of the Russian Mennonites*, pp. 84ff.

38. In the history of the Mennonites, it may be that the failure of the American Congress to enact the special legislation was of little importance. One group had already decided on a Canadian relocation, and others came to the United States nonetheless (Smith, *Coming of the Russian Mennonites*, p. 90).

Senator Edmunds later lent his name to the two federal acts (the Edmunds Act of 1882 and the Edmunds-Tucker Act of 1887) which, in effect, enforced the *Reynolds* decision.

39. R. T. Ely and G. S. Wehrwein, *Land Economics* (Madison: University of Wisconsin Press, 1964), p. 101.

40. Ibid., giving the Amana Society as an example.

41. Samuel J. Tilden, "Considerations in Regard to the Application of the Shakers for Certain Special Privileges," in *The Writings and Speeches of Samuel J. Tilden*, ed. John Bigelow (New York: Harper & Brothers, 1885), 1:95.

42. See account in Hinds 1908, p. 371.

43. *State v. Amana Society*, 132 Iowa 304 (1906), holding that the Amana Society had not exceeded its powers as a religious corporation. The case "is unique in the history of the communistic societies in that action was brought not by a member or ex member, nor even by a world heir, but by a resident and taxpayer of Iowa country." Bertha Shambaugh, *Amana That Was and Amana That Is* (1932; reprint ed., New York: Arno, 1976), p. 878.

44. "History of the Church at Mt. Lebanon, New York, No. 17, Believers Before the Legislature," *The Manifesto*, November 1890, reporting that a committee investigated and said that persons aggrieved should present their complaints, but that there was no further action.

45. Ohio Statutes, 1811, ch. 8, pp. 13–16, January 11, 1811: "An Act providing for the relief and support of women

who may be abandoned by their husbands, and for other purposes."

46. Kentucky Statutes, 1812 (in *Digest of the Statute Law of Kentucky, 1834*, pp. 124-26): "An Act concerning alimony and separate maintenance of wives and children abandoned by their husbands and fathers." Compare bill rejected in New Hampshire (reprinted in R. F. Upton, "Franklin Pierce and the Shakers," pp. 11-12): "An Act for the better protection of married women and children."

See also the Maine Statute of 1830 regulating divorce (ch. 456).

47. For an account of this legislative inquiry, see *The Other Side of the Question in Three Parts*. [1. an explanation of the Proceedings of Eunice Chapman and the Legislature against the United Society Called Shakers in the State of New York. 2. A Refutation of the False Statements of Mary Dyer against the Said Society in the State of New Hampshire. 3. An Account of the Proceedings of Abram Van Vleet, Esq. and His Associates against the Said Society at Union Village Ohio comprising a General Vindication of the Character of Mother and the Elders against the Attacks, of Public Slander—the Edicts of a Prejudiced Party and the Misguided Zeal of Lawless Mobs], compiled by Wright, Morrell, Houston & Serring (Union Village, 1819); see also Nelson M. Blake, "Eunice Against the Shakers," *New York History* 91 (1960): 359-78.

48. *The Other Side of the Question*, "Remonstrance," pp. 30-37. An attack on the Shakers in Ohio (1817) complained that the Shakers were "holding numbers of our young, innocent, free born citizens in bondage" and that the Shakers were "instilling the most abominable principles into every mind that can be duped or deluded by their vile sophistry." See *The Other Side of the Question*, p. 118, where the charges are reprinted by the Shakers, and answered.

See also Memorial to the Senate of the State of New York, from Stanton Buckingham, Stephen Wells, Justice Harwood and Chauncey Copley, Shaker Trustees, Watervliet, March 18, 1845, protesting a bill which would have prevented the binding of minor children to the Shakers.

Where legislatures responded to this issue they sometimes included provisions for the issuance of a writ of habeas corpus. The term refers to a method for bringing parties before the court. The central question on a writ of habeas corpus is not guilt or innocence, but legality or illegality of confinement. See New York Statute (McKinney's Consolidated Law of New York Domestic Relations Law, sec. 71); also Kentucky Statutes 405:070.

49. The council objected to the legislative bill in the Eunice Chapman case because it not only dissolved the marriage of the Chapmans, but also provided that in case a parent joined the Shakers, the authorities might award custody to that parent who stayed outside the society, even though, by the general law of the state, "applicable alike to all classes of men excepting slaves," the custody and control of infant children belonged exclusively to their father. Since, under the provisions of the bill, the father could be divested of these rights solely because he had joined the Shakers, the bill constituted a deprivation of rights merely because one was a Shaker. If the legislators could do this, "they have an equal right for the same cause, to disfranchise him of every other privilege, or to banish him, or even to put him to death." There was no evidence, the council found, of licentiousness on the part of the Shakers, or acts inconsistent with the peace and safety of the state. (In Council of Revision, February 27, 1818, pp. 1-4.) The divorce case (with child-custody issues) of Eunice Chapman in New York, and the somewhat similar case of Mary Dyer in New Hampshire, were among the most celebrated instances of individual anti-Shaker agitation. On Mary Dyer, see Edward D. Andrews, *The People Called Shakers: A Search for the Perfect Society* (New York: Dover, 1953; new enlarged ed., Magnolia, Mass.: Peter Smith, 1963), pp. 208-10; see *Dyer v. Dyer*, 5 N.H. 271 (1830); also *Fitts v. Fitts*, 46 N.H. 184 (1865).

50. Report of the Select Committee on the Subject of the Shakers, State of New York, in Assembly (April 2, 1849) (No. 198), p. 11.

51. Ibid., p. 13. In 1852, following a report from the Shak-

ers on the value of their holdings, the permissible limit was raised. (See Andrews, *The People Called Shakers*, p. 218.)

52. See *The Investigator: or a Defense of the Order, Government and Economy of the United Society Called Shakers Against Sundry Charges and Legislative Proceedings Addressed to the Political World by the Society of Believers at Pleasant Hill, Ky.* (Lexington: Smith & Palmer, 1828), reprinted in *Constitution of the United Society of Believers (called Shakers) Containing Sundry Covenants and Articles of Agreement, Definitive of the Legal Grounds of the Institution* (1833; reprint ed., New York: AMS, 1978) (hereafter cited as AMS *Constitution*).

53. Ibid., p. x, reprinting (at pp. viii-x) "An act to regulate civil proceedings against certain communities having property in common" (Kentucky, 1828).

54. Ibid., p. iii.

55. Ibid., p. iv.

56. Arndt M. Stickles, *The Critical Court Struggle in Kentucky, 1819-1829* (published under the auspices of the Graduate Council, Indiana University, 1929), p. 55.

57. Speech of Robert Wickliffe in the Senate of Kentucky, January 1831, in *The Investigator* (Lexington: 1828; reprinted N.Y. 1846), pp. 57-83.

58. Ibid. (*Investigator*, 1828, 1846), p. 75.

59. Ibid., p. 81. See also *Merrifield v. Shakers*, 30 Ky. 496 (1832), Robert Wickliffe representing the Shakers.

60. *Report of the Examination of the Shakers of Enfield and Canterbury, before the New-Hampshire Legislature, at the November Session, 1848, including the Testimony at Length; several extracts from Shaker Publications; the Bill which passed the House of Representatives; the Proceedings in the Pillow case: Together with the Letter of James W. Spinner* (Concord: Ervin Tripp, 1849). See also Richard F. Upton, "Franklin Pierce and the Shakers: A Subchapter in the Struggle for Religious Liberty," *Historical New Hampshire* 23 (1968): 3-18.

61. Quoted in *The Investigator*, in AMS *Constitution*, p. 15.

62. Ibid. See also the account in Arndt 1:363ff; also Arndt

1:485 on a later request for legislative intervention at the time of the schism (1832).

63. *The Investigator,* in AMS *Constitution,* pp. 15-16.

64. Ibid., p. 16.

65. Ibid.

66. Ibid.

67. Ibid., p. 17.

68. "Oneida Community," *The Circular,* February 4, 1867.

69. See Robertson, *Oneida Community Profiles,* pp. 115ff; Robert Allerton Parker, *A Yankee Saint: John Humphrey Noyes and the Oneida Community* (New York: G. P. Putnam's Sons, 1935), pp. 187-89; also *The Circular,* December 12, 1864.

70. "Oneida Community," *The Circular,* February 4, 1867.

71. *American Socialist,* September 4, 1879.

72. "Oneida Communism," *The Nation,* September 14, 1879.

73. See generally Maren Lockwood Carden, *Oneida: Utopian Community to Modern Corporation* (1969; New York: Harper Torchbooks, 1971). On Noyes, see also Robert David Thomas, *The Man Who Would Be Perfect: John Humphrey Noyes and the Utopian Impulse* (Philadelphia: University of Pennsylvania Press, 1977).

74. George Cannon, "A Review of the Decision of the Supreme Court of the United States in the Case of Geo. Reynolds v. the United States" (Salt Lake City: Deseret News Printing and Publishing Establishment, 1879), pp. 39-40; see also Laurence Tribe, *American Constitutional Law* (Mineola, N.Y.: Foundation Press, 1978), p. 854.

75. Compare the criminal provision of the 1811 Ohio statute, above.

76. This is, however, sometimes suggested.

77. *State ex rel. Stephen Ball v. Anna Hand* (1848) *Western Law Journal* 238. MacLean provides this information on the Ball litigation. On October 6, 1847, it was held that the father, Stephen Ball, would lose the children because "the law of Ohio was if a man joined the Shakers, he forfeited all right and title to his children." A further proceeding resulted in a split decision, 2-2. The case was then assigned to Judge John-

son [Johnston?], who decided against the father. An appeal to the state supreme court (April 19, 1848) resulted in a decision, over two dissents, that joining the Shakers deprived individuals "of their natural right to their children." MacLean's description of the case is under the heading "Judicial Persecution." John P. MacLean, *Shakers of Ohio: Fugitive Papers Concerning the Shakers of Ohio, With Unpublished Manuscripts* (Columbus: F. J. Heer, 1907), p. 256.

On the Millerite (adventist) excitement, see Whitney R. Cross, *The Burned-Over District: The Social and Intellectual History of Enthusiastic Religion in Western New York, 1800–1850* (1950; New York: Harper Torchbooks, 1965), p. 287: "Probably well over fifty thousand people in the United States became convinced that time would run out in 1844, while a million or more of their followers were skeptically expectant."

Note that (as counsel for Ball argued) Stephen Ball's case was not covered by the Ohio statute.

78. *Ball v. Hand*, p. 239.

79. Ibid., p. 243.

80. Ibid., 244.

81. Ibid., p. 242.

82. *People v. Pillow*, 1 Sand. (Sup. Ct.) 672 (1848), argument at p. 675. This case was one of several proceedings involving William Pillow and his family. See also *Fowler v. Hollenbeck and Pillow* 9 (Barb.) N.Y. 309 (1850).

Among the Shakers associated with the Pillow controversy was Daniel Boler, presumably the same Daniel Boler whose custody had been in dispute some time earlier in Kentucky. See Julia Neal, *By Their Fruits* (Chapel Hill: University of North Carolina Press, 1947), pp. 50–51; also Thomas Whittaker, O.S.B., "From Jasper Valley to Holy Mount: The Odyssey of Daniel Boler," *Shaker Quarterly* 10, no. 2 (Summer 1970): 35–45; see also "Trial of the Shakers . . ." in *Report of the Examination of the Shakers of Enfield and Canterbury*, pp. 90ff.

83. *People v. Pillow*, argument at p. 676.

84. Ibid., p. 678.

85. Ibid.

86. Ibid., p. 679.

87. *People ex rel. Barbour v. Gates*, 43 New York 40 (1870), p. 47.

88. Ibid., p. 48. See also: *Matter of M'Dowle*, 8 J. R. (N.Y.) 328 (1811); *Curtis v. Curtis*, 71 Mass. 535 (1855).

89. See Robert Nozick, *Anarchy, State and Utopia* (New York: Basic Books, 1974), p. 14.

90. See on this point, in general: Lon Fuller, *The Problems of Jurisprudence* (1949; Brooklyn: Foundation Press, 1974), pp. 708ff; also: Introduction ("Contract as a Principle of Order"), Friedrich Kessler and Grant Gilmore, *Contracts: Cases and Materials*, 2nd ed. (Boston: Little, Brown, 1970). See also: Harry W. Jones, "The Jurisprudence of Contracts," *Cincinnati Law Review* 44 (1975), pp. 43-54: " . . . perhaps the 'illegal bargain' cases should not be taught in contracts at all, but rather in constitutional law as the inseparable first cousins of the cases on federalism and delegation of legislative power" (p. 54).

Chapter 4

Free and Binding Contract

Restatement of Contracts 2d (St. Paul, Minn.: American Law Institute, 1973).

Thomas Hobbes, *Leviathan*, from *Hobbes: Selections*, ed. F. J. E. Woodbridge (New York: Scribners, 1930, 1958), pp. 272-73.

1. Friedrich Kessler and Grant Gilmore, *Contracts: Cases and Materials*, 2nd ed. (Boston: Little, Brown, 1970), p. 1.

2. Towner 1, October 23, 1879.

3. *The Exposition Continued in Answer to Sundry Inquiries and Objections*, "The Claims of Withdrawing Members Considered," in AMS *Constitution*, p. 25.

4. Hervey Elkins, *Fifteen Years in the Senior Order of Shakers: A Narrative of Facts concerning that Singular People* (Hanover, 1853), p. 21.

5. Etienne Cabet, "History and Constitution of the Icarian Community," tr. Thomas Teakle, *Iowa Journal of History and Politics* 15 (1917): 248.

6. Towner 1, October 23, 1879.

7. Noyes, *Strange Cults [American Socialisms]*, pp. 35–40.

8. Charles A. Reich, "The New Property," *Yale Law Journal* 73 (1964): 771.

9. See Hinds 1908, pp. 522–30.

10. Quoted in James Dombrowski, *The Early Days of Christian Socialism in America* (New York: Columbia University Press, 1936), p. 147. A variant appears in Albert Fried, *Socialism in America: From the Shakers to the Third International: A Documentary History* (Garden City, N.Y.: Doubleday Anchor, 1970), p. 359.

11. Shaker *Circular Epistle*, in AMS *Constitution*, p. 77.

12. Ibid.

13. Towner 1, October 23, 1879.

14. Ibid.

15. Ibid.

16. Ibid.

17. While the law developed other ideas about the basis of enforcement of contract (e.g., reliance—see Sec. 90, *Restatement of Contracts*), it is enough for our purposes to say that the utopian contracts were perceived as supported by consideration, strictly defined.

18. J. H. N. [John Humphrey Noyes], "An Appeal," *The Circular*, December 9, 1867.

19. "Shaker Societies: Their Purpose and Maintenance," *The Shaker*, June 1872, p. 41.

20. Ibid. But one early Shaker covenant did authorize return of original property. See 1810 Ohio covenant in AMS *Constitution*, pp. 1–2.

21. Durbin Ward in the *Shaker Income Tax Application* (1869), pp. 15–16.

22. Ibid. This factual picture does not, however, appear to have been presented to the courts. Compare *Grosvenor infra*.

23. Noyes, "An Appeal."

24. No litigation on this point is at hand. But see the idea of counterclaim *infra*.

25. Lawrence Friedman, *Contract Law in America* (Madison: University of Wisconsin Press, 1965), p. 20.

Chapter 5

Covenant As Contract

1. H. Richard Niebuhr, "Religious Institutions, Christian," *Encyclopaedia of the Social Sciences* (1931), p. 271, noting the existence of these "extreme features" in the nineteenth century Mormons.

2. Franklin H. Littell, prefatory essay to Charles Nordhoff, *The Communistic Societies of the United States: From Personal Visit and Observation* (1875; reprint ed., New York: Schocken, 1966), p. x. See also Franklin H. Littell, *The Origins of Sectarian Protestantism: A Study of the Anabaptist View of the Church* (New York: Macmillan, 1964).

3. Edmund Morgan, *Visible Saints: The History of a Puritan Idea* (Ithaca, N.Y.: Cornell University Press, 1963), p. 25.

On the legalism of the American Puritan tradition, and the emphasis on the idea of covenant, see particularly Perry Miller, *Errand into the Wilderness* (Cambridge, Mass.: Harvard University Press, 1956), ch. 3; see also Champlin Burrage, *The Church Covenant Idea: Its Origin and Its Development* (Philadelphia: American Baptist Publishing Society, 1904).

4. *Testimony of Christ's Second Appearing, As Exemplified by the Principles and Practice of the True Church of Christ: History of the Millennial Church . . . Published by the United Society Called Shakers*, 4th ed., p. 449 (thereafter cited as *Testimony of Christ's Second Appearing*). See also John H. Morgan, "Religious Communism: The Shaker Experiment in Christian Community," *Shaker Quarterly* 12 (Winter 1973): 119, 124.

5. Shaker Covenant Hymn, 1813, from AMS *Constitution*, pp. 94-95 (first three verses of ten):

Come ye souls that are sincere, the gospel to pursue
Now your faith you may declare, & what
you mean to do
Are you pleas'd with what is done,
To introduce Emanuel's reign?
Yea I am, and each for one, may freely say—Amen.

Can you in this work rejoice, because it saves from sin?
Was it your delib'rate choice that freely
bro't you in?
Is it your good faith alone
That holds you like a golden chain?
Yea it is, and each for one, may freely say,—Amen.

Does the cov'nant you have sign'd a right'ous
thing appear?
Is it your unwav'ring mind, in it to persevere?
In its bonds however tight
Are you determin'd to remain?
Yea I am—Then we'll unite and jointly say Amen.

On Shaker music and dance, see Edward Deming Andrews, *The Gift to Be Simple: Songs, Dances and Rituals of the American Shakers* (1940; reprint ed., New York: Dover, 1962).

6. "The Shaker Covenant," *The Shaker*, February 1877, p. 13.

7. Ibid.

8. Karl J. R. Arndt, *A Documentary History of the Indiana Decade of the Harmony Society, 1814-1824*, 1:1814-1819 (Indianapolis: Indiana Historical Society, 1975), p. xi.

9. See discussions of the commitment mechanisms "sacrifice" and "investment," in Rosabeth Moss Kanter, *Commitment and Community* (Cambridge, Mass.: Harvard University Press, 1972), pp. 80ff.

10. Quoted in Constance Noyes Robertson, *Oneida Community Profiles* (Syracuse, N.Y.: Syracuse University Press, 1977), pp. 82-83.

11. Frederick W. Evans, *Shakers: Compendium of the Origin, History, Principles, Rules and Regulations, Government and Doctrines of the United Society of Believers in Christ's Second Appearing,* 4th ed. (1867; reprint ed., New York: AMS, 1975), p. 42.

12. See the Harmonist explanation for their change in relation to refunds, below.

13. *A Brief Exposition of the Established Principles, and Regulations of the United Society of Believers Called Shakers* (Albany, 1830; Watervliet, Ohio, 1832), p. 8, reprinted in AMS *Constitution.*

14. Ibid.

15. *The Other Side of the Question* (1819), p. 3.

16. Franklin H. Littell, "The Anabaptist Doctrine of the Restitution of the True Church," *Mennonite Quarterly Review* 24 (January 1950): 36. Professor Littell notes that while this may sometimes have meant merely social ostracism among the sixteenth century Anabaptists, "generally it meant the loss of privileges within the brotherhood" (p. 37).

17. Matthew 18:15-17.

18. Ernst Troeltsch, *The Social Teaching of the Christian Churches,* tr. Olive Wyon (New York: Harper, 1931), p. 331. On the Shakers as a sect, see Henri Desroche, *The American Shakers: From Neo-Christianity to Presocialism,* tr. John K. Savacool (Amherst: University of Massachusetts Press, 1971).

19. Philip Schaff, excerpted in Milton Powell, ed., *The Voluntary Church: American Religious Life, 1740-1865, Seen through the Eyes of European Visitors* (New York: Macmillan, 1967), p. 150. For a discussion of church/sect differences in the American context see H. Richard Niebuhr, *The Social Sources of Denominationalism* (1929; New York: Meridian, 1972).

20. Shaker hymn, in AMS *Constitution,* p. 95. Does "justice" in the last line refer to natural justice? To the result of some early case like *Heath v. Draper* (1810)?

Chapter 6

The Social Contract

Karl N. Llewellyn, "What Price Contract?—An Essay in Perspective," *Yale Law Journal* 40 (1931): 736–37.

1. John Locke, *Second Treatise on Civil Government*, ch. 8, "Of the Beginning of Political Society" (Chicago: Gateway, 1955), p. 78.

2. Hancock Covenant of 1830, preamble, in John S. Williams, *The Shaker Religious Concept, together with the Covenant* (Old Chatham, N.Y.: Shaker Museum Foundation, 1959).

3. Pleasant Hill Constitution, p. [i], reprinted in AMS *Constitution.*

4. *Investigator*, p. iv, reprinted in AMS *Constitution.*

5. Ibid.

6. Ibid.

7. See John Marshall's dissent in *Ogden v. Saunders*, 25 U.S. 213 (1827), pp. 337, 342ff.

8. Frederick Pollock and Frederic W. Maitland, *History of English Law Before the Time of Edward I*, intro, S. F. C. Milson, 2 vols. (London: Cambridge University Press, 1968), 2:233.

9. Quoting Isaiah 28:15.

10. Quoted in Vernon L. Parrington, *Main Currents in American Thought*, vol. 2, *The Romantic Revolution in America: 1800–1860* (1927; New York: Harcourt, Brace, 1954), p. 403.

11. Quoted in Robert Allerton Parker, *A Yankee Saint: John Humphrey Noyes and the Oneida Community* (New York: G. P. Putnam's Sons, 1935), p. 49.

12. Ibid.

13. See Robert S. Fogarty, "Oneida: A Utopian Search for Religious Security," *Labor History* 14 (1973): 202, who suggests that the influence has been exaggerated. See also Peter

Brock, *Radical Pacifists in Antebellum America* (Princeton, N.J.: Princeton University Press, 1968), p. 88.

14. Hinds 1908, p. 182.

15. Ibid.

16. John Humphrey Noyes, *The Berean: A Manual for the Help of Those Who Seek the Faith of the Primitive Church* (Putney: Office of the Spiritual Magazine, 1847), p. 503.

17. Ibid., p. 504

18. *The Perfectionist*, November 1843, quoted in John McKelvie Whitworth, *God's Blueprints: A Sociological Study of Three Utopian Sects* (Boston: Routledge & Kegan Paul, 1975), p. 153.

19. *Circular Epistle*, 1829, reprinted in AMS *Constitution*, p. 77.

20. Icarian Constitution, art. 8, art. 9, in Etienne Cabet, "History and Constitution of the Icarian Community," tr. Thomas Teakle, *Iowa Journal of History and Politics* 15 (1917): 248.

21. Constitution of 1833, art. 11, in George B. Landis, "The Society of Separatists of Zoar, Ohio," *American Historical Association Annual Report* (1898), p. 216: Landis referred to the communistic societies as "experiments in government by compact" (p. 165). The Shaker covenant also invokes the outside legal system. The preamble recites that the covenant "shall stand as a lawful testimony, of our religious and social compact before all men, and all cases of question and law" (Hancock Covenant of 1830, in Williams, *Shaker Religious Concept*, p. 16). See also covenant provisions relating to the duties of the trustees. Thus: trustees were to "make all just and equitable defense in law, for the protection and security of the consecrated and united interest" (Hancock Covenant of 1830, sec. 2, in Williams, *Shaker Religious Concept*, p. 22). Compare Pleasant Hill Church covenant, 1814, in AMS *Constitution*, p. 84. See also Ira Drew, "Legal Decisions of Common Law of the United States," Alfred, Maine, September 30, 1865, responding to questions concerning trustees who violate their obligations.

22. W. H. Dixon, *New America* (Philadelphia: Lippincott, 1867), 2:108.

23. Icarian Constitution, p. 269, "A Statement of Motives," introducing "Regulations for the General Assembly."

Chapter 7

Turning Away

Reprinted in Albert Shaw, *Icaria: A Chapter in the History of Communism* (1884; reprint ed., Philadelphia: Porcupine, 1972), p. 198.

1. J. H. N. [John Humphrey Noyes], "Nathaniel Hawthorne," *The Circular*, May 30, 1864. Noyes had "no faith in the permanence of Hawthorne's reputation."

2. Ibid.

3. Arthur Bestor, *Backwoods Utopias: The Sectarian Origins and the Owenite Phase of Communitarian Socialism in America, 1663-1829*, 2nd enlarged ed. (Philadelphia: University of Pennsylvania Press, 1950, 1970), p. 55.

4. Edward D. Andrews, *The People Called Shakers: A Search for the Perfect Society* (New York: Dover, 1953; new enlarged ed., Magnolia, Mass.: Peter Smith, 1963), quoting Covenant of 1795, p. 63.

5. See text in *Schriber v. Rapp*, 5 Watts (Pa.) 351 (1836), p. 357.

6. "Secession from the Community," *The Circular*, May 23, 1864; Zoar Contract (1817) in George B. Landis, "Society of Separatists of Zoar, Ohio," *American Historical Association Annual Report* (1898), p. 205.

7. "Secession," *The Circular*, May 23, 1864.

8. G. K. Chesterton, *Orthodoxy* (1908; reprint ed., Westport: Greenwood, 1974), p. 212 (the language is used in a different context).

9. Hinds 1878, p. 107.

10. Marguerite Melcher, *The Shaker Adventure* (Cleveland: Press of Case Western Reserve University, 1941), p. 93.

11. Ibid., p. 241.

12. Ibid.

13. Caleb Dyer, a son of Mary Dyer, before the legislature of New Hampshire (1848), *Examination of the Shakers*, p. 71.

14. Maren Lockwood Carden, *Oneida: Utopian Community to Modern Corporation* (1969; New York: Harper Torchbooks, 1971), pp. 70-80.

15. Edgar B. Nixon, "The Society of Separatists of Zoar" (unpublished dissertation, Ohio State University, 1933), p. 185.

16. Arndt 1, ch. 32.

17. *The Shaker,* June 1872, p. 41.

18. Albert Shaw, *Icaria,* p. 75.

19. Ibid.

20. *Summary View of the Millennial Church or United Society of Believers Commonly Called Shakers* (Albany, N.Y., 1823), p. vii.

21. "Secession," *The Circular,* May 23, 1864.

22. Ibid.

23. Edward Brinley, "The Apostate," *The Circular,* January 30, 1865.

24. J. H. N. [John Humphrey Noyes], "A Human Parasite," *The Circular,* November 14, 1864.

25. *The Shaker,* June 1872, p. 41.

26. Edward D. Andrews, *The People Called Shakers,* p. 193.

27. Zechariah Chafee, "Internal Affairs of Associations Not for Profit," *Harvard Law Review* 43 (1930): 993.

28. Ibid.

29. Arndt 2, p. 60 (re Nachtrieb).

30. Melcher, *Shaker Adventure,* p. 93.

31. *Brief Exposition,* in AMS *Constitution,* p. 8.

32. Quoted in Nixon, "Society of Separatists of Zoar," p. 187.

33. *An Icarian Communist in Nauvoo: Commentary by Emil Vallet,* ed. and with an introduction by H. Roger Grant (Springfield: Illinois State Historical Society, 1971) (pamphlet no. 6), p. 34.

34. Charles Nordhoff, *The Communistic Societies of the United States: From Personal Visit and Observation* (1875; rev. reprint ed., New York: Schocken, 1966), p. 406.

35. Ibid., pp. 394-5.

36. Hon. John Brethett of Kentucky, quoted in *A Brief Exposition,* in AMS *Constitution,* p. 36.

37. Aristotle, *Politics*, tr. T. A. Sinclair (Baltimore: Penguin, 1962), p. 64.

38. In these cases, the "exit" option was very costly, and the "voice" option might be equally so. See generally Albert O. Hirschman, *Exit, Voice, and Loyalty: Responses to Decline in Firms, Organizations, and States* (Cambridge, Mass.: Harvard University Press, 1970).

39. *The Shaker*, June 1872, p. 41.

40. Ibid.

41. J. H. N. [John Humphrey Noyes], "Meaning of the Mills War," *The Circular*, February 6, 1865. Compare this with an attitude in which those who are excommunicated are always viewed as "potentially penitent." See Emil Oberholzer, *Delinquent Saints: Disciplinary Action in the Early Congregational Churches of Massachusetts* (New York: Columbia University Press, 1956), p. 38.

42. J. H. N. [John Humphrey Noyes], "An Appeal," *The Circular*, December 9, 1867.

Chapter 8

The Bargain

Reprinted in Albert Shaw, *Icaria: A Chapter in the History of Communism* (1884; reprint ed., Philadelphia: Porcupine, 1972).

1. Quoted in George Woodcock, *Anarchism: A History of Libertarian Ideas and Movements* (New York: Meridian, 1962), p. 458.

2. Quoted in Noyes, *Strange Cults [American Socialisms]*, pp. 99-100. On Warren, see George B. Lockwood, *The New Harmony Movement* (1905; reprint ed., New York: Dover, 1971), ch. 21; Noyes, *Strange Cults [American Socialisms]*, p. 94ff.

3. Quoted in Arthur Bestor, *Backwoods Utopias: The Sectarian Origins and the Owenite Phase of Communitarian Socialism in America, 1663-1829*, 2nd enlarged ed. (Philadelphia: University of Pennsylvania Press, 1950, 1970), p. 209.

4. Max Weber, *The Theory of Social and Economic Organization*, tr. A. M. Henderson and Talcott Parsons (New York: Free Press, 1947), p. 361.

5. Ibid.

6. Karl N. Llewellyn and E. Adamson Hoebel, *The Cheyenne Way: Conflict and Case Law in Primitive Jurisprudence* (Norman: University of Oklahoma Press, 1941), p. 28. See generally Leopold Pospisil, *Anthropology of Law: A Comparative Theory* (New York: Harper & Row, 1971), ch. 4.

7. Karl J. R. Arndt, *Documentary History of the Indiana Decade of the . armony Society, 1814-1824*, vol. 1:1814-1819 (Indianapolis: Indiana Historical Society, 1975), p. xvi.

8. Arndt 1:74-75; see Arndt 1:562, 593 for other references to rules.

9. Ibid., 1:75.

10. Quoted in "Scraps and Talks," *The Circular*, December 2, 1868.

11. Bertha Shambaugh, *Amana That Was and Amana That Is* (1932; reprint ed., New York: Arno, 1976), p. 243.

12. See: Edward D. Andrews, *The People Called Shakers: A Search for the Perfect Society* (New York: Dover, 1953; new enlarged ed., Magnolia, Mass.: Peter Smith, 1963), pp. 243-89; Theodore E. Johnson, "The Millennial Laws of 1821," *Shaker Quarterly* 7, no. 2 (Summer 1967): 35-38. Theodore E. Johnson, "Rules and Orders for the Church of Christ's Second Appearing[;] Established by the Ministry and Elders of the Church[;] New Lebanon, New York[;] May 1860," *Shaker Quarterly* 11, no. 4 (Winter 1971).

For a well-known description of the Shaker statutes by an apostate, see Hervey Elkins (1853) quoted in Charles Nordhoff, *The Communistic Societies of the United States: From Personal Visit and Observation* (1875; rev. reprint ed., New York: Schocken, 1966), pp. 177-78: "Not a single action of life, whether spiritual or temporal . . . but that has a rule for its perfect and strict performance."

13. Johnson, "Millennial Laws," p. 45.

14. See Icarian Constitution, in Etienne Cabet, "History and Constitution of the Icarian Community," tr. Thomas Teakle, *Iowa Journal of History and Politics* 15 (1917): 251-69.

15. Quoted in Robert V. Hine, *California's Utopian Colonies* (New York: Norton, 1973).

16. Quoted in Hinds 1908, p. 234.

17. John McKelvie Whitworth, *God's Blueprints: A Sociological Study of Three Utopian Sects* (Boston: Routledge & Kegan Paul, 1975), p. 30.

18. Ibid.

19. Similar accusations were made about the Masons after the abduction of William Morgan in 1826.

20. Quoted in Noyes, *Strange Cults [American Socialisms]*, p. 5.

21. Hinds 1878, p. 36.

22. Ibid., p. 37.

23. George B. Landis, "The Society of Separatists at Zoar, Ohio," *American Historical Association Annual Report* (1898), p. 190.

24. Nordhoff, *Communistic Societies*, pp. 49-50.

25. Ibid., pp. 54-55.

26. [John Humphrey Noyes], *Mutual Criticism* (1876; reprint ed., Syracuse, N.Y.: Syracuse University Press, 1975). See introduction by Murray Levine and Barbara Bunker: *Mutual Criticism* "may most likely be attributed to John Humphrey Noyes."

27. Ibid.

28. Nordhoff, *Communistic Societies*, pp. 290ff.

29. Morris A. Hillquit, *History of Socialism in the United States*, 5th ed. (1910 [1st ed. 1903]; reprint ed., New York: Dover, 1971), p. 46. Nordhoff writes that the man "whom I will call Charles" (p. 290) was criticized for a number of shortcomings. Noyes is quoted as criticizing Charles for a "selfish love"—the desire to form an exclusive intimacy with the woman carrying his child (p. 292).

30. [Henry James], *The Nation*, January 14, 1875. Note the perception of the utopians as standing on a line with the rest of American society rather than in opposition to it. One can only speculate on the intention, if any, behind "Henry."

31. Clara Endicott Sears, *Gleanings from Old Shaker Journals* (New York: Houghton Mifflin, 1916), pp. 275-76.

32. William Hebert, "A Visit to the Colony of Harmony in Illinois" (1825), reprinted in *Cooperative Communities: Plans and Descriptions: Eleven Pamphlets, 1825-1847* (New York: Arno, 1972), pp. 3-4.

33. Eugen Ehrlich, *Fundamental Principles of the Sociology of Law*, tr. Walter L. Moll (1936; reprint ed., New York: Arno, 1975), pp. 73-74.

34. J. A. Corcoran, "Excommunication," *American Catholic Quarterly Review* 12 (January-October 1887): 663.

35. Levi Bimeler's newspaper is reprinted in E. O. Randall, *The Separatist Society of Zoar: An Experiment in Communism—From Its Commencement to Its Conclusion*, first published in *Ohio Archaeological and Historical Quarterly* 8, no. 2 (1899), pp. 55-68. Three issues were published, and a fourth prepared in part, when Bimeler was threatened with expulsion unless he stopped publishing. The fourth issue of his paper was not published or given to the public (except by Randall). In abandoning the paper, Bimeler acted on advice of counsel (Nixon, "Society of Separatists of Zoar" [unpublished dissertation, Ohio State University, 1933], p. 224).

Levi Bimeler, the schoolteacher at Zoar, was educated outside the society. Randall reports this as the "only instance in which a member had been sent away or been permitted to leave temporarily for the purpose of being educated" (p. 44). By contrast, Oneida sent a number of its people to outside schools, and T. W. Higginson remarked that "the young men whom they send to Yale College, and the young women whom they send for musical instruction to New York, always return eagerly and devote their lives to the Community." This, he noted, "proves a good deal." T. W. Higginson, *Woman's Journal*, March 2, 1872, p. 65.

36. J. H. N. [John Humphrey Noyes], "Meaning of the Mills War," *The Circular*, February 6, 1865.

37. Robert Parker, *A Yankee Saint: John Humphrey Noyes and the Oneida Community* (New York: G. P. Putnam's Sons, 1935), p. 223.

38. Fayette Mace, *Familiar Dialogues on Shakerism: In Which the Principles of the United Society Are Illustrated and Defended* (Concord, N.H.: William White, 1838), p. 79.

39. *The Investigator*, AMS *Constitution*, p. vi. The Whitby petition was for himself and others, among them apparently "Samuel Banta" (see p. vii).

40. Ibid., p. 12.

41. Ibid.

42. Arndt 1:358.

43. Reprinted in Shaw, *Icaria*.

44. Nixon, "Society of Separatists of Zoar," p. 58.

45. Ibid.

46. *Brief Exposition*, p. 9, in AMS *Constitution*; also Frederick W. Evans, *Shakers: Compendium of the Origin, History, Principles, Rules and Regulations, Government and Doctrines of the United Society of Believers in Christ's Second Appearing*, 4th ed. (1867; reprint ed., New York: AMS, 1975), pp. 45ff.

47. Evans, *Shakers*, p. 45.

48. Ibid., pp. 48-49.

49. Ibid.

50. Ibid., p. 50.

51. Ibid.

52. *Exposition Continued*, p. 28, in AMS *Constitution*.

53. See Landis texts, and particularly articles 7 and 11 of the 1824 compact, and article 11 of the 1833 Constitution. Hinds quoted a Zoar spokesman who indicated that of the 126 members, only 72 were of the second (higher) class.

54. See Arndt texts of the Harmonist articles of 1805 (1:72-73); 1821 (1:198-99); 1827 (1:355-56); and 1836 (1:571-72) (voiding refund provision of earlier contracts). Texts also appear in *Schriber v. Rapp* (1805; 1821; 1827); 5 Watts (Pa.) 351 (1836).

55. Hinds 1908, pp. 310-11. There was interest allowed for the period from the adjustment of the account to the repayment, as well as the possibility of a gratuity to the seceding member (Article VIII, Amana Constitution [1859], in Shambaugh, *Amana*, p. 289).

56. Bestor, *Backwoods Utopias*, pp. 173-74; p. 174, n. 51.

57. See also Rosabeth Moss Kanter, *Commitment and Community* (Cambridge, Mass.: Harvard University Press, 1972), p. 82.

Chapter 9

Settlements

Karl N. Llewellyn, "What Price Contract?—An Essay in Perspective," *Yale Law Journal* 40 (1931): 730–31.

1. J. H. N. [John Humphrey Noyes], "An Appeal," *The Circular*, December 9, 1867.

2. Ibid.

3. This point is clearer in the 1875 Oneida covenant than in the 1864 version. The early Oneida contract read:

On the admission of any member, all property belonging to him or her becomes the property of the Association. A record of the estimated amount will be kept, and in case of the subsequent withdrawal of the member, the Association, according to its practice heretofore, will refund the property or an equivalent amount. This practice however stands on the ground, not of obligation, but of expediency and liberality; and the time and manner of refunding must be trusted to the discretion of the Association. While a person remains a member, his subsistence and education in the Association are held to be just equivalents for his labor; and no accounts are kept between him and the Association, and no claim of wages accrues to him in case of subsequent withdrawal.

"Secession from the Community," *The Circular*, May 23, 1864, reprinting terms of admission dating from 1848.

4. See above text.

5. "Secession," *The Circular*, May 23, 1864.

6. Ibid.

7. Hinds 1878, p. 124.

8. "Secession," *The Circular*, May 23, 1864.

9. See generally Charles Rosenberg, *The Trial of Assassin Guiteau: Psychiatry and Law in the Gilded Age* (Chicago: University of Chicago Press, 1968). Also, *Report of the Proceedings*

in the Case of the United States vs. Charles J. Guiteau (Washington, D.C.: U.S. Government Printing Office, 1882).

10. Rosenberg, *Trial of Assassin Guiteau,* p. 20.

11. John Humphrey Noyes, *Guiteau vs. Oneida Community* (in the National Archives, Washington, D.C.), pp. 8-9; see also Rosenberg, *Trial of Assassin Guiteau,* pp. 108-9.

12. Noyes, *Guiteau vs. Oneida Community.* Guiteau suggested as to his release that "The Oneida Community is a *despotism* and all Contracts made therein are *void*" (Rosenberg, *Trial of Assassin Guiteau,* p. 542).

13. Noyes, *Guiteau vs. Oneida Community.*

14. The church relation does "not prohibit the trustees of said joint interest or property from doing justice to such persons in case they should finally conclude to withdraw; and it has been an invariable rule with the trustees, to make donations to the full amount of property that such persons have brought in, or become heir to, on their withdrawal." *State of New York In Assembly April 4, 1849, No. 198, Report of Select Committee on the Subject of the Shakers,* p. 7. Some doubt is cast on the invariability of the Shaker practice (that is, in all societies) by a case like *Gass and Bonta,* which concerns property brought in and not returned. See also John McKelvie Whitworth, *God's Blueprints: A Sociological Study of Three Utopian Sects* (Boston: Routledge & Kegan Paul, 1975), p. 31; Samuel J. Tilden, "Considerations in Regard to the Application of the Shakers for Certain Special Privileges," in *The Writings and Speeches of Samuel Tilden,* ed. John Bigelow (New York: Harper & Brothers, 1885), 1:96.

15. *Brief Exposition,* in AMS *Constitution,* p. 12.

16. Ibid.

17. Marguerite Melcher, *The Shaker Adventure* (Cleveland: Press of Case Western Reserve University, 1941), p. 242.

18. Hinds 1878, pp. 15-16.

19. Quoted in Arndt 1:572.

20. Hinds 1878, p. 27.

21. Edgar B. Nixon, "The Society of Separatists of Zoar" (unpublished dissertation, Ohio State University, 1933), p. 60.

22. Arnold Van Gennep, *The Rites of Passage*, tr. Monika B. Vizedom and Gabrielle L. Caffee (Chicago: University of Chicago Press, 1961), p. 113.

23. Ibid., p. 114.

24. Hinds 1878, pp. 124–25.

25. Quoted in Arndt 1:355.

Chapter 10

An Expensive Evil

Georg Simmel, *Conflict* (tr. Kurt H. Wolff), in Simmel, *Conflict and the Web of Group Affiliations* (New York: Free Press, 1964), p. 37.

J. H. N. [John Humphrey Noyes], quoted in C. N. Robertson, *Oneida Community: The Breakup, 1876–1881* (Syracuse, N.Y.: Syracuse University Press, 1972), p. 292.

1. I Corinthians 6:5–7.

2. *Testimony of Christ's Second Appearing*, p. 448.

3. "Secession from the Community," *The Circular*, May 23, 1864.

4. On hostility to lawyers in eighteenth century American religious tradition, see Alan Heimert, *Religion and the American Mind: From the Great Awakening to the Revolution* (Cambridge, Mass.: Harvard University Press, 1966), pp. 180ff. For later anti-legalism, see P. W. Grayson, "Vice Unmasked," in Perry Miller, *The Legal Mind in America: From Independence to the Civil War* (Ithaca, N.Y.: Cornell Paperbacks, 1962); also Perry Miller, *The Life of the Mind in America from the Revolution to the Civil War* (New York: Harvest Books, 1965), pp. 99–104.

5. Thomas More, *Utopia*, ed. Edward Surtz, S.J. (New Haven: Yale University Press, 1964), p. 114.

6. Quoted in Christopher Hill, *The World Turned Upside Down: Radical Ideas During the English Revolution* (Baltimore: Penguin, 1972), p. 269; on lawyers, see p. 271.

7. Edward Bellamy, *Looking Backward, 2000-1887* (1888; New York: Modern Library, 1951), pp. 164-68. Bellamy was a lawyer but did not practice. (See introduction by Robert L. Shurter, p. xi.)

8. See Zoar articles in George B. Landis, "The Society of Separatists of Zoar, Ohio," *American Historical Association Annual Report* (1898), pp. 208, 213.

9. Hinds 1908, p. 591.

10. Etienne Cabet, "History and Constitution of the Icarian Community," tr. Thomas Teakle, *Iowa Journal of History and Politics* 15 (1917): 248.

11. J. H. N. [John Humphrey Noyes], "An Appeal," *The Circular*, December 9, 1867. The Perfectionists acknowledged their debt to lawyers in their Second Annual Report of 1850. Of the "three learned professions which rule society"—that is, doctors, priests, and lawyers—"the lawyers are far the most liberal toward us." The result was that "the very men into whose hands the intolerance of society is most likely to throw us, are the men who are most likely to prove liberal mediators between us and society." Quoted in J. H. N. [John Humphrey Noyes], "The Parasite—no. 3," *The Circular*, November 28, 1864.

12. Quoted in Edward D. Andrews, *The People Called Shakers: A Search for the Perfect Society* (New York: Dover, 1953; new enlarged ed., Magnolia, Mass.: Peter Smith, 1963), p. 59.

13. On litigation at Owen's New Harmony between Owen and his associate, William MacClure (quickly settled but "gleefully reported in hostile papers throughout the country"), see Arthur Bestor, *Backwoods Utopias: The Sectarian Origins and the Owenite Phase of Communitarian Socialism in America, 1663-1829*, 2nd enlarged ed. (Philadelphia: University of Pennsylvania Press, 1950, 1970), p. 197.

14. See Simmel, *Conflict*, p. 65.

15. James Dombrowski, *The Early Days of Christian Socialism in America* (New York: Columbia University Press, 1936), pp. 164-65.

16. Kai Erickson, *Wayward Puritans: A Study in the Sociology of Deviance* (New York: Wiley, 1966), p. 60.

17. John P. MacLean, *Shakers of Ohio: Fugitive Papers Concerning the Shakers of Ohio, With Unpublished Manuscripts* (Columbus: F. J. Heer, 1907), pp. 69-70.

18. Ibid.

19. J. H. N. [John Humphrey Noyes], "An Appeal," *The Circular*, December 9, 1867.

20. David Quinn, "A Review and Comparison of the Two Decisions Pronounced by Judge McLean in the Case of *Goesele et al. v. Bimeler et al.*," Cincinnati, Ohio, 1853.

21. Aaron Williams, *The Harmony Society at Economy, Penn'a founded by George Rapp, A.D. 1805* (Pittsburgh: W. S. Haven, 1866), p. 88.

22. Noyes, "An Appeal."

23. Towner 9, December 18, 1879.

24. "Shaker Societies: Their Purpose and Maintenance," *The Shaker*, June 1872, p. 41.

25. *Brief Exposition*, p. 13, in AMS *Constitution*.

26. Anna White and Leila Taylor, *Shakerism: Its Meaning and Message* (1904; reprint ed., New York: AMS, 1972), p. 121. The Cuyahoga County litigation was started by a sister who had been with the society for fifteen years, then withdrew and married. She sued for services during membership. See MacLean, *Shakers of Ohio*, pp. 149-50.

For an account of an early Harmonist suit for wages (Müller), see Aaron Williams, *Harmony Society*, p. 83; also Karl J. R. Arndt, *Documentary History of the Indiana Decade of the Harmony Society, 1814-1824*, vol. 2: 1820-1824 (Indianapolis: Indiana Historical Society, 1975), pp. 348-49, 672-73.

27. Quoted in Henri Desroche, *The American Shakers: From Neo-Christianity to Presocialism*, tr. John K. Savacool (Amherst: University of Massachusetts Press, 1971), pp. 280, 284.

28. Hinds 1878, p. 16.

29. Ibid., p. 34.

Chapter 11

Judgments on Utopia

1. Towner 10, December 31, 1874, and December 25, 1879.

2. Ibid.

3. For settlements at Zoar, see Edgar B. Nixon, "The Society of Separatists of Zoar" (unpublished dissertation, Ohio State University, 1933), pp. 51-52; see also "Suing the Shakers," *New York Times*, June 26, 1888, reporting a suit to recover $1,000, concluded with a compromise of $800. (She had signed the covenant while under age.) For a Harmonist compromise, see Arndt 1:562; for settlement of the "Mills War" at Oneida, see Robert Allerton Parker, *A Yankee Saint: John Humphrey Noyes and the Oneida Community* (New York: G. P. Putnam's Sons, 1935), p. 223.

4. One early Shaker case, *Heath v. Draper* (New Hampshire, 1810), is available in Shaker materials. (*The Investigator*, reprinted in AMS *Constitution*, p. 39, citing the *National Intelligencer* of December 1, 1827.) The suit was for property and wages. The plaintiff did not recover.

5. Karl N. Llewellyn, *The Bramblebush* (Dobbs Ferry, N.Y.: Oceana, 1960), p. 38. See also G. Edward White, "The Appellate Opinion as Historical Source Material," *Journal of Interdisciplinary History* 1 (1971): 491-509.

6. Roscoe Pound, *An Introduction to the Philosophy of Law* (New Haven: Yale University Press, 1954), pp. 64ff. On equity, see Lon Fuller, *Basic Contract Law* (St. Paul, Minn.: West, 1947), pp. 27-31; Ellen A. Peters, *Commercial Transactions: Cases, Text and Problems on Contracts Dealing with Personality, Realty and Services* (Indianapolis: Bobbs-Merrill, 1971), pp. 75-77.

7. Pound, *Philosophy of Law*, p. 65.

8. The plaintiffs were not, however, children outside the community claiming a violation of the support obligation. On

support, see *Waite v. Merrill*, 4 Me. 102 (1826), p. 122. (See also discussion of legislative interventions, above, pp. 45ff.) On possible attack by a creditor, see *Schriber v. Rapp*, 5 Watts (Pa.) 351 (1836), p. 361; Underwood, dissenting, in *Gass and Bonta*, 2 Dana [32 Ky.] 170 (1834), p. 190.

9. Edward Gibbon, *The Triumph of Christendom in the Roman Empire*, ed. J. B. Bury (chs. 15–20 of *The History of the Decline and Fall of the Roman Empire*) (New York: Harper Torchbooks, 1958), p. 51. On this level, the problem of the second-generation utopians was not at all unique to nineteenth century America.

Shaker conceptions of the consecration of property did not involve the disinheriting of heirs.

5. Any person becoming a member must rectify all his wrongs, and, as fast and as far as it is in his power, discharge all just and legal claims, whether of creditors or filial heirs. . . .

6. No difference is to be made in the distribution of parental estate among the heirs, whether they belong to the society or not; but an equal partition must be made as far as may be practicable and consistent with reason and justice.

7. If an unbelieving wife separate from a believing husband, by agreement, the husband must give her a just and reasonable share of the property; and if they have children who have arrived to years of understanding sufficient to judge for themselves, and who chuse to go with their mother, they are not to be disinherited on that account. Tho the character of this Institution has been much censured on this ground; yet we boldly assert that the rule above stated has never, to our knowledge, been violated by this Society.

Brief Exposition, in AMS *Constitution*, pp. 6–7. Also, *The Investigator*, in AMS *Constitution*, p. 28; also, Henri Desroche, *The American Shakers: From Neo-Christianity to Presocialism*, tr. John K. Savacool (Amherst: University of Massachusetts Press, 1971), p. 198.

10. *Gass and Bonta* involved an original contribution. See also *Ruse v. Williams*, 14 Ariz. 445 (1913)

11. Argument in *Grosvenor*, 118 Mass. 78 (1875), p. 89.

12. See Ellyn C. Ballou, "Prentiss Mellen, Maine's First Chief Justice: A Legal Biography," *Maine Law Review* 28 (1977): 317.

13. Simon Greenleaf, lawyer and court reporter in Maine, continued in practice during that time (see above, p. 128). In 1833 he was offered the Royall Professorship at Harvard Law School by Justice Joseph Story, the Dane Professor of Law at Harvard. There Greenleaf prepared *A Treatise on the Law of Evidence* (1842) and a work called *Examination of the Testimony of the Four Evangelists by the Rules of Evidence Administered in Courts of Justice, with an Account of the Trial of Jesus* (1846). See also Arthur E. Sutherland, *The Law at Harvard: A History of Ideas and Men, 1817-1967* (Cambridge, Mass: Harvard University Press, 1967).

14. *Anderson v. Brock*, 3 Me. 243 (1825), p. 248. Compare this description and that of Zoar given by John McLean (pp. 141-42) with the description of the Amish offered in *Wisconsin v. Yoder*, 406 U.S. 205 (1972), pp. 216ff.

15. *Easum v. Bohon*, 180 Ky. 451 (1918). There is some indication in *Gass and Bonta* that the majority did not believe that the community's maintenance and support was legal consideration. On this question see *Easum v. Bohon*, noting that "even if the language of that opinion be regarded as sufficient to indicate the court's view that no consideration existed for the donation of the property, we would be disinclined to follow it (p. 462)."

16. Joseph Underwood (1791-1876). Born in Virginia, he graduated from Transylvania University in 1811. He studied law in Lexington, Kentucky (under Robert Wickcliffe) and was admitted to practice in 1813. He was appointed associate justice of the Court of Appeals in 1828, resigning in 1835. In 1847 he was elected to the United States Senate, remaining until 1853. Four years before his dissent in *Gass and Bonta v. Wilhite* (1834), in *Shain v. Markham*, 4 Marshall (27 Ky.) 578 (1830), Justice Underwood considered a problem arising out

of a charge of assault and battery brought by a former Shaker against Shakers who had ordered him to leave the Shaker property and then physically expelled him (new trial ordered).

17. Aaron Williams, *The Harmony Society at Economy, Penn'a founded by George Rapp, A.D. 1805* (Pittsburgh: W. S. Haven, 1866), p. 84.

18. Ibid.

19. See Stanley I. Kutler, "John Bannister Gibson: Judicial Restraint and the 'Positive State,' " *Journal of Public Law* 14, no. 1 (1965): 181-97.

20. Edgar B. Nixon, "The Society of Separatists of Zoar" (unpublished dissertation, Ohio State University, 1933), pp. 190-200.

21. For accounts of a seceders' march on Economy, see Arndt 1:524ff; Williams, *Harmony Society,* pp. 78ff.

22. On John McLean as an anti-slavery judge, see Robert Cover, *Justice Accused: Antislavery and the Judicial Process* (New Haven: Yale University Press, 1975), pp. 243ff. The case was *Ohio v. Carneal* (1817) (Ervin Pollack, ed., *Ohio Unreported Judicial Decisions Prior to 1823* [Indianapolis: A. Smith, 1952], p. 139), quoted in Cover, *Justice Accused,* p. 244.

On McLean generally see Francis Weisenburger, *The Life of John McLean: A Politician on the Supreme Court of the United States* (Columbus: Ohio State University Press, 1937).

23. On McLean and the Methodists, see Weisenburger, ch. 12. Early in his career, McLean had been the printer of the Shaker book *The Testimony of Christ's Second Appearing* (1808) (see Weisenburger, p. 7). In 1856, the day before the *Nachtrieb* decision was to come down, he had dinner with the leader of the Harmonists (Arndt 2:59).

24. David Quinn, "A Review and Comparison of the Two Decisions Pronounced by Judge McLean in the Case of *Goesele et al. v. Bimeler et al.,*" Cincinnati, Ohio, 1853, pp. 10, 11. The document is addressed not to John McLean but to "Roger B. Taney, John Catron, Peter V. Daniel, Samuel Nelson, Robert C. Grier, and Benjamin Curtiss."

25. Williams, *Harmony Society,* p. 87.

26. See Frank Otto Gatell, "Robert C. Grier," in *The Justices of the United States Supreme Court. 1789-1969: Their*

Lives and Major Opinions, ed. Leon Friedman and Fred L. Israel, 4 vols. (New York: Chelsea House, 1969), 2:873.

27. The Grier opinion is followed by this note: "In a case brought by another complainant against these same defendants, there being imperfect evidence of any expulsion, and the defendants by their answer 'conceding the complainant's perfect right and liberty to return to the enjoyment of all the privileges, benefits, and advantages contemplated by the association, he discharging the duties incumbent on him as a member of it,' the court refused to grant the complainant any relief, but dismissed his bill with costs." *Lemix v. Harmony Society* (unreported).

For another case dealing with events surrounding the signing of a release, see *Goodrich v. Walker*, 1 Johns 250 (1800). The appellate court agreed with the trial court that the weight of the evidence on duress was "in favor of the defendant Shakers, and that the plaintiff ought not to recover."

For a full discussion of the background of the *Nachtrieb* case, see Arndt 2, ch. 3.

28. Quoted in George B. Landis, "The Society of Separatists of Zoar, Ohio," *American Historical Association Annual Report* (1898), p. 195. We are told that one of the losing Zoarites was accepted back into the community and a pension given to two others (p. 196).

29. Each of the sisters received $50. F. W. S. [Francis Wayland-Smith], *The Circular*, October 11, 1875. On Roxalana Grosvenor, see Clara Endicott Sears, *Gleanings from Old Shaker Journals* (New York: Houghton Mifflin, 1916); also Thomas Swain, "The Evolving Expressions of the Religious and Theological Experiences of a Community," *Shaker Quarterly* 12, no 1 (Spring 1972).

30. John Wells (1819-1875) was admitted to the bar in 1841, and appointed to the Supreme Judicial Court of Massachusetts in 1866. See obituary notice of John Wells, *American Law Review, 1875-1876* (Boston: Little, Brown, 1876), pp. 365-70.

31. Roxalana L. Grosvenor, *The Shakers' Covenant (Never Before Published) With a Brief Outline of Shaker History* (Boston: W. C. Allan, 1873), p. ii.

32. The plaintiffs argued that the authorities referred to in the covenant were the Shaker leaders at Mount Lebanon. The Massachusetts court said that its understanding of the covenant was that the authorities referred to were those of this society, and not the authority at Mount Lebanon.

33. No Perfectionist was drafted because "the Mansion House stood at the border of Madison and Oneida counties, and each county's recruiting officer decided that the Community lay within the jurisdiction of the other." Maren Lockwood Carden, *Oneida: Utopian Community to Modern Corporation* (1969; New York: Harper Torchbooks, 1977), p. 84. The anecdote is telling.

34. E.g. *Davis v. Beason*, 133 U.S. 333 (1889), p. 343.

35. The headnote is not a part of the opinion. Compare Grier's statement: "Whether the society be governed by prophet, priest, king or majority, they are subject to the law of the land" (*Nachtrieb v. Harmony Settlement*, 17 Fed. Cas. 1139 (1855), p. 1145).

36. Karl Marx and Friedrich Engels, *The Communist Manifesto*, in Karl Marx, *The Revolutions of 1848*, Political Writings, vol. 1, ed. David Fernback (New York: Vintage Books, 1974), p. 96. Desroche quotes comments of Friedrich Engels (1845) on the Shakers: "As far as they are concerned the laws of the country do not exist, and indeed they could be abolished without anyone in the community knowing the difference, since these peaceful people have never caused anyone to be sent to prison" (p. 295). But it is not true that for them the laws of the country did not exist. See above, *passim*.

37. " . . . the legal relation which is being litigated shows distorted features which are quite different from, and foreign to, the same relation when it is in repose. Who would judge our family life or the life of our societies by the law-suits that arise in the families or in the societies?" Eugen Ehrlich, *Fundamental Principles of the Sociology of Law*, tr. Walter L. Moll (1936; reprint ed., New York: Arno, 1975), p. 495.

38. F. R. Aumann, "A Minor Prophet in Iowa," *The Palimpsest* 8 (1927): 253–60.

39. Ibid., p. 255.

40. *Scott v. Thompson*, 21 Iowa (Withrow) 599 (1866), appendix. On John Dillon, see *Dictionary of American Biography*.

Chapter 12

Law-Ways

Morris Raphael Cohen, "The Basis of Contract," *Harvard Law Review* 46 (1933): 562.

Karl N. Llewellyn, *The Bramblebush* (Dobbs Ferry, N.Y.: Oceana, 1960), p. 59; on "law-ways" see Karl N. Llewellyn and E. Adamson Hoebel, *The Cheyenne Way: Conflict and Case Law in Primitive Jurisprudence* (Norman: University of Oklahoma Press, 1941).

1. On the "instrumental" conception of law as a tool to shape society, see Morton J. Horwitz, *The Transformation of American Law, 1780–1860* (Cambridge, Mass.: Harvard University Press, 1977), pp. 16–30.

2. Grant Gilmore, *The Ages of American Law* (New Haven: Yale University Press, 1977), p. 15. See generally Karl N. Llewellyn, *The Common Law Tradition: Deciding Appeals* (Boston: Little, Brown, 1960), p. 36, describing the "grand style" of pre-Civil War adjudication.

3. James Willard Hurst, *Law and the Conditions of Freedom in the Nineteenth Century United States* (Madison: University of Wisconsin Press, 1956), p. 18.

4. Friedrich Kessler and Grant Gilmore, *Contracts: Cases and Materials*, 2nd ed. (Boston: Little, Brown, 1970), p. 4.

5. Walton H. Hamilton, "Freedom of Contract," *Encyclopaedia of the Social Sciences* (1931), p. 450.

6. *Coppage v. Kansas*, 236 U.S. 1 (1914), p. 17.

7. Ibid.

8. Hinds 1878, *Oneida Contract*, appendix.

9. *Waite v. Merrill*, 4 Me. 102 (1826), pp. 119–20.

10. Ibid., p. 120.

11. Ellyn C. Ballou, "Prentiss Mellen, Maine's First Chief Justice: A Legal Biography," *Maine Law Review* 28 (1976): 369.

12. *Gass and Bonta*, dissent, 2 Dana [32 Ky.] 170 (1834), p. 202.

13. Ibid.

14. *Schriber v. Rapp*, 5 Watts (Pa.) 351 (1836), p. 360. See also p. 362: "No one who has witnessed the workings of fanaticism in the strongest and most cultivated minds will presume to set bounds to it; or to say that the absurdity of a dogma is evidence of the insincerity of him who professes to believe it."

15. *Grosvenor v. United Society of Believers*, 118 Mass. 78 (1875), p. 91.

16. *Watson v. Jones*, 13 Wall. 679 (1871), p. 728.

17. *Gonzales v. Archbishop*, 280 U.S. 1 (1929), p. 16. See also *Serbian Eastern Orthodox Diocese v. Milivojevich*, 426 U.S. 696 (1976).

18. *People v. Ruggles*, 8 Johns (N.Y.) 290 (1811).

19. *Vidal v. Girard's Executors*, 2 How. 127 (1834); for a discussion of the Christian-nation problem, see Leo Pfeffer, *Church, State, and Freedom*, rev. ed. (Boston: Beacon, 1967), p. 243. On Girard's will in the twentieth century, see Elias Clark, "Charitable Trusts, the Fourteenth Amendment and the Will of Stephen Girard," *Yale Law Journal* 66 (1957): 980.

20. Ibid., *Vidal v. Girard's Executors*, p. 200.

21. Quoted and discussed in Ann Douglas, *The Feminization of American Culture* (New York: Avon, 1977), p. 17.

22. *Mormon Church v. United States*, p. 49.

23. Greenleaf, "Memoir of the Life and Character of the Late Chief Justice Mellen," 17 Me. 467 (1841), p. 476.

24. Grier obituary notice, *Albany Law Journal*, October 14, 1870, p 295.

25. Francis Weisenburger, *The Life of John McLean: A Politician on the Supreme Court of the United States* (Columbus: Ohio State University Press, 1937), pp. 175ff.

26. Wells obituary notice, *American Law Review* (1875–1876), p. 369.

27. See Robert Cover, *Justice Accused: Antislavery and the Judicial Process* (New Haven: Yale University Press, 1975).

28. See Jerome Frank, *Courts on Trial: Myth and Reality in American Justice* (Princeton, N.J.: Princeton University Press, 1949), pp. 146ff.

29. Argument for Zoar, *Goesele v. Bimeler*, 55 U.S. 589 (1852), p. 597.

30. *Goesele v. Bimeler*, 10 Fed. Cas. 528 (1851), p. 532.

31. *Schriber v. Rapp*, 5 Watts (Pa.) 351 (1836), p. 364.

32. Thomas Case, "Spiritual Whoredom Discovered in a Sermon before the House of Commons" (1647), quoted in Christopher Hill, *The World Turned Upside Down: Radical Ideas During the English Revolution* (Baltimore: Penguin, 1972), p. 100.

33. William Strong, *Two Lectures Upon the Relation of Civil Law to Church Polity, Discipline and Property* (New York: Dodd & Mead, 1875), pp. 35–36.

34. *Ball v. Hand* (1848) *Western Law Journal* 238.

35. *Anderson v. Brock*, 3 Me. 243 (1825), p. 248.

36. *Heath v. Draper* (in AMS *Constitution*, reprinted in *The Investigator*, p. 41).

37. *Ellis v. Newbrough*, 6 N.M. 181 (1891), pp. 182–83; 27 Pac. 490 (1891), pp. 490–91. (The case involved the Faithists. See Hinds 1908, pp. 452–55.)

38. Ibid., p. 491.

39. Frankfurter, dissenting in *West Virginia v. Barnette*, 319 U.S. 624 (1943), p. 653.

40. Ibid., p. 654.

41. *Prince v. Massachusetts*, 321 U.S. 158 (1944).

42. *Wisconsin v. Yoder*, 406 U.S. 205 (1972).

43. See generally Kent S. Bernard, "Churches, Members and the Role of the Courts: Toward a Contractual Analysis," *Notre Dame Lawyer* 51 (1976): 545, and particularly pp. 558–59, n. 76.

44. Richard T. Ely, *Property and Contract in Their Relation to the Distribution of Wealth*, 2 vols. (1914; reprint ed., Port Washington, N.Y.: Kennikat, 1971), 2:562.

45. *Lochner v. New York*, 198 U.S. 45 (1905), p. 53.

46. *Gasely v. Separatists*, 13 Ohio 144 (1862), p. 155.

47. Harmony Contract (1805), in Arndt 1:74; *Schriber v. Rapp*, 5 Watts (Pa.) 351 (1836), p. 358.

48. J. H. N. [John Humphrey Noyes], "An Appeal," *The Circular*, December 9, 1867. The analogy to the family is strengthened by a reading of the support obligation of the husband as reciprocating the original transfer to him of his wife's wealth. See Joseph Story, *Commentaries on Equity Jurisprudence, As Administered in England and America* (1836; reprint ed., New York: Arno, 1972), p. 646; also, Monrad G. Paulsen, "Support Rights and Duties Between Husband and Wife," *Vanderbilt Law Review* 9 (1956): 709.

49. T. W. H. [Higginson], *Woman's Journal*, March 2, 1872, p. 65.

50. See Morton Keller, *Affairs of State: Public Life in Late Nineteenth Century America* (Cambridge, Mass.: Harvard University Press, 1977), pp. 467ff., for a discussion of the marriage contract.

51. *Cropsey v. Sweeney*, 27 Barb. 310 (N.Y. 1858), p. 315. See generally H. C. Havighurst, "Services in the Home—A Study of Contract Concepts in Domestic Relations," *Yale Law Journal* 41 (1932): 386.

52. Pierrepont Noyes, *My Father's House: An Oneida Boyhood* (New York: Farrar & Rinehart, 1937), p. 173. The expulsion nightmare is included in a chapter on the events of 1880 called "Joint-Stock Looms."

53. "Developments in the Law: Judicial Control of Actions of Private Associations," *Harvard Law Review* 76 (1963): 1010.

54. Argument for the Harmony Society, in *Nachtrieb v. Harmony Settlement*, 17 Fed. Cas. 1139 (1855), p. 1143 (A. W. Loomis for the society).

55. *Nachtrieb v. Harmony Settlement*, 17 Fed. Cas. 1139 (1855), p. 1145.

56. See John R. Commons, *Legal Foundations of Capitalism* (Madison: University of Wisconsin Press, 1924), p. 284, linking the prohibition of specific performance to the Thir-

teenth Amendment. See also Albert V. Dicey, *Lectures on the Relation Between Law & Public Opinion in England, During the Nineteenth Century* (London: MacMillan, 1905), p. 151.

57. See *Mary Clark, a woman of color*, 1 Indiana (1821), 139. Mary Clark was a servant by indenture who had voluntarily bound herself to work for twenty years. She now worked involuntarily and asked the court to release her from detention, which it did.

58. Ibid., p. 141.

59. Ibid.

60. Noyes, above, p. 89.

61. Arndt 1:49.

62. Ibid.

63. Lon Fuller, "Two Principles of Human Association," in *Voluntary Associations*, ed. J. Roland Pennock and John W. Chapman (Nomos, no. 11) (New York: Atherton, 1969), p. 29.

64. Zechariah Chafee, "Internal Affairs of Associations Not for Profit," *Harvard Law Review* 43 (1930): 1029.

65. Ibid.

Chapter 13

Who Can Choose?

David Hume, "Of The Original Contract," in *Social Contract*, ed. Sir Ernest Barker (New York: Oxford University Press, 1962), p. 156.

1. Letter, July 14, 1816, in Arndt 1:216–17.

2. Towner 1, March 23, 1874, and October 23, 1879.

3. On utopian and common law images of man, see Maxwell Bloomfield, *American Lawyers in a Changing Society: 1776–1876* (Cambridge, Mass.: Harvard University Press, 1976), pp. 32ff.

4. Raymond Firth, *Symbols: Public and Private* (Ithaca, N.Y.: Cornell University Press, 1973), p. 368.

5. Ibid.

6. John Donne, Holy Sonnets, no. 14.

7. Translation of Wurzel, *Das juristische Denken* (1904), p. 82, in Lon Fuller, *Basic Contract Law* (St. Paul, Minn.: West, 1947), pp 75-76.

8. Ibid.

9. Ibid.

10. See generally Roscoe Pound, *Jurisprudence* (St. Paul, Minn.: West, 1959), vol. 4, ch. 25, "Persons."

11. *Waite v. Merrill*, 4 Me. 102 (1826), p. 103.

12. Frederick W. Evans, *Shakers: Compendium of the Origin, . istory, Principle, Rules and Regulations, Government and Doctrines of the United Society of Believers in Christ's Second Appearing*, 4th ed. (1867; reprint ed., New York: AMS, 1975), p. 43.

13. W. D. Howells, "A Shaker Village," *Atlantic Monthly* 37 (1876): 705.

14. Samuel J. Tilden, *The Writings and Speeches of Samuel Tilden*, ed. John Bigelow (New York: Harper & Brothers, 1885), p. 95.

15. Pierrepont Noyes, *My Father's House*, p. 3; see also Arndt 2:42:43.

16. Pierrepont Noyes, *My Father's House*, p. 113.

17. Ibid., p. 126.

18. Ibid., p. 162.

19. Lawrence M. Friedman, *A History of American Law* (New York: Simon & Schuster, 1973), ch. 4, pp. 209ff.

20. John Dawson, "Economic Duress: An Essay in Perspective," *Michigan Law Review* 45 (1947): 262.

21. Ibid., p. 263.

22. Ibid., p. 266.

23. *Restatement of Contracts* (St. Paul, Minn.: American Law Institute, 1932), sec. 497.

24. *Schriber v. Rapp*, 5 Watts (Pa.) 351 (1836), pp. 363-64.

25. Ibid., p. 364. Avoidance of a release on the ground of oppression was argued by counsel for Nachtrieb. See *Baker v.*

Nachtrieb, 15 Lawyers' Edition 528 (1856), p. 529, argument of Edwin Stanton.

26. *Schriber v. Rapp,* 5 Watts (Pa.) 351 (1836), p. 364.

27. W. D. Howells, *The Leatherwood God* (New York: Century, 1916), based on Taneyhill's "The Leatherwood God" (Ohio Valley Historical Series, no. 7, 1871), an account of "one of the most interesting and curious episodes in the history of the Ohio Valley."

28. Howells, *Leatherwood God,* pp. 149–50.

29. Ibid., pp. 172–73.

30. Ibid., p. 173.

31. *United States v. Ballard,* 322 U.S. 78 (1944).

32. Ibid., p. 90.

33. Ibid., pp. 92–93.

34. Ibid., pp. 93–95.

35. Edward D. Andrews, *The People Called Shakers: A Search for the Perfect Society* (New York: Dover, 1953; new enlarged ed., Magnolia, Mass.: Peter Smith, 1963), p. 206; John P. MacLean, *Shakers of Ohio: Fugitive Papers Concerning the Shakers of Ohio With Unpublished Manuscripts* (Columbus: F. J. Heer, 1907), p. 77.

36. Andrews, *The People Called Shakers,* p. 206.

37. *Reynolds v. United States,* 98 U.S. 145 (1879), p. 164.

38. *Cantwell v. Connecticut,* 310 U.S. 296 (1940), pp. 303–4.

39. Philip B. Kurland, *Religion and the Law: Of Church and State and the Supreme Court* (Chicago: Aldine, 1961), p. 22.

40. See Laurence H. Tribe, *American Constitutional Law* (Mineola, N.Y.: Foundation Press, 1978), p. 838.

41. William James, *Varieties of Religious Experience: A Study in Human Nature* (New York: Mentor, 1958), p. 24.

42. Ibid.

43. Ibid. The free exercise issues here do not relate to private psychiatric counseling, but to cases of state involvement on the civil or criminal side.

44. On spiritualism at Oneida, see Hinds 1878, pp. 126–27.

Chapter 14

What Can Be Chosen?

Thomas More, *Utopia*, ed. Edward Surtz, S.J. (New Haven: Yale University Press, 1964), p. 108.

1. By analogy, for example, with *Columbia Nitrogen Co. v. Royster Co.*, 451 F. 2d 3 (1971).

This question could be dealt with in the contract. The Zoar constitution of 1833 provided that "all unintelligibleness, equivocation, or deficiency which peradventure might exist in this constitution, shall always be construed and treated in favor of the society, and never to the advantage of individual members." George B. Landis, "The Society of Separatists of Zoar, Ohio," *American Historical Association Annual Report* (1898), p. 217.

2. The court said that there was no recognition of such a right at Oneida; that such a right was disclaimed; and that, in any case, the plaintiff could not make any claim to the settlement, since his letter said that he did not want to invoke the well-established practice.

3. Quoted in Jacobus ten Broek, *Equal Under the Law* (1951 [orig. title: *The Antislavery Origins of the Fourteenth Amendment*]; reprint ed., New York: Collier, 1965), p. 177.

4. Richard T. Ely, *Property and Contract in Their Relations to the Distribution of Wealth*, 2 vols. (1914; reprint ed., Port Washington, N.Y.: Kennikat, 1971), 2:714, discussing peonage contracts at pp. 715ff.

See also Anthony T. Kronman and Richard Posner, *The Economics of Contract Law* (Boston: Little, Brown, 1979), pp. 256–60. Also *Horwood v. Millar's Timber and Trading Co. Ltd.* 1 K. B. 305 (1917) (oppressive contract with moneylender).

5. Morris Raphael Cohen, "The Basis of Contract," *Harvard Law Review* 46 (1933): 587.

6. Albert V. Dicey, *Lectures on the Relation Between Law & Public Opinion in England, During the Nineteenth Century.* (London: MacMillan, 1905), pp. 151–52.

7. Is there a possible conflict between a First Amendment freedom to bind oneself and a Thirteenth Amendment prohibition of involuntary servitude? Would a court enforce a service now involuntary in fact (the believer having decided that he wanted to withdraw his service) on the theory that the original contract was a protected (enforceable) exercise of religion?

8. William Faux, *Memorable Days in America, Being A Journal of a Tour to the United States, November 27, 1818, July 21, 1820*, vol. 11 of *Early Western Travels: 1784–1846*, ed. Reuben Gold Thwaites (Cleveland: Arthur H. Clark, 1905), p. 249; quoted in Raymond Lee Muncy, *Sex and Marriage in Utopian Communities* (Baltimore: Penguin, 1974), p. 237. See also Arndt 1:276–77.

9. Charles Rosenberg, *The Trial of Assassin Guiteau: Psychiatry and Law in the Gilded Age* (Chicago: University of Chicago Press, 1968), p. 554. Guiteau felt strongly enough about the comparison to argue the slavery point in front of Frederick Douglass, who had escaped from slavery in 1838 and had published his autobiography in 1845. From 1881 to 1886, Frederick Douglass served as Recorder of Deeds for the District of Columbia.

10. Argument for plaintiff in *Goesele v. Bimeler*, 55 U.S. 589 (1852), p. 590 (David Quinn, representing the Goeseles).

11. Argument for plaintiff in *Gasely v. Separatists*, 13 Ohio 144 (1862). The argument of David Quinn (1859) is quoted in George B. Landis, "The Society of Separatists of Zoar, Ohio," *American Historical Association Annual Report* (1898), p. 195.

12. "[W]e further agree to apply all our strength, good will, diligence and skill *during life* to the general benefit of the society and satisfaction of said directors" (1824 Zoar Articles, Landis, "Society of Separatists at Zoar, Ohio," p. 207). See also Article 6 of the Zoar Constitution of 1833: "[W]e likewise agree to apply all our strength, good will, industry, and skill *for life* to the general benefit of said society and to the satisfaction of the trustees" (ibid., p. 214, emphasis added).

13. Argument for the plaintiff in *Gasely v. Separatists*, 14 Ohio 144 (1862). Argument of David Quinn (1859) quoted in Landis, "Society of Separatists at Zoar," p. 192.

14. David Quinn, "Review," p. 27.

15. Argument for plaintiff, *Waite v. Merrill*, 4 Me. 102 (1826), p. 113.

16. Ibid.

17. *Gass and Bonta*, 2 Dana [32 Ky.] 170 (1834), p. 202.

18. *Nachtrieb v. Harmony Settlement*, 17 Fed. Cas. 1139 (1855), p. 1145.

19. See *Burt v. Oneida*, 137 N.Y. 346 (1893), p. 360.

20. Charles Nordhoff, *The Communistic Societies of the United States: From Personal Visit and Observation* (1875; rev. reprint ed., New York: Schocken, 1966), pp. 417–18.

21. Although the issue had been resolved by the time of the appellate proceeding, there was in *Grosvenor* a question of whether, in fact, there had been an expulsion. In the *Grosvenor* case, the defendant Shakers had argued (defendant's answer filed April 7, 1873, original in Social Law Library, Boston) that Roxalana Grosvenor was not expelled but had "voluntarily left and removed from said order or family" (p. 4). By the time of the appeal (defendant's points, March 1875), the defendants conceded the expulsion, but argued its validity (p. 1).

22. Oneida's contract distinguished in its language between the cases of the voluntarily withdrawn member and the member expelled for just cause (see Hinds 1878, appendix). Hinds merged the two categories in the term "seceder" (Hinds 1878, p. 124).

23. Towner 9, December 18, 1879; for a Perfectionist response, see F. W. S. [Francis Wayland-Smith], *The Circular*, October 11, 1875. In his discussion of the *Grosvenor* case, Towner notes that the case was heard twice. The first time, the judge held that there was no cause of action. "For reasons not necessary to be here stated," Towner says, the case was reheard. The second judge held that under the covenant the plaintiffs had no case and directed a jury verdict for the Shakers.

24. Towner 10, December 25, 1879.

25. Ibid.

26. See Section VII, Special Contracts, "Law on Expulsion and Withdrawal from the Icarian Community," 1879, quoted

in Albert Shaw, *Icaria: A Chapter in the History of Communism* (1884; reprint ed., Philadelphia: Porcupine, 1972).

27. J. H. N. [John Humphrey Noyes], "An Appeal," *The Circular*, December 9, 1867.

28. Argument for plaintiff, in *Grosvenor v. United Society of Believers*, 118 Mass. 78 (1875), p. 89.

29. Argument for appellee (Nachtrieb) in *Baker v. Nachtrieb*, 15 Lawyers' Edition 528 (1856), p. 529.

30. Argument for plaintiff in *Burt v. Oneida*, 137 N.Y. 346 (1893), p. 348.

31. Mark de Wolfe Howe, *The Garden and the Wilderness: Religion and Government in American Constitutional History* (Chicago: University of Chicago Press, 1965), p. 34.

32. Zechariah Chafee, "Internal Affairs of Associations Not for Profit," *Harvard Law Review* 43 (1930): 1018.

33. *Bonacum v. Harrington*, 65 Neb. 831 (1902), 91 N. W. 886, p. 887. Cf: *Gray v. Christian Society*, 137 Mass. 329 (1884) (Holmes, J.). See generally, "Developments," Private Associations, *Harvard Law Journal* 76 (1963): 1026ff.

Conclusion

1. On utopianism and messianism, see Martin Buber, *Paths in Utopia* (Boston: Beacon, 1958), pp. 8-9.

2. *Schriber v. Rapp*, 5 Watts (Pa.) 351 (1836), p. 360.

3. See *Pierce v. Society of Sisters*, 268 U.S. 510 (1925): "The fundamental theory of liberty upon which all governments in this Union repose excludes any general power of the State to standardize its children by forcing them to accept instruction from public school teachers only" (p. 535). On children, see Robert Nozick, *Anarchy, State and Utopia* (New York: Basic Books, 1974), p. 330. See also Kenneth Henley, "Children and the Individualism of Mill and Nozick," *The Personalist* 59, no. 4 (1978): 415-19. Of course, there are also limits on parental authority. Thus: "Parents may be free to become martyrs themselves. But it does not follow they are

free, in identical circumstances, to make martyrs of their children before they have reached the age of full and legal discretion when they can make that choice for themselves" (*Prince v. Massachusetts*, 321 U.S. 158 (1944), p. 120).

4. "Some of the most glaring inequalities in American life have always been economic; and yet, on the whole, a remarkably small proportion of the debates on equality recurring throughout American history has been taken up by such questions as the redistribution of wealth or any effective re-evaluation of the criteria by which economic rewards are allotted." J. R. Pole, *The Pursuit of Equality in American History* (Berkeley: University of California Press, 1978), p. xi.

5. This essay has suggested the historical existence of a structure similar to that described by Robert Nozick, which permits, within a libertarian and laissez-faire framework, separate communities of a quite different character. Nozick, pp. 320ff. See also John Rawls, *A Theory of Justice* (Cambridge, Mass.: Harvard University Press, 1971), on a social union of social unions (pp. 527ff).

INDEX

TABLE OF CASES